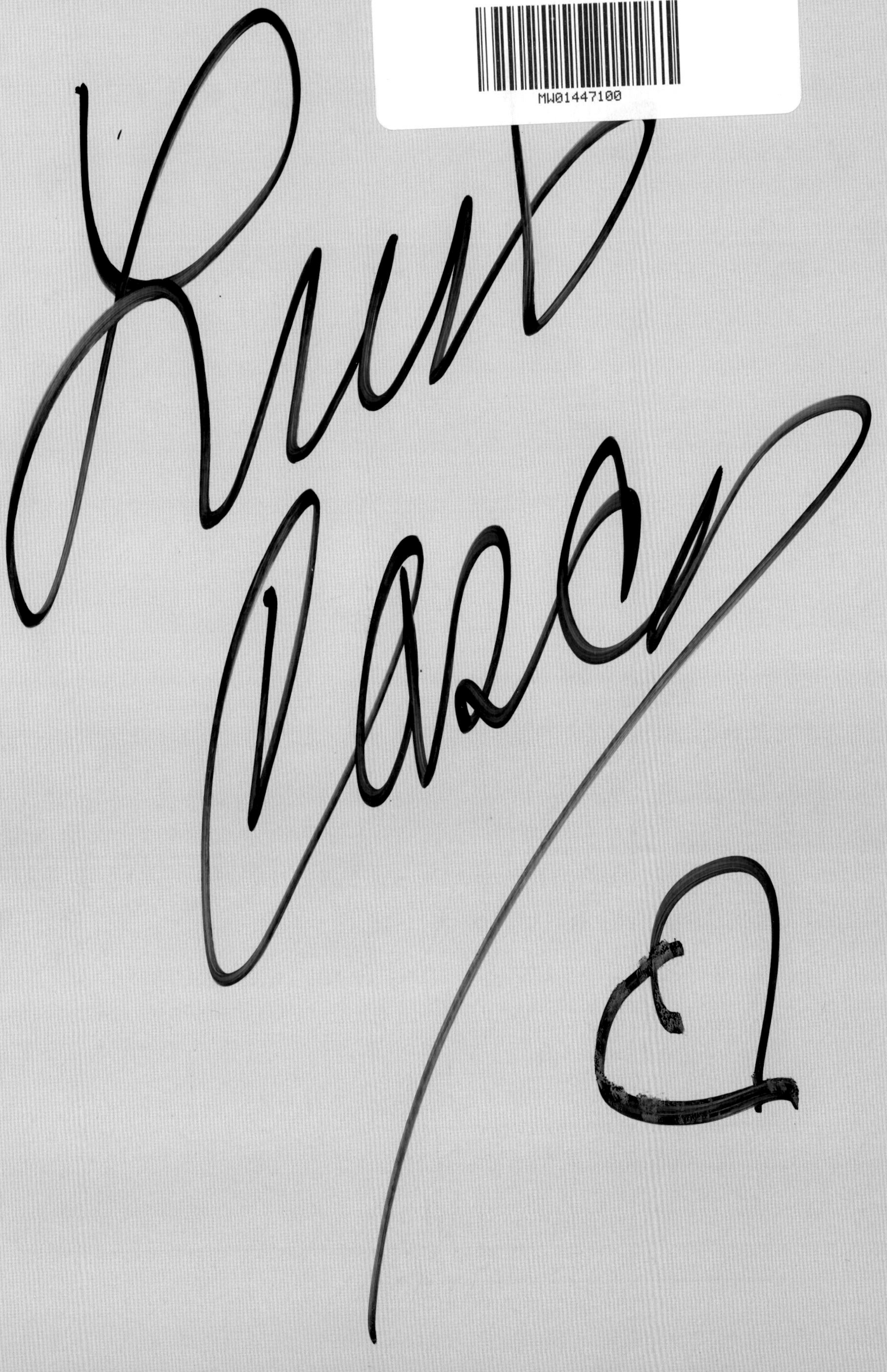

Copyright ©2018 by Luis Casco
All rights reserved. No part of this book may be reproduced in any form or by any electronic or mechanical means, including information storage and retrieval systems, without permission in writing from the publisher, except by a reviewer who may quote brief passages in a review.

ISBN 978-0-9864145-6-5
Printed in China

Luis Casco *Creative Director / Writer*
The Sagami Group *Producer*
Lorraine Young *Beauty Photographer*
Stephen Kamifuji *Designer*
Susan Linney *Copy Editor*

Luis Casco *Makeup*
Preston Wada *Hairstylist*
Veronica Soto *Makeup Assistant*
Frank Sebastian *Makeup Assistant*
Tino Portillo *Wardrobe Stylist*
Abigail Nieto *Wardrobe Stylist*
Veronica Soto *Manicurist*

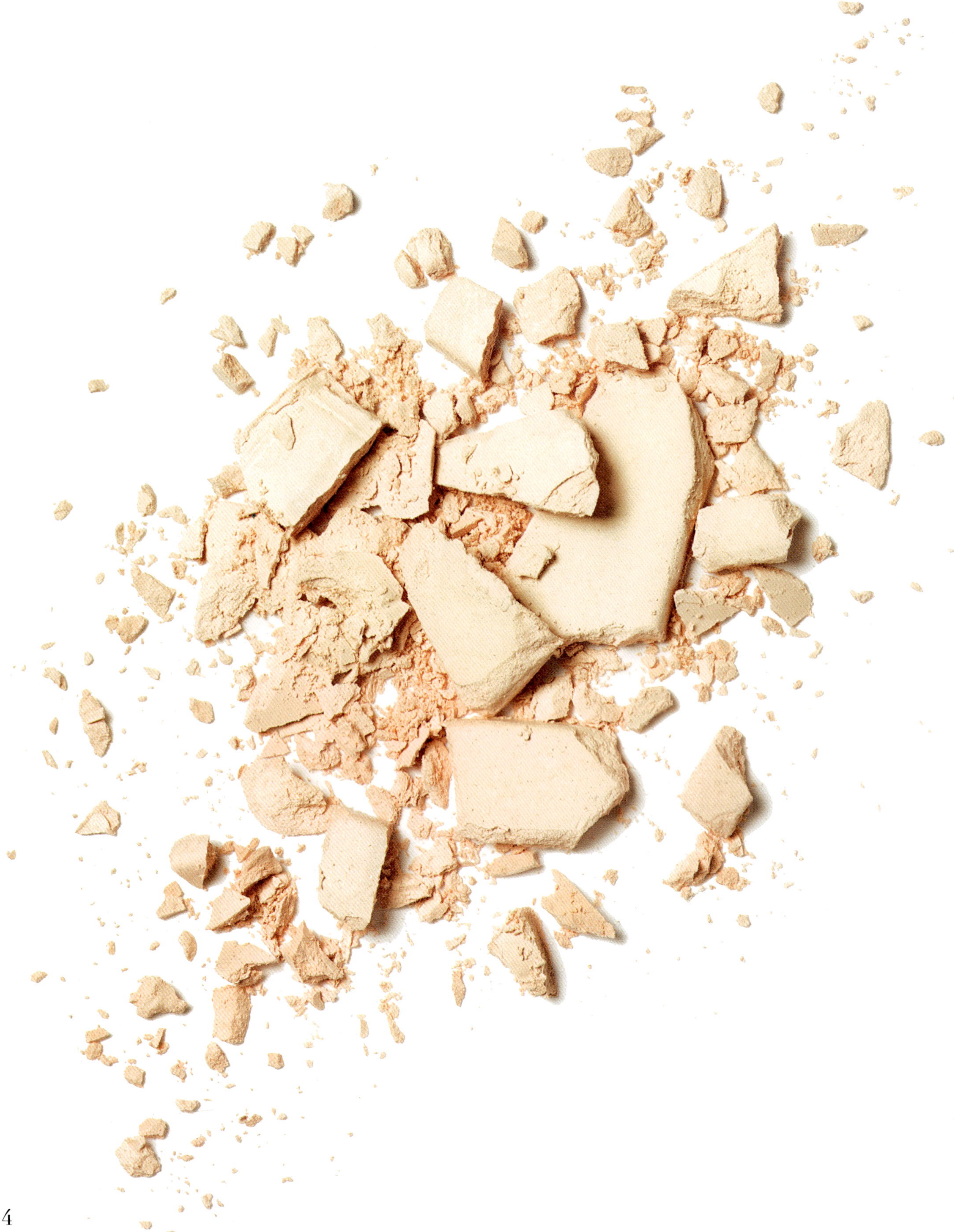

In his first book, celebrity makeup artist Luis Casco gave readers exclusive pro tips for amping up their selfie game. Now, he's sharing exclusive insider secrets for creating #RealLifeWorthy looks that are flawless up-close and in person — no filter required.

Born and raised in San Salvador, El Salvador, Luis discovered his love for makeup and color at a young age. Now internationally renowned, he has worked with some of the biggest names in the business, including Heidi Klum, Charlize Theron, and Christy Turlington, and his work has appeared in countless fashion magazines, from *Harper's Bazaar* to *Vogue*. A dynamic force on social media (follow him @luiscascomakeup!), Luis has amassed tens of thousands of followers and is passionate about helping his fans create industry-inspired looks that are easy to achieve.

CHAPTER

Preface	LUIS CASCO	10
	WHY #BEAUTYUNFILTERED?	18
01	**FACE THE FACTS:** ESSENTIAL TIPS FOR FLAWLESS #UNFILTERED SKIN	19
02	**ACE THE BASE:** CREATING A #SEAMLESS COMPLEXION	34
03	**MASTER THE SHADES:** COLOR THEORY 101	48
04	**THE EYES HAVE IT** #LUSCIOUS LIDS & PERFECT LINES	54
05	**PERFECT #ARCHITECTURE:** BUILDING BROWS THAT WOW	76
06	**IN A WINK:** AMAZING #EYELASHES	80
07	**BLUSH BASICS:** CHEEK & CHIC	84
08	**CHISELED CHEEKBONES:** #CONTOURING & HIGHLIGHTING	90
09	**GIMME SOME LIP:** PERFECTING YOUR POUT	96
10	**TOOLS OF THE TRADE:** APPLICATION, #UNFILTERED	100
11	**A MAN FOR ALL SEASONS:** EASY GROOMING TIPS THAT MAKE ALL THE DIFFERENCE	104
12	**TURN BACK THE CLOCK:** TOP TIPS FOR A YOUNGER LOOK	108

TABLE OF CONTENTS

TABLE OF CONTENTS

CHAPTER 13

50+ NEW UNFILTERED LOOKS

GORGEOUS AT ANY AGE: 3 LOOKS FOR A YOUNGER YOU
1. SOFT NEUTRAL — 116
2. WORKING OVERTIME — 118
3. PAINTING THE TOWN — 120

ONE GIRL FOUR LOOKS
4. NATURAL BEAUTY — 124
5. SOFT CHIC — 126
6. SMOKEY — 128
7. SULTRY GLAM — 130

THE NEUTRALS
8. GLOWING BEIGE — 134
9. SWEET MATTE — 136
10. SHEER NEUTRAL — 138
11. SLATE NEUTRAL — 139
12. RADIANT! — 140
13. SHEER BRONZE — 142
14. SUMMERTIME — 143

BEAUTY SCHOOL: #UNFILTERED
15. COMING UP ROSY — 146
16. YOU GLOW, GIRL — 148
17. CHARMING — 150
18. SOFT METALS — 152

EYELINER LOOKS
19. PERFECT LINE — 156
20. CHARCOAL LINE — 158
21. COLORFUL LINE — 160
22. PRECISE LINE — 162
23. GRAPHIC LINE — 164

A POP OF COLOR
24. OMBRÉ — 168
25. TEAL GAZE — 170
26. HOT PINK — 172
27. BURNT CORAL — 174
28. SPARKLING VIOLET — 176
29. BOLD RED — 178

SMOKEY LOOKS
30. SMOKEY GRAY GAZE — 182
31. COPPER SMOKE — 184
32. AQUA SMOKE — 185
33. VIOLET SMOKE — 186
34. ICY GRAY SMOKE — 188

THE METALS
35. GOLDEN GARNET — 192
36. GOLDEN TOPAZ — 194
37. ROSEGOLD — 196
38. SPARKLING PEWTER — 198
39. BLUE PEARL — 200

THE PARTY LOOKS
40. CLASSIC CHIC — 204
41. 24-KARAT MAGIC — 206
42. GARNET GOLD — 207
43. PARTY GLOW — 208
44. BRONZE SMOKE — 210

THE BRIDAL LOOKS
45. PRETTY IN PINK — 214
46. SOFT ROMANCE — 216
47. BITTEN LIP — 217
48. CANDLELIGHT — 218
49. SWEET CHAMPAGNE — 219

THE RUNWAY LOOKS
50. ADDICTED TO LOVE — 222
51. AU COURANT — 224
52. MESMERISING — 226
53. DRAW THE LINE — 228
54. CATWALK GIRL — 229

THANK YOU — 231

LUISCASCO

As a kid growing up in El Salvador, I learned about the transformative effect of makeup by watching my mom perfect her glam routine. She's always been a chameleon, someone with an active social and philanthropic life, whose style is always evolving. I grew up watching her totally transform herself with different looks, from short blonde Mia Farrow hair to long Raquel Welch locks. She was never afraid to experiment with color, use plenty of mascara, and finish everything off with a bold swipe of lipstick.

Clockwise from above: My mom and dad at a gala; my mom at the presidential house in El Salvador; my mom in her debutante look; my first passport photo with mom (I was already a world traveler at three years of age); my mom wearing a Chinese cheongsam and her favorite red lipstick.

I started to create my own transformations as soon as I could get my hands on a camera. When I was about 12 years old, I began using a polaroid camera to take pictures of my sister and her friends. I would style them, teach them how to pose, and of course do their hair and makeup. Once I was in high school, I took my interest to the next level by taking a photography class, which inspired me to shoot pictures with my friends. We'd spend weekends transforming ourselves into our own new-wave versions of Morrissey and Siouxsie Sioux (or so we thought :), putting together outfits, designing our own hair and makeup, and finding cool locations where we could shoot.

During my college years, I moved with my family to Houston and started taking fashion design classes. I got a job working as an assistant to someone who would become my mentor — Linda Gillan Griffin, the then Fashion Editor of the *Houston Chronicle*. Linda had impeccable taste, major industry contacts, and really helped kick-start my career. I was only about 22 years old, but she put me in charge of the photo shoots for her weekly section of the newspaper. I scouted locations, booked models, and got designers to send us their clothes. And yes, I also did hair and the makeup!

Linda was friends with many major designers of the time. As her protégée, I was able to work with legends such as Bob Mackie and Bill Blass, doing makeup for the models in their Houston trunk and runway shows. That's how my career was born.

In the mid 1990s, Linda and I traveled to Paris to attend some of the most high-profile fashion shows for designers like CHANEL and YSL. The first show I worked was CHANEL, and it was so exciting. All of the supermodels came out in motorcycle boots; Linda Evangelista even entered runway on a motorcycle! The backstage scene was the most exciting world to me and I loved watching the "girls" switch from one designer look to another. I also loved seeing them ride the metro and walk the streets in their own clothes, but with impeccable hair and amazing makeup. It really was love at first sight! So I moved to Paris and became an art director of sorts, doing tests with photographers and falling in love with the art of makeup. This was a time when there was NO retouching of photographs — except for huge campaigns and major magazine covers.

To this day, working fashion shows and creating different looks are my favorite things to do. New York Fashion Week and all of its international iterations are my top priority, which is why I've been the Lead Makeup Artist on *Project Runway* for the last four years doing what I love — creating transformations!

In 2015, I wrote a book called *#Beautiful* in which I explored the concept of selfies and how to look best while taking them. It felt so timely as the word had just been added to the Oxford English Dictionary and was even coined as the Word of the Year. The majority of pictures in *#Beautiful* are real selfies that were taken by different women using my smartphone. I wanted to teach my fans what I had learned instinctively over the years — that with the proper photo angles, poses, and makeup looks, anyone can look stunning in a selfie.

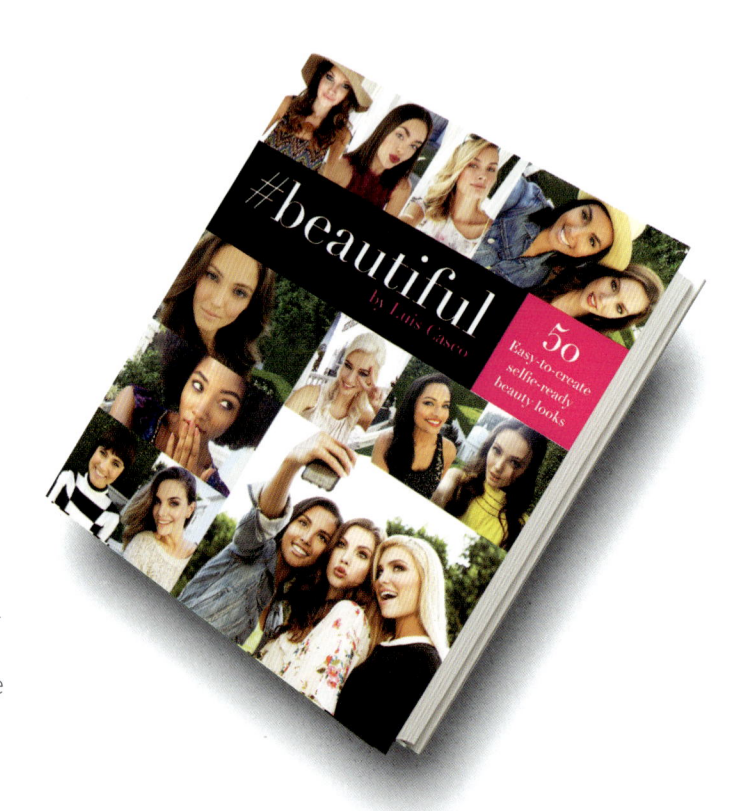

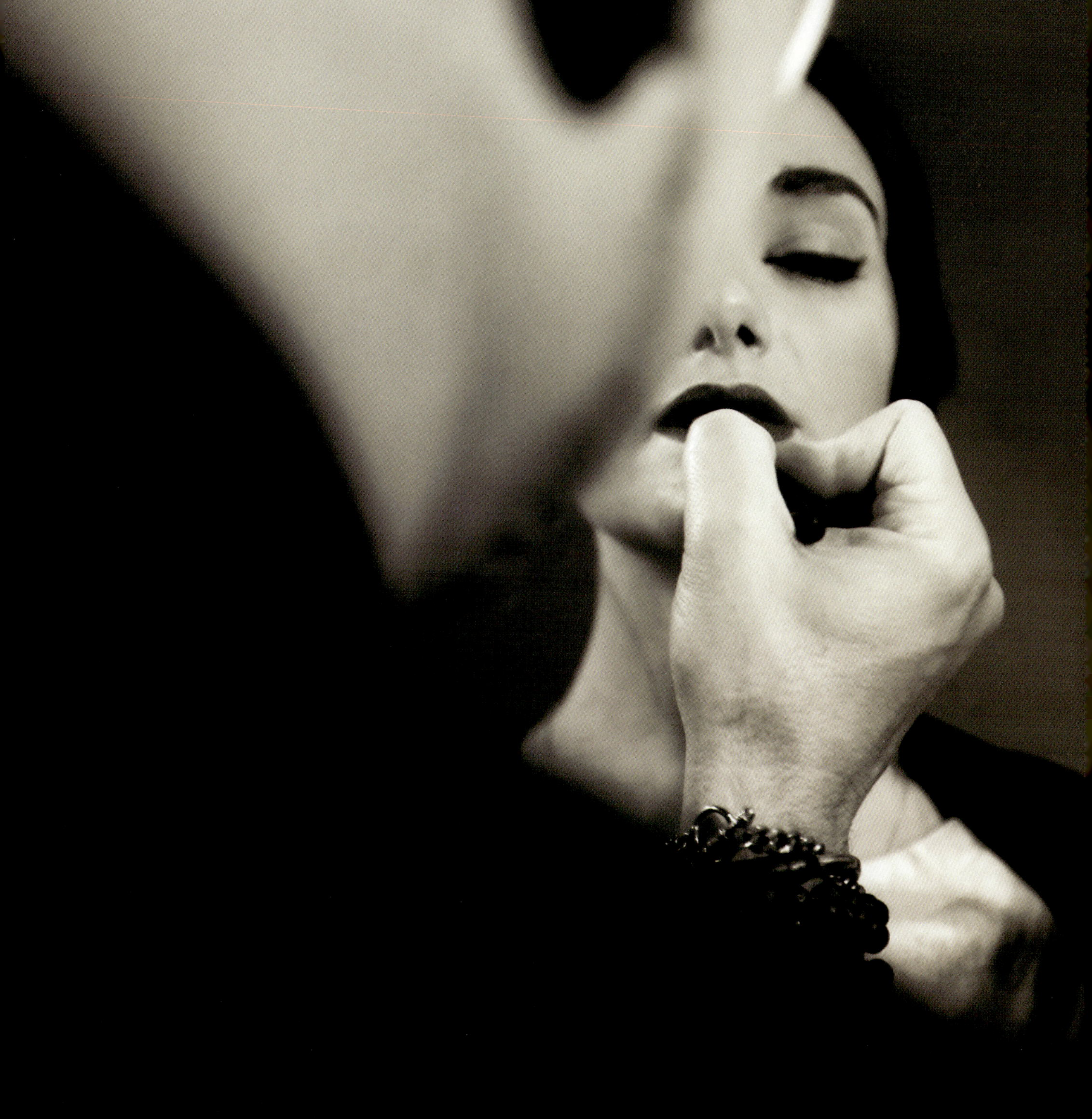

#BEAUTY *UNFILTERED* IS ALSO ABOUT *LOOKING STUNNING* — NOT JUST IN A SELFIE BUT IN *REAL LIFE, TOO.*

After 25-plus years as a makeup artist, I've learned that even the most basic makeup techniques can seem incredibly challenging for the average person to carry out.

Which is why I've written this book — to show how you can create your own transformations, no filter required. To teach you how makeup and a little trick here and there can make a huge difference in the way you look and feel. The tips in this book are real, they work, and whether you're a makeup novice, a skilled beginner, or an experienced glamour girl, I hope you love them and use them.

Because in real life, there are no filters.

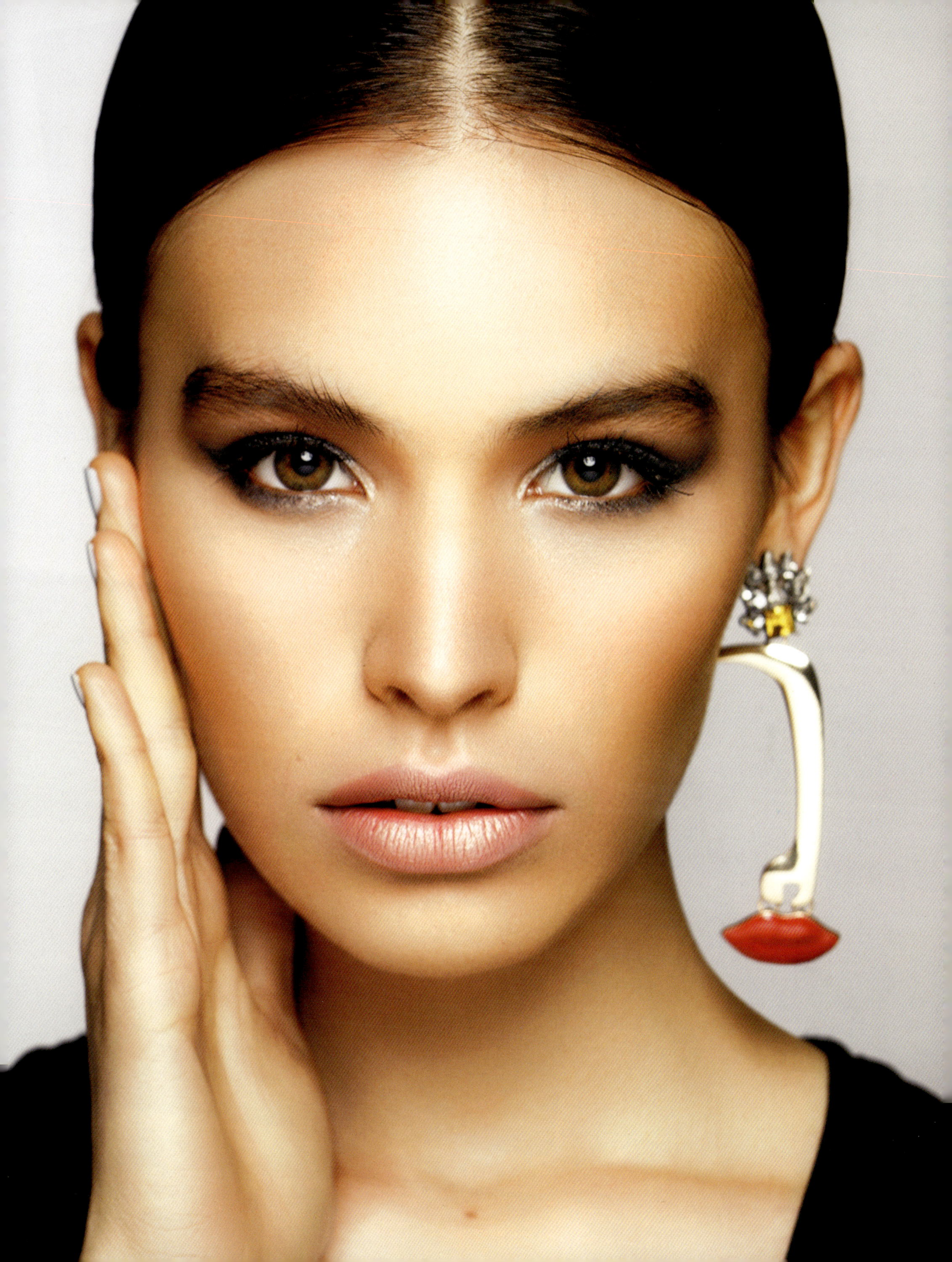

THE MOST BEAUTIFUL FACE *IN* THE WORLD

When I was a young artist working in Paris, I got a call one evening from my agent with news that I'd booked a job with Paulina Porizkova. At the time, Paulina was considered by everyone in the know to be the most beautiful woman in the world. She was one of the highest-paid supermodels and appeared on countless magazine covers, from *Vogue* to *Cosmopolitan*. She was thought to have the most beautiful and symmetric face and eyes. Even my mom, who at that time spoke very little English and only watched Spanish language TV and read mags like *Vanidades* and *¡Hola!,* knew who she was. It was a big moment for me.

The next morning, as I chatted with Paulina at the photo studio in Paris and began prepping her face, I realized that even the most beautiful woman in the world had her flaws. There were some issues that I would definitely have to address. Understand, this was before the age of digital retouching. Even with great lighting and perfect features, a supermodel still needed some pretty terrific makeup to bring it all together, and that meant the pressure was on me.

I tell you this to illustrate the point that everyone has flaws and issues, even the "most beautiful woman in the world." But with makeup and the right application techniques, any woman can look gorgeous. In this book, I'll show you how.

Me and Paulina Porizkova at Pin-Up studios in Paris circa the mid '90s

A polaroid of my work on Paulina Porizkova. Paris, 1990s

My first Harper's Bazaar cover.

Soon after I arrived in Paris, I worked on this shoot for Madame Figaro. *It was shot right after a couture show, just outside of the Louvre...my first editorial ever.*

My first photo in Marie Claire

My first photo in Vogue España

I lived and worked in over 15 countries for the first 10 years of my career.

17

WHY #BEAUTY UNFILTERED?

I want to make it clear that personally, I love social media (feel free to follow me everywhere @luiscascomakeup! :) I use it as a way to promote positive, all-inclusive, and hopefully attainable beauty looks. #BeautyUnfiltered came to be because I wanted to remind my fans and followers that not everything we see on social media is real, and that some photos really should come with a disclosure that reads *"FILTERED!"* I mean, anything "on fleek" usually denotes an unrealistic standard. That "holographic" highlighter, for instance, will look amazing in a perfectly lit photo, but in person? Odds are it will appear as though you have a blinding, unblended stripe of shine on top of your cheeks!

Don't get me wrong, we all like to look our best in photos. And once we realize that it just takes an easy tweak with the smartphone to enhance our appearance, it becomes even more tempting to cheat. But what happens when people see you in real life? You might be *#InstaWorthy*, but are you *#RealLifeWorthy?* That is where this book comes in.

Today's standards of beauty are largely measured by social media content. Beauty gurus, makeup artists, celebrities, and everyday people are posting their makeup "hacks, hauls and transformations," which are instantly devoured by an increasingly eager audience. Some posts become instant trends and some dissipate quickly (remember the "feathered brow?"). But overall, *#InstaBeauty* is where it all seems to start nowadays. Of course fashion, street style, and celebrity still have a say in what we deem beautiful, but even those standards are evolving with the rise of social media.

#BeautyUnfiltered is all about real beauty and looking your best in person. I encourage you to go ahead and transform yourself in any way you want, but also keep in mind that unless you constantly travel with a lighting crew (or never go outside!), the results should be believable when you're up close and personal. That's why I felt it necessary for me — someone the media has called a "selfie guru" — to come up with this book. I hope you find plenty of easy-to-implement makeup and skincare tips, and that they become your own real-life filters.

On any given day, I can be working on magazine editorials, beauty campaigns, celebrity shoots, red carpet events, and runway shows. I consult with makeup brands and help out with product development and trendspotting. Now I have taken all of this knowledge and poured it into *#BeautyUnfiltered*. It is my own recipe book of sorts. I give you the basics, and it's up to you to adjust them to your taste. Just remember that it's all about looking great in pictures and in person. It's all about embracing *#NoFilterBeauty*.

CHAPTER 1

FACE THE FACTS:

ESSENTIAL TIPS FOR FLAWLESS #UNFILTERED SKIN

Throughout my career, I've been fascinated by the look and health of skin, as well as the ongoing evolution of skincare products. I remember working with a very well-known Hollywood actress who used to be a model and whose skin was not in good shape. This was during the 90s, back when all we had to do was use foundation and powder to camouflage and cover, cover, cover. Well, that was then and this is now. I saw this actress not too long ago and her skin had completely changed; it was radiant and literally looked flawless. I asked her what her secret was, and she said it was simple — ***regular facials, the right products, and healthy living.***

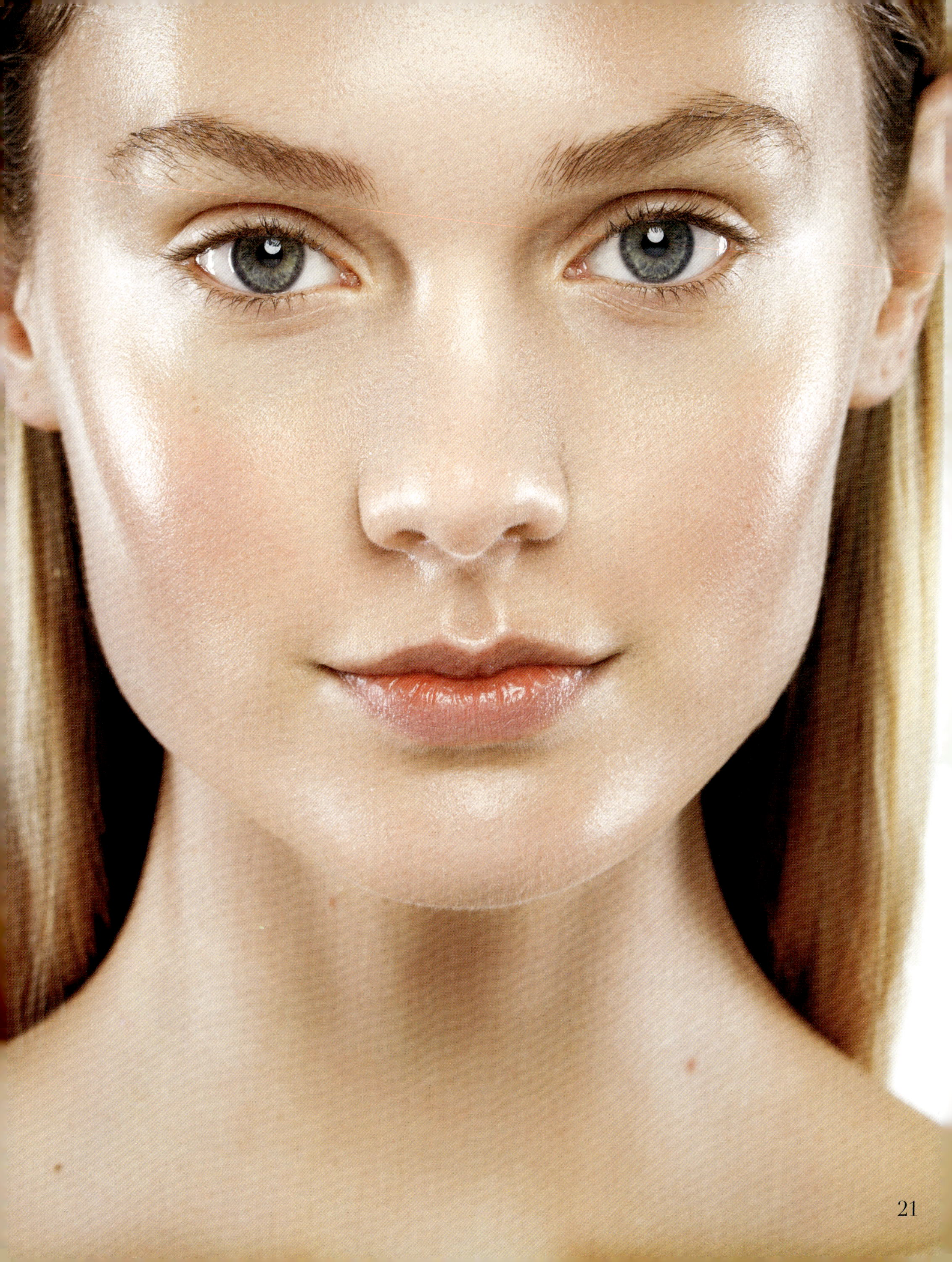

HERE, I SHARE WHAT I'VE LEARNED

I am continuously amazed by all of the new advances in skincare technology. I have had the privilege of meeting with many prominent skin specialists and scientists, so I know firsthand that when used correctly and regularly, these breakthrough products can totally transform the look of your skin.

I also share what has worked for me and my clients. Ingredients, quality, and perseverance are all integral parts of a good skincare routine. And good genes don't hurt either! :)

Consider your skin type and remember that everyone's skin is different. Following are some basic skin types and the common concerns that come with them:

Normal:
Not prone to acne, not prone to spots, has a healthy balance of hydration and oil production.

Oily:
Shiny, acne-prone skin, may have enlarged pores.

Dry:
Skin that's tight and dehydrated. May feel itchy and flaky in certain areas. Wrinkles tend to be more visible.

Sensitive:
Easily irritated, turns red, is very sensitive to certain skincare ingredients.

Combination:
Oily on the t-zone (the forehead, nose, and chin), with dry patches around the rest of the face.

"The key to getting great results from your skincare routine is to know your skin's needs."

Stress and lack of sleep greatly affect the look of your skin and can lead to breakouts, redness, bumps, and more. Whatever you can do to relax — whether it's amping up your yoga or meditation practice, curling up with a good book, or making sure you get your eight hours each night — will show in your skin. While working in Asia, I became fascinated with relaxing facial massages. The ritual can really help you relax and unwind. Turn the page for a simple and quick version that I love to use on my clients. I also use it on myself during long flights. I usually put a little lavender or essential oil on my wrists and use a moisturizer on my face for extra hydration. Start incorporating this face massage into your skincare routine now. The circular upward motions will help any skincare product do a better job. And the added circulation will show up on your face — it's easy and you can do it yourself!

THE PERFECT PAMPERING FACIAL

Follow the arrows and use your fingertips to lightly massage in these directions. You can do this when applying serums or moisturizer. It helps to apply them evenly and it feels like you are pampering yourself at the same time.

1. Start by massaging the jaw area from your lips and chin to the outer edge of your face.

2. Follow by massaging the cheeks, using an upward and outward motion.

3. Massage the under-eye area, moving toward the forehead.

4. Massage the forehead with upward motions.

5. Massage the neck with upward motions.

6. Repeat as needed.

7. Relax!

25

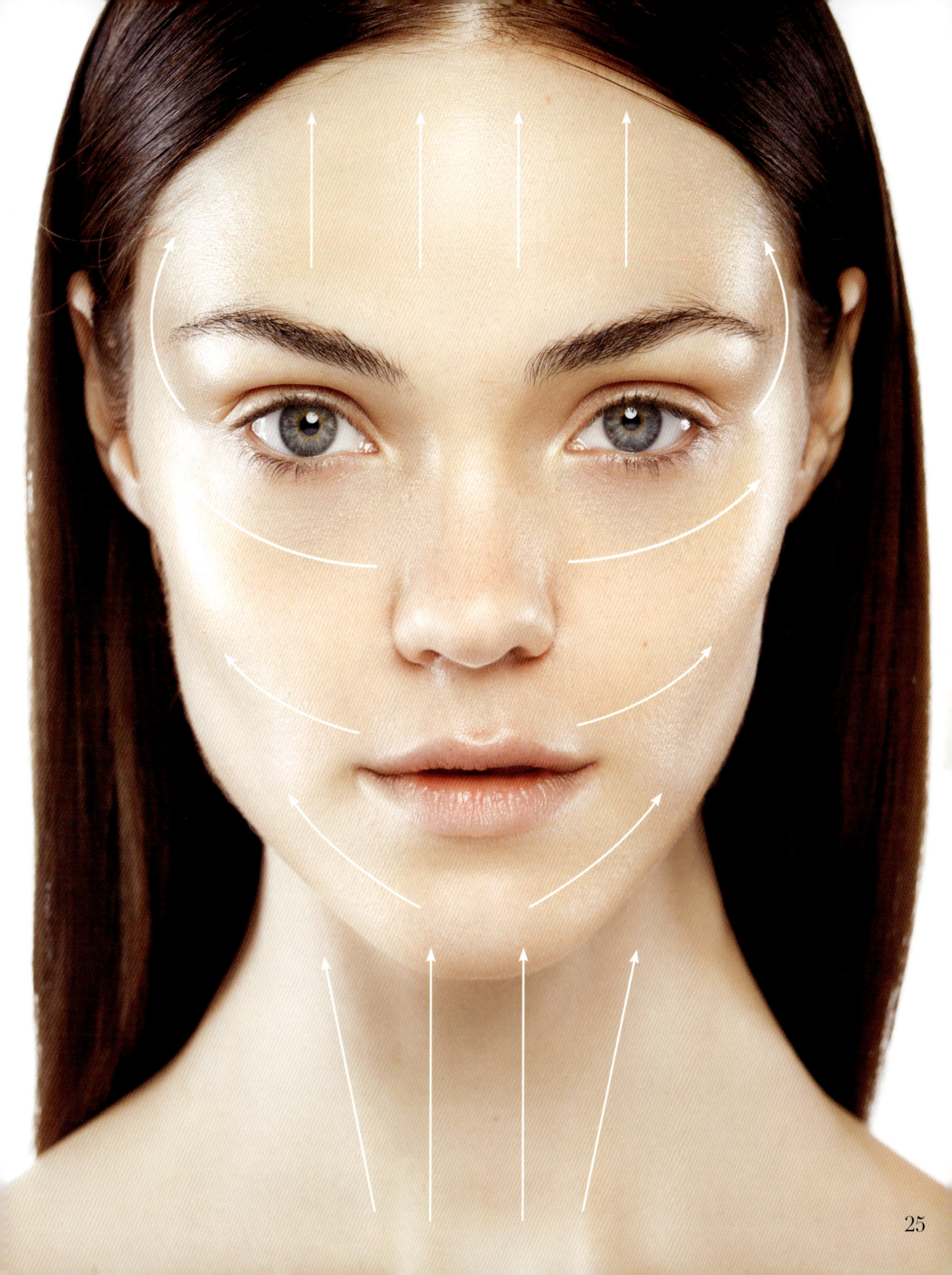

COVER UP!

SPF creams are essential, as every skin type can be affected by UVA/UVB rays. Spots, wrinkles, dehydration, and sensitivity are just some of the issues caused by sun exposure. And let's not forget skin cancer! When outdoors, remember to reapply sunscreen frequently, and to use water- and sweat-resistant formulas.

ANTIOXIDANTS ARE A *MUST*

Free radicals have been proven by scientists to heighten the effects of aging, damage skin cells, and increase the risk of skin disease. The perfect antidote for protecting against and reducing this damage? Antioxidants! Get them from a diet rich in fruits and vegetables (vitamins C and A); nuts, seeds, lean meats, and fish (vitamin E and selenium); and avocados (niacin). You should also look for those ingredients in your skincare products, along with botanicals that help shield against skin damage.

"Even if your skin is a deep tone that doesn't normally get sunburned, it is essential that you protect it from harmful ultraviolet A and B rays."

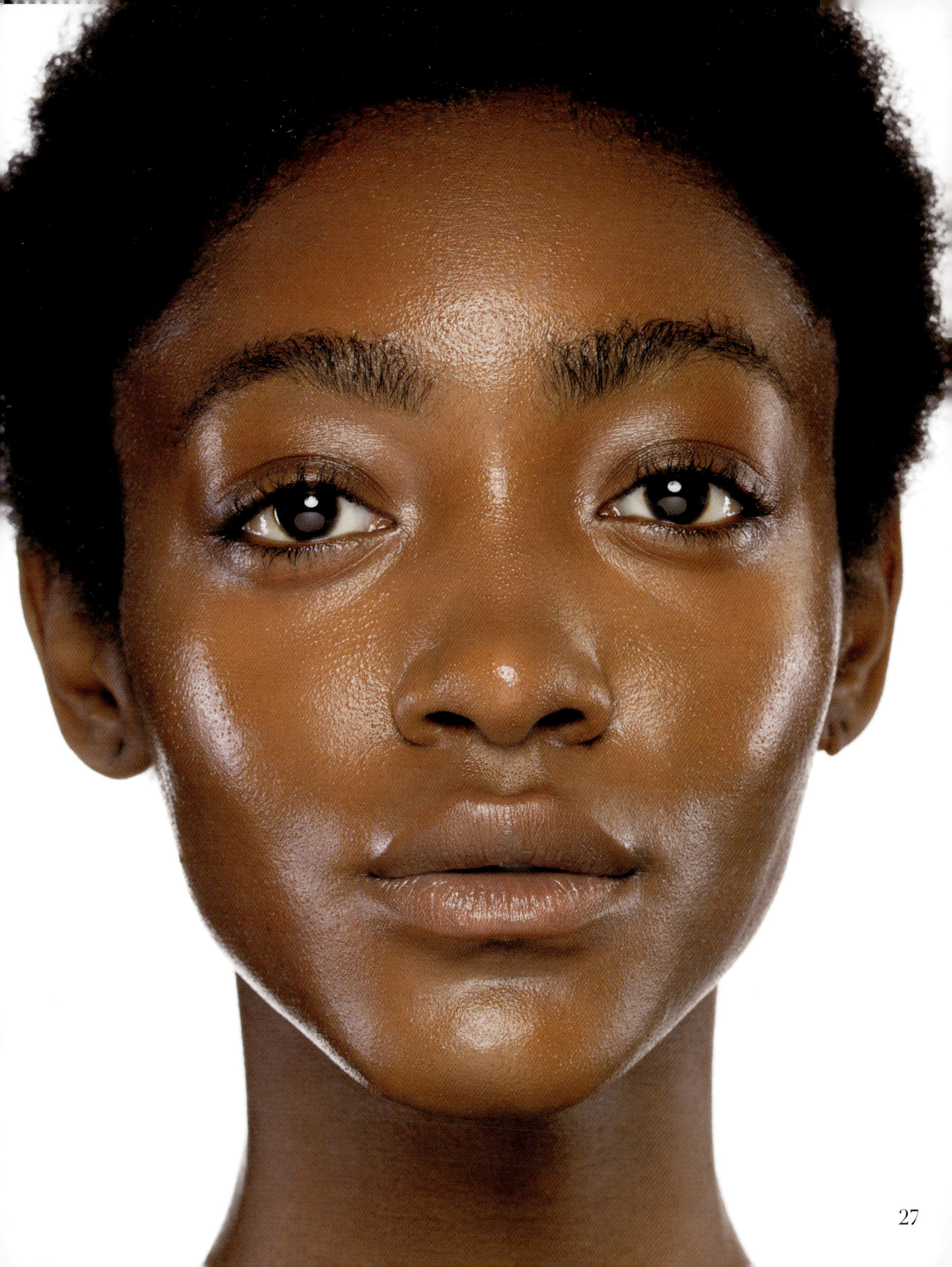

SERUMS WORK!

Serums usually contain more of the active ingredients that are so critical to preventing and treating skin damage. They're potent, technologically advanced, and should be the first thing you apply to your skin after cleansing (and before moisturizing). Think of serums as an extra skincare boost, one that's packed with potent peptides, antioxidants, and vitamins.

CONSIDER A MOISTURIZER'S TEXTURE

"Hyaluronic acid is one of my favorite ingredients for giving skin an extra boost of hydration."

Dry skin benefits from moisturizers that have creamy textures, while oilier complexions respond better to lighter lotions. Keep in mind that you might need to adjust your moisturizer type during certain seasons or after sun exposure. Use common sense and remember that it's okay to up the ante at different times of the year.

Think From the Inside Out
What you eat can have a big effect on your skin. If you struggle with redness and irritation, try taking fish oil or probiotic supplements. Probiotics are the naturally occurring "good bacteria" that live in your gut. Increasing this "good bacteria" helps the digestive system fight inflammation, which can be the cause of many skin issues. The omega 3 fatty acids in fish oil are known to boost skin hydration and help prevent acne.

Hydrate
The first thing I do when working on a face? Hydrate it! I am always amazed at how many of us walk around with dry, dehydrated skin. Aggressors such as the environment, smoking, or drinking alcohol and/or too much caffeine can dry up your skin and encourage premature aging. The bottom line? Drink plenty of water and always use a hydrating face cream, no matter what your skin type.

"I compare using serums to drinking a cold-pressed vegetable juice or adding an extra vitamin boost to your morning shake."

NO STRIPPING ALLOWED!

Some people like their skin to feel "squeaky clean" after they wash it, but lots of times this means that they are over-exfoliating — and in turn drying out — their skin. You should pay special attention to cleansers, masks, and face creams that have ingredients that can strip the skin of essential oils, such as retinol or salicylic acid. Always use these products in moderation.

Limit face peels and heavy masks to once or twice a week, and remember not to go crazy with your cleansing regime. Also, hot water dries your skin, so use lukewarm water to wash your face. If your skin feels very tight after cleansing, you are most likely scrubbing it too hard or using the wrong product for your skin type.

Day vs Night Formulas
There are many differences between day and night skincare formulas, but here are the basics (and why you should use them in the proper order).

Day creams usually contain SPF and ingredients that protect and retain skin firmness, as well as restore your skin's natural moisture levels. Look for the right formula for your skin type.

Night creams promote the recovery of skin while you sleep. They are restorative and include ingredients that work best at night, such as retinol, certain antioxidants, and peptides.

"Vitamin C is a great ingredient that helps to protect and repair collagen. It's also a great skin brightener. Try to get it in its purest form, such as a powder, ampule, or square that you open and use immediately, as vitamin C oxidizes quickly."

EYE CREAMS WORK

Dark circles, dryness, and puffiness are the common issues that eye creams combat. People always want to know how to conceal dark under eye circles; I always start by asking if they are using an eye cream. Odds are they are not, which is a big mistake. With continued use, eye creams smooth fine lines and decrease dark circles, which means your concealer has to do much less work!

"Make vitamin C a part of your skincare routine. You will see a difference. It's worked for me and everyone I've recommended it to."

YES, IT'S FOR GUYS, TOO!

Face It — Guys Need Skincare, Too.
An easy regimen that starts with a facial cleanser, and is followed by a serum and a moisturizer with SPF, is essential.

"It is crucial for men to use the right moisturizer after shaving in order to prevent redness and irritation."

Never Too Young to Start
Teenagers have to deal with so many changes, and often it's hard for them to stick to a good skincare routine. If you're a teen and you struggle with blemishes, or are prone to dry or oily skin, it's important that you cleanse and moisturize regularly — it's not enough to simply cover up problem areas with makeup and slather your skin with over-drying anti-acne cream. Be consistent, diligent and patient, and your efforts will pay off.

Look for oil-free cleansers that are gentle enough to use twice a day. Avoid products that contain harsh chemicals — not only will they make your skin feel tight and dry, but they'll also cause your skin to produce excess oil (and that's the last thing you want!).

Appropriate moisturizers for younger skin are lightweight and oil-free. Look for non-comedogenic formulas that soothe the skin and won't clog pores.

If you have acne-prone skin, look for products that contain a small amount of salicylic acid, which helps fight acne by reducing redness and unblocking clogged pores.

"Keep it simple and pay attention to your skin's needs. Develop a solid skincare routine and stick with it — you will thank yourself later!"

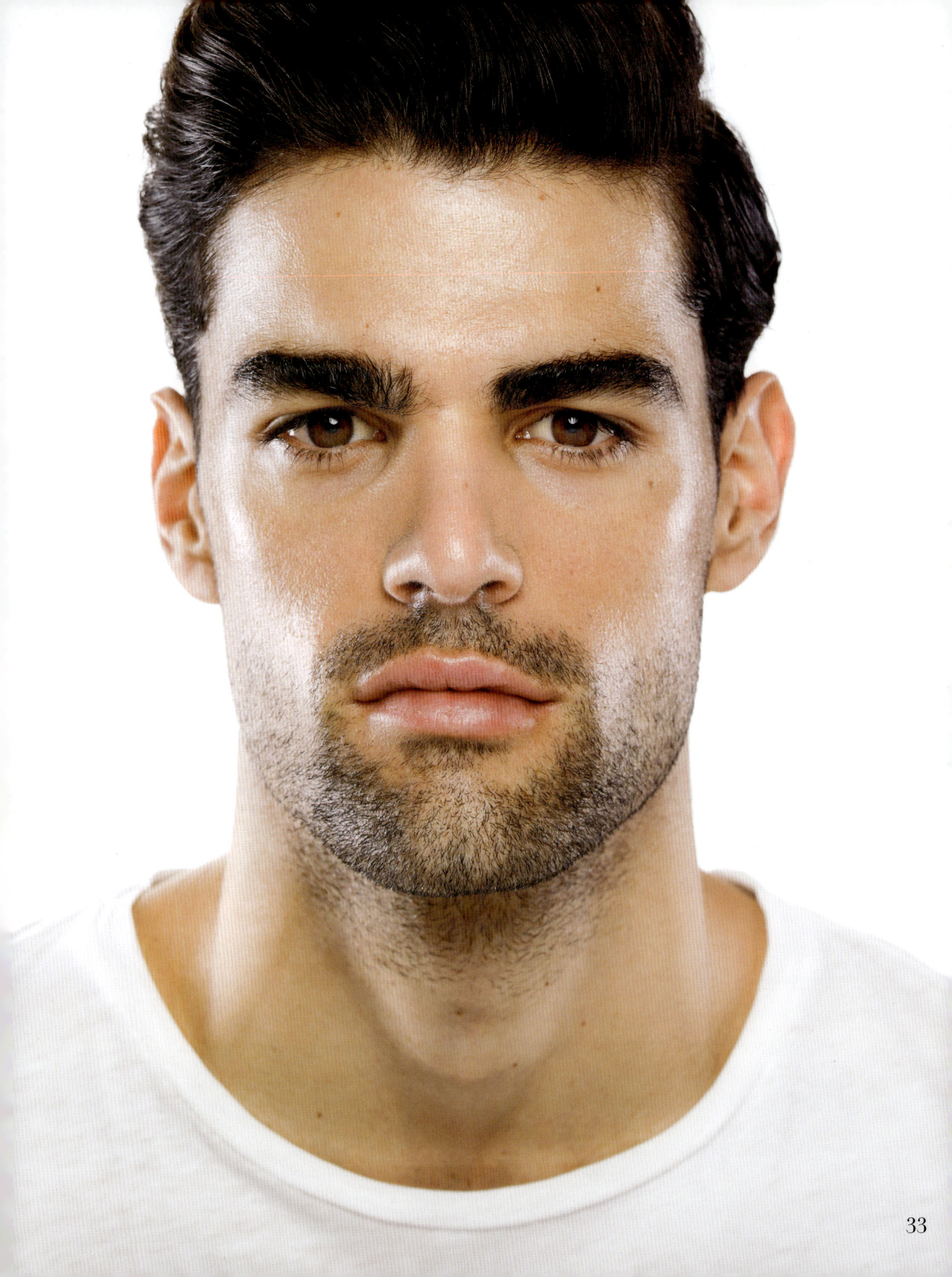

CHAPTER 2

ACE THE BASE: *CREATING A #SEAMLESS COMPLEXION*

35

"WHAT IS THE NUMBER ONE MAKEUP MISTAKE?"

That's one of the most frequently asked questions I receive. My answer usually involves foundation — people tend to either use too much or the wrong shade.

The goal of foundation is to smooth out skin discolor-ation and imperfections, and create a seamless look on your face. Which means that you want your foundation to look like your own skin — only better! In order to do that, you need to know a little bit about the different foundation formulas and how to select the one that's right one for you.

Foundation Type

Liquid

Mineral Powder

Cream-to-Powder

BB/CC Creams

Stick/Cream Foundations

Tinted Moisturizer

What Does It Do Best?	**How Do You Apply It?**
Comes in light, medium, and full-coverage, as well as matte and dewy formulas. They are suited for all skin types.	Use a brush or sponge for full-coverage; a wet sponge or your fingertips for a more sheer look. Usually about a quarter size is sufficient for the whole face. Spread from the center of the face toward the jawline and the forehead.
Provides light to medium coverage. Works best on skin that's sensitive, acne-prone and/or has rosacea.	Apply with a brush and spread onto the face in circular motions. Start at the center of the face and apply light layers, if needed.
Designed to control oil and give the complexion a matte appearance. Glides on like a cream, but dries to a powder finish. Creates medium-to-full coverage and works best on oily skin.	Apply with clean fingers or a sponge. You can also use a foundation brush to blend and diffuse the product in certain areas on the face.
"Beauty Balms" and "Complexion Correctors" offer light coverage replete with good-for-your-skin ingredients, as well as SPF. They're the perfect product if you don't require too much coverage but want to even out skin tone.	You can use your fingers, a brush, or a sponge—it depends on the kind of coverage you are looking for. The point of these balms is that are easy to apply, so use whatever tool works best for you! Make sure that the shade you choose is not too light, as SPF can have a lightening effect on the skin. The best way to test this is to try the shade on and let it sit on your skin for a few minutes to make sure it's a good match.
Foundation sticks usually provide the most coverage, but can look a bit unnatural. They are often used on stage or as special effects makeup. Apply sparingly and mix with a little moisturizer to make the coverage appear more natural.	For heavy coverage, apply with a dry sponge, then use your fingers or a damp sponge to blend. You can also use a foundation brush for a lighter application. Just remember to blend well, as stick formulas can look cakey and mask-like if they are not diffused properly. Stick foundations are also great for covering dark hyperpigmentation, scars, or discoloration.
These are ideal for a no-makeup look or for someone who likes natural-looking coverage with a sheer finish.	Apply with your fingertips, the same way you would apply your daily moisturizer.

TAKING IT TO THE *NEXT LEVEL*

Think of the following two steps as the base and top coats that you'd apply to your nails. They may seem like extra work, but using them will seal your look and give your makeup major staying power.

Foundation Primers
A primer may feel like an annoying extra step in your beauty routine, but the truth is that they are essential for improving the look of your makeup and making it last. There are color correcting primers, as well as formulas with added silicon for smoothing fine lines and imperfections.

Finishing and Setting Sprays
A finishing spray is designed to keep your makeup from melting, whether you're dealing with a hot, humid summer day or you're dancing up a sweat. It's also great for toning down over-powdered skin, and will help shimmer stay in place on your eyes and cheeks. Apply the finishing spray over your face in a "t" motion (for the t-zone) and an "x" shape (for the rest of the complexion) to make sure you cover the whole face.

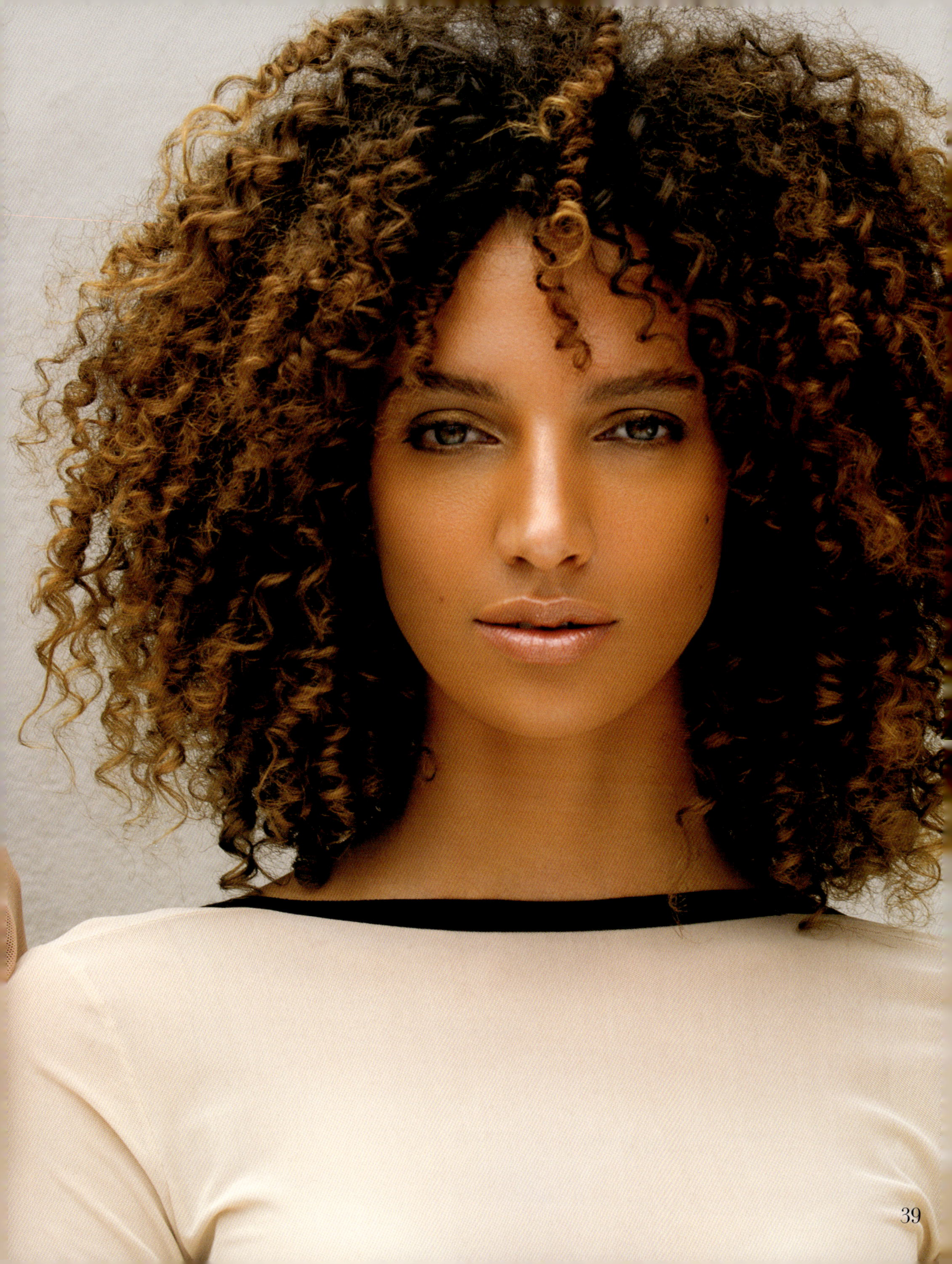

THE PERFECT MATCH

"How do I find the perfect foundation shade?"
This is another one of those questions that I'm asked all the time. The answer involves a few essential, tried-and-true tricks.

Find the Right Light
When looking for a matching foundation, try to test them in the best light possible. Ideally, you want to have a sunny window behind you and a mirror in front of you. The goals is to find one or two shades that seamlessly sink into your skin, so that the foundation appears to be a part of your natural complexion.

Know Your Undertone
Determining your skin's undertone, which is the color of your skin from beneath the surface, is essential for finding the right foundation. There are three different types:

Cool (Ivory):
Your skin turns bright pink or red when out in the sun without protection; your complexion is ruddy and has hints of blue and/or pink. Look for foundation in Ivory or Porcelain shades. Veins on wrist are usually blue or purple.

Neutral (Beige):
Your skin has no obvious pink or sallow undertones; its natural color is more evident. Try mixing foundations.

Warm (Bronze):
Your skin stays the same, freckles, or tans when out in the sun; your complexion skews yellow, sallow, peachy, or golden.

Porcelain	Ivory	Warm Ivory
Beige	Warm Beige	Natural
Golden	Almond	Chestnut

MY FIVE FOUNDATION APPLICATION TIPS

1. Pick at least three shades of foundation. With a Q-tip, apply one line of each foundation shade just below and in front of the ear. The shade that disappears into your skin will be your true match. It's important to note that most people need to try a few shades of foundation, as results may vary depending on the time of year and the condition of the skin. It's always good to have a couple of options.

2. Compare the shade to the rest of your body and make sure that your face matches.

3. The higher the pigment of your skin (the more bronze it is in color), the more hues you'll have in your complexion. For instance, it is very common for darker-skinned women to have skin that's lighter in the center of the face and darker around the perimeters. In this case, you'll want to find complementary foundation shades with the same undertones that are just a little bit darker or lighter, and blend them into your main foundation.

4. Slow down! In order to find an accurate match, you want the shades that you are testing to settle into the skin. So wait a few seconds and let the the color sit before making a decision.

5. The higher the level of coverage (yes this is very much an #unfiltered tip!), the more important it is to find a close match that looks natural. Don't rely on selfies to match your foundation — make sure you perform these steps in person and in natural light.

Skin Matching Tips

- Wear white or hold a sheet of white paper under your chin so that you don't have any color reflecting onto your complexion as you try to match foundation shades.

- Just below and in front of the ear is my favorite place to test out foundation shades, as this is where the neck and the jawline meet.

- Don't test around scars or blemishes. You want to match the overall shade of your complexion, so steer clear of problem areas that may be discolored.

FOUNDATION APPLICATION 101

Dot It
On clean and moisturized skin, dot a dime-sized amount of foundation onto any place that needs more coverage — usually the nose, chin, and/or forehead.

Blend It
Start at the middle of the face and move outward. Use a foundation brush, a sponge, or your fingers. Blend with downward strokes, which will help to flatten tiny facial hairs. Blend, blend, and did I say blend?

Seal It
Add concealer, apply blush and/or bronzer, and follow with a light dusting of powder on the t-zone. Follow with a light mist of a finishing spray for a look that lasts.

Conceal It
I like to begin with foundation and follow with concealer for a perfect and flawless application. Foundation helps cover imperfections, so you will need less concealer when foundation is applied first.

that's slightly lighter (to highlight). If you have specific areas of concern, then you should also include a corrector to help counteract these problem spots. I know it seems like a lot of products, but if used correctly, you will only need a tiny bit of each. And with practice, you'll be able to apply them very quickly and reap the benefits almost instantly!

Two Steps to Expert Concealing

1. Correct
Start by using a corrector to neutralize problem areas. A peach or salmon shade works great for light-to-medium skin tones, while a deeper yellow/orange color will help with deeper skin tones. Follow by using concealer on top of the correction.

Color Corrector Basic Shades and What They Do

Green Neutralizes red

Lavender Brightens dark areas

Yellow Neutralizes blue/purple

2. Conceal
Use a concealer that's as close to your natural skin tone as possible, which will help hide imperfections on the face. These products offer a little more coverage than foundation; using a shade that's close to your skin tone will cover, rather than highlight, any problem areas.

CONCEALER

- When covering up dark circles or imperfections, think of concealing and highlighting as two separate steps.
- One of the major mistakes people make when covering up dark under eye circles is to use a concealer that looks too light under their eyes. While it's true that your concealer should be one to two shades lighter than your skin tone, that only applies when you have no dark spots to cover up. In my opinion, women should have two concealers: one that's close to their skin tone (to conceal) and one

POWDER

A powder's main purpose is to set creams and lotions. They prevent product from settling into fine lines, or slipping and rubbing off of the skin. Whether translucent or pressed, my favorite way to apply powder is to dip a large brush onto the product. Tap the excess and apply it to the t-zone. You can also use a powder puff, which will allow you to "press" the product onto the skin for a matte look. Make sure you buff it out with a brush to give the skin a more natural look.

Blotting papers are also a great tool — I use them all of the time. They are perfect for touch-ups, especially on hot days, and also help prevent powder build-up on the face.

Pick Your Powder

Translucent

Translucent powders are usually colorless and are all about texture. They are great for controlling shine and setting foundation. They contain very little pigment and give the skin a sheer look, which makes them ideal for most skin tones. Apply by pressing the powder on with a powder puff, then blend it out with a large powder brush.

Pressed

Pressed powders are more opaque and provide more coverage. It's important to avoid creating patchy looking skin, so make sure you blend pressed powder thoroughly into the skin with a large powder brush.

Illuminating

These are light-reflecting powders that give skin dimension and create a soft-focus effect. Use sparingly, as shimmery formulas tend to highlight skin imperfections. If your complexion isn't looking its best, opt for minimal shimmer.

FAKING THE TAN!

Getting a sun-kissed look is easy when you apply a bronzer to the areas of your face that the sun naturally hits. This includes the forehead, the bridge of the nose, and the tops of cheekbones. Select a color that's just a shade darker than your skin tone.

To avoid giving the skin a muddy look, use a clean brush to apply. Blend thoroughly for a natural-looking hue, and apply bronzer before cheek color to create a warm and sexy glow.

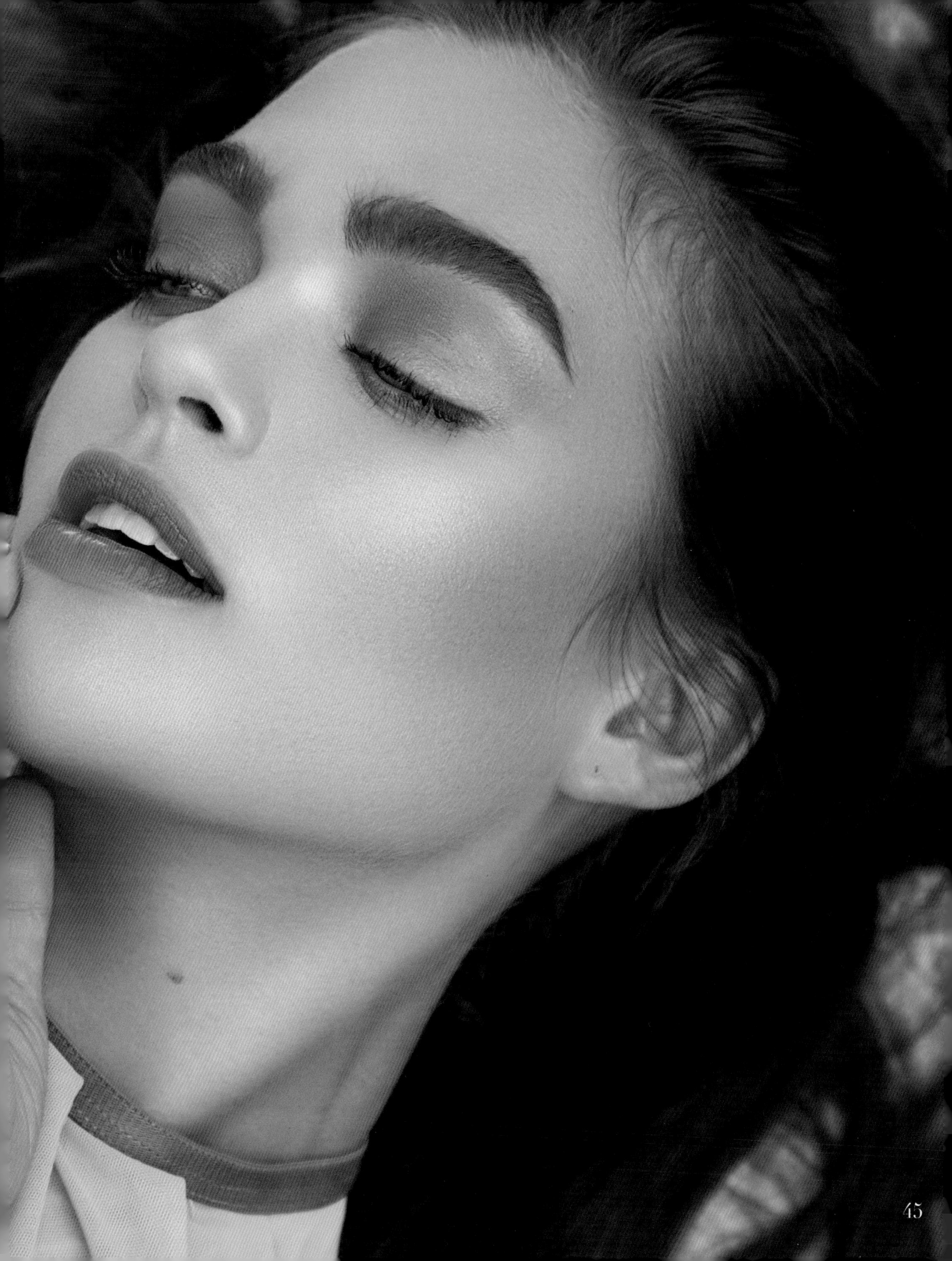

BRONZING
IN A BOTTLE

Matte bronzer is best if you're looking for a dewy, sparkle-free option. They're great for warm complexions, as well as oily skin and/or deep skin tones. They're also excellent for contouring. Apply with a large brush and blend well.

Illuminating bronzer gives you an overall warm glow, and is best for creating a radiant finish. Remember that the deeper your skin tone, the less shimmer you'll want. I love mixing an illuminating bronzer with a cheek color for a beautiful, lit-from-within look. Use a cheek brush to blend on the tops of the cheeks; dust whatever product is left on the temples and décolletage.

Powder foundation (loose or pressed) works really well to create warmth on the skin. Use a color that's about two shades warmer than your skin tone and apply the same way you'd apply a bronzer. The product is easy to blend and will often look

Liquid foundation or CC cream can give the skin a warm glow, however they can be tricky to apply as an overall bronzer unless you carry the color down to the body and find formulas that are transfer free. Make sure you apply to moisturized skin or mix with a moisturizer or body lotion to achieve a streak-free effect.

Self-tanners and spray-tan products give you an overall bronzed glow that can look very natural and be applied over the entire body. The key is to find the perfect shade for your skin (see the section on undertones for help). In my opinion, the most natural self-tanning effect is created when a professional airbrushes the whole body. Exfoliating prior to self-tanning is key to preventing patchy color.

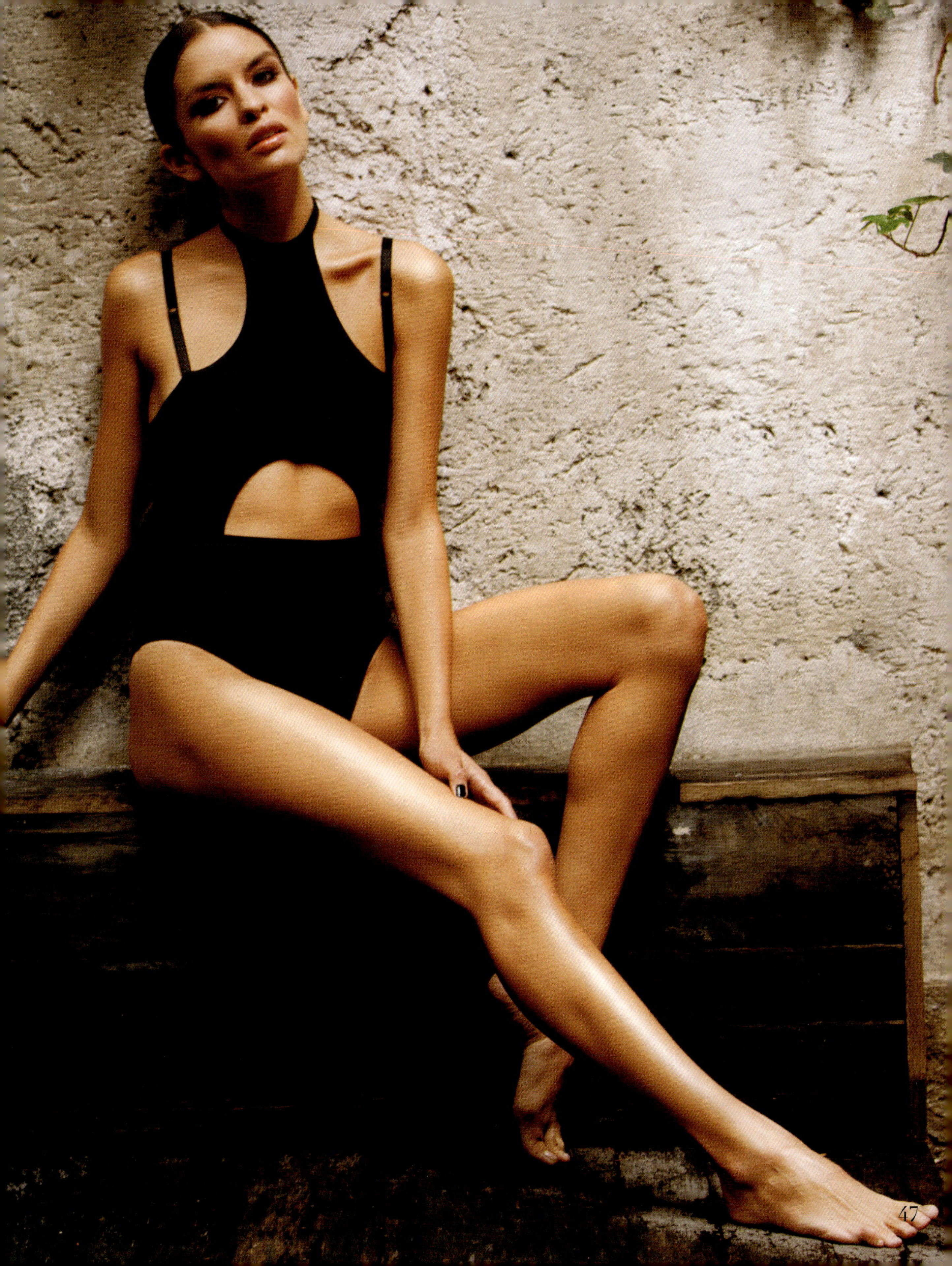

CHAPTER 3

MASTER THE SHADES
COLOR THEORY 101

Here's a quote by Picasso that a friend of mine shared with me when we were discussing color. I love it and believe that it's true.

"LEARN THE RULES LIKE A PRO, SO YOU CAN BREAK THEM LIKE AN ARTIST."
—PABLO PICASSO

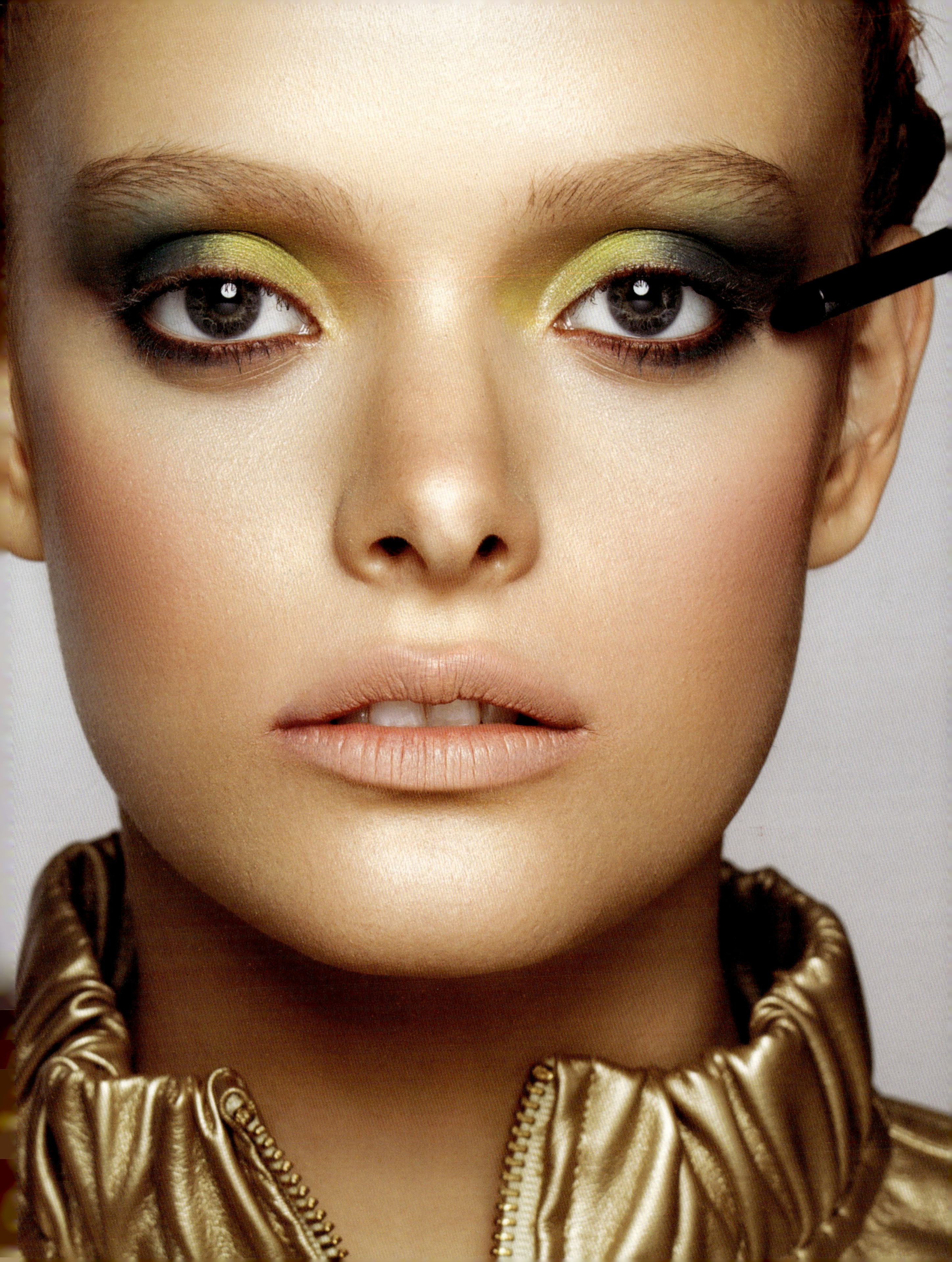

I LOVE COLOR...

It's a key part of my everyday life. Living in Los Angeles gives me the opportunity to enjoy a rainbow of gorgeous shades each day. My house has more windows than walls, and I get so much joy from looking at the sky, the trees, the water, and the overall change in light that occurs naturally throughout the day. Art is also a big source of color inspiration for me; I love clean, white environments filled with fun, bright artwork. My favorite piece? An Andy Warhol screenprint from the 1970s. It's of a geisha and combines shades of pink, blue, green, and black in striking contrast. I literally look at it every day and it fills me with joy.

This is how color works for me — I'm inspired by how it makes me feel at any given moment. Whether it's something I wear or a shade that surrounds me, I am always aware of the power that color can have on a person, and how it affects others and their perception of you.

In the next few pages, I will go over some basic guidelines about the visual effects of certain colors, and how they can be used to enhance your skin tone and eye color. But while you read them, keep my friend's quote in mind. Because while these tips do work, I also encourage you to tap into your inner creativity and think outside the box. There's nothing wrong with being a #rulebreaker and breaking boundaries. In the end, *#BeautyUnfiltered* is all about understanding your own personality and knowing what makes YOU feel good — that is how you should look at color. Know what works, but also know that it's okay to break the rules and experiment with ANY color you want!

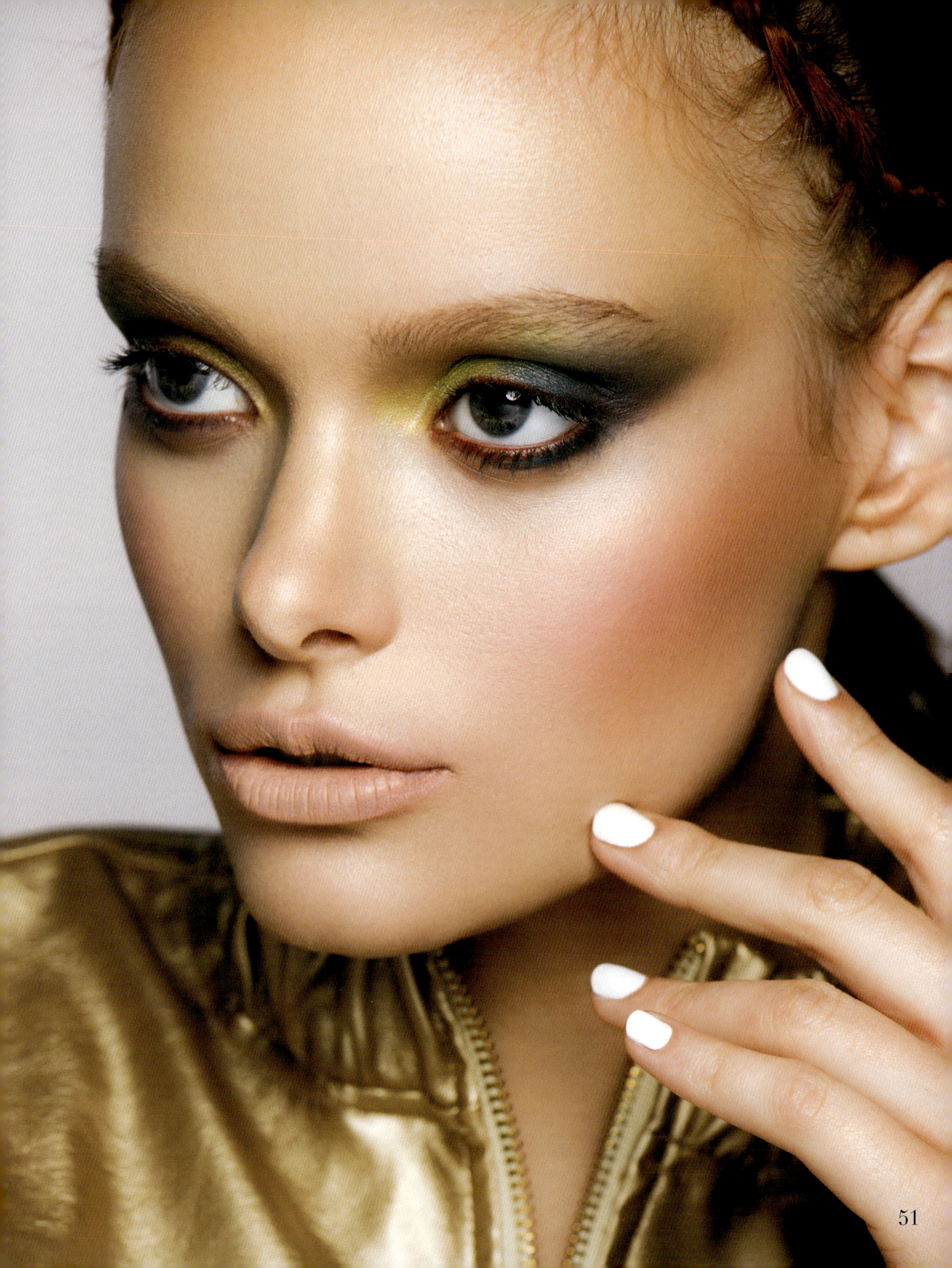

WHAT *IS* IT?

THE COLOR WHEEL

The original color wheel was based on the primary colors: red, yellow and blue. It was created by Sir Isaac Newton in 1666 and is still widely used today. A color wheel can have as few as six shades and as many as 24, 48, 96 or more.

Why Was It Invented?
A color wheel is a visual tool designed to help identify harmonious color combinations. Understanding these color relationships will help you create makeup looks that are both natural-looking and complementary.

What Can It Tell Me?
Here are the very basics to remember:
- Warm colors make up the top half of the wheel.
- Cool colors make up the bottom half of the wheel.
- Opposite colors on the wheel create contrast and appear brighter than their counterparts. They stand out and show each other off.
- Colors next to each other on the wheel usually work harmoniously together.
- Adding white to any shade will make it appear softer.
- Adding black to any shade will make it appear darker.

Using the Color Wheel to Create Your Own Palette

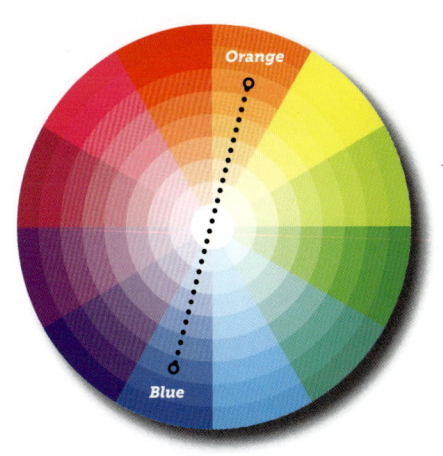

Complementary Color
Colors that are opposite each other on the color wheel are considered complementary colors

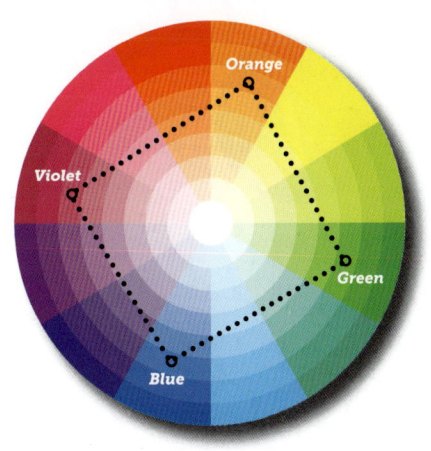

Square Color
The square color scheme is similar to the rectangle, but with all four colors spaced evenly around the color circle.

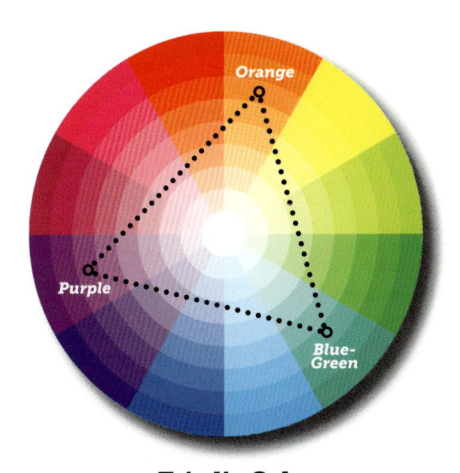

Triadic Color
A triadic color scheme uses colors that are evenly spaced around the color wheel

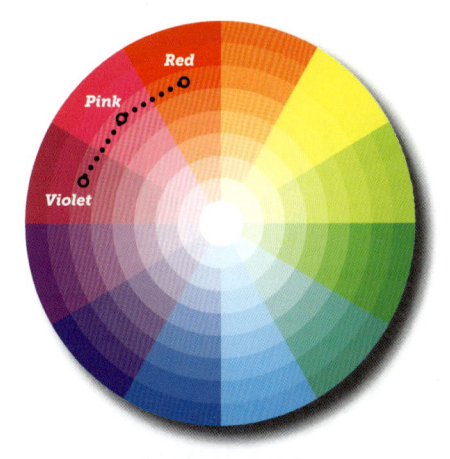

Analogous Color
Analogous color schemes use colors that are next to each other on the color wheel.

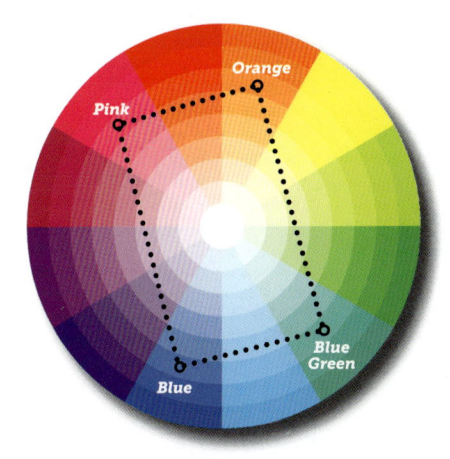

Rectangle (tetradic) Color
The rectangle or tetradic color scheme uses four colors arranged into two complementary pairs.

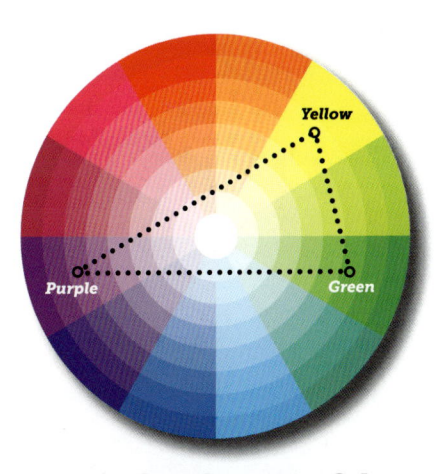

Split-Complementary Color
This color scheme is a variation of the complementary scheme—adding the two colors adjacent to its complement.

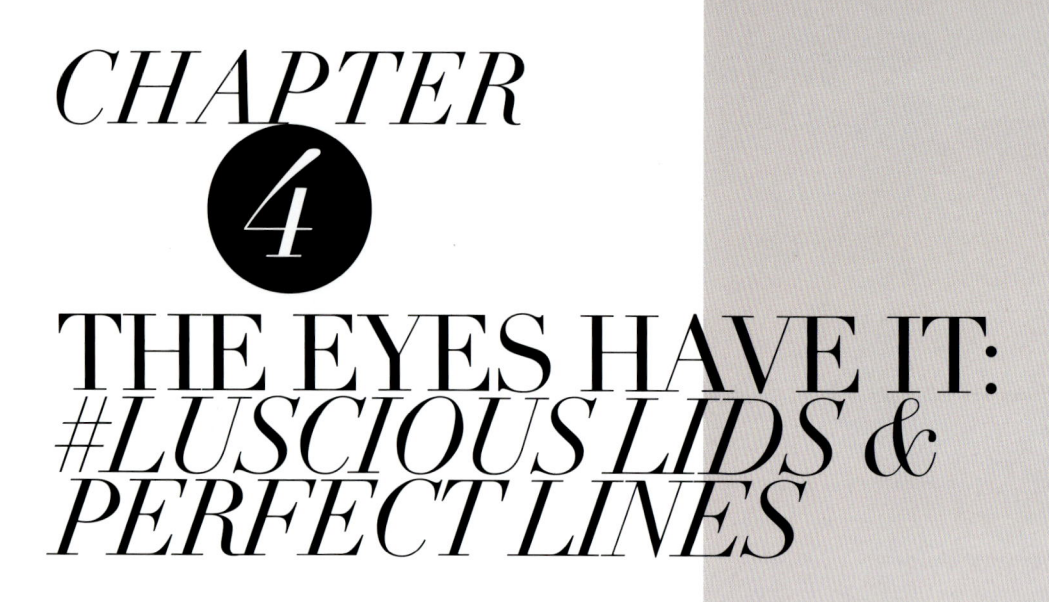

CHAPTER 4
THE EYES HAVE IT: #*LUSCIOUS LIDS* & *PERFECT LINES*

BASICS FOR CREATING YOUR OWN COLOR PALETTES

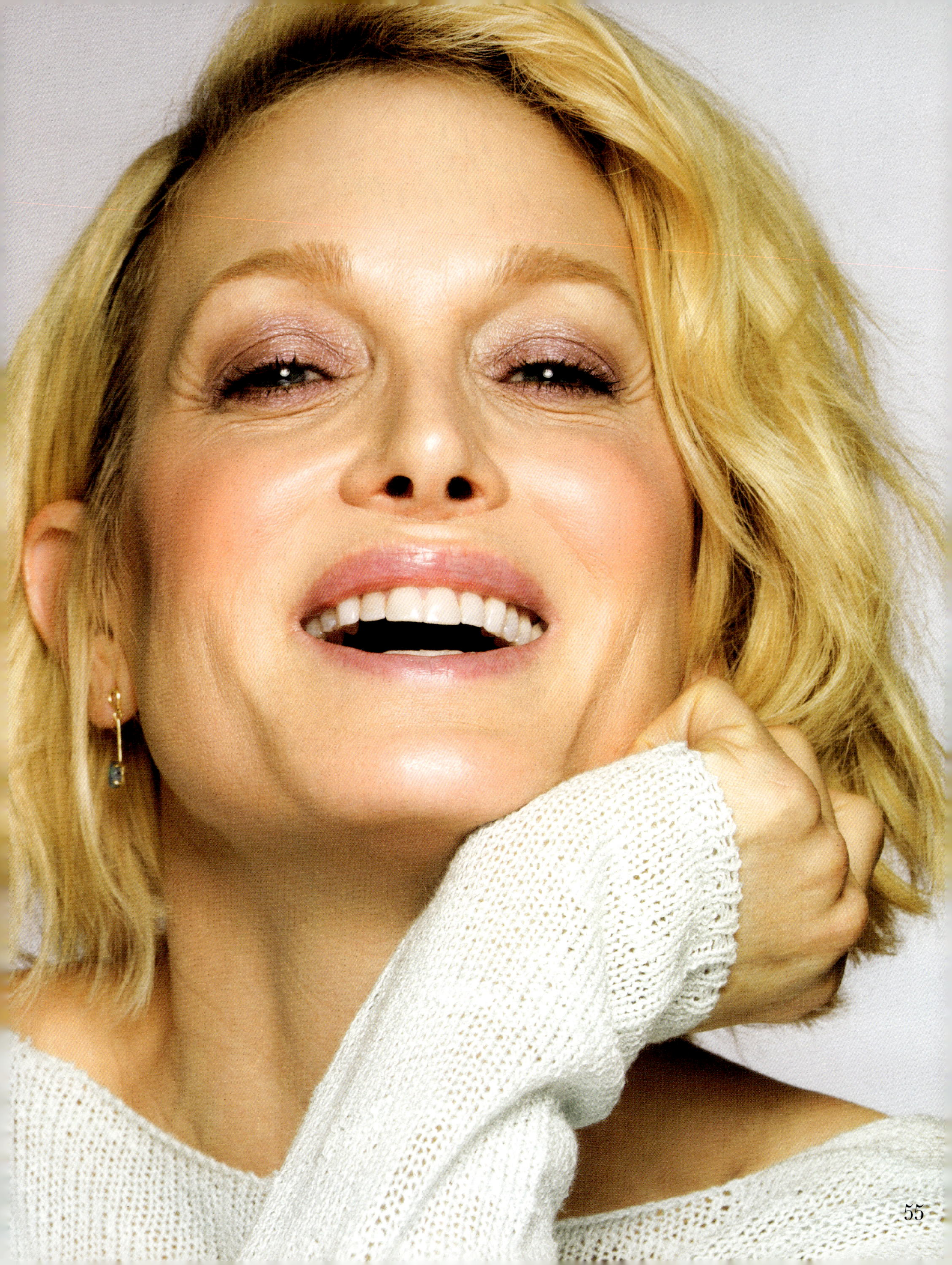

EYE SHADOW SHADOW *FOR YOUR EYE COLOR*

BROWN EYES

Of all eye colors, brown can pull off the most options when it comes to shades. Smoky blue, purple and violet are great Complementary colors (opposite on the color wheel). They will create contrast and make the eyes stand out. Analogous colors (next to each other on the color wheel) like copper and gold will bring out light flecks in the color of the eyes and create a beautiful lighter, sparkle. I'd advise staying away from pastels around brown eyes.

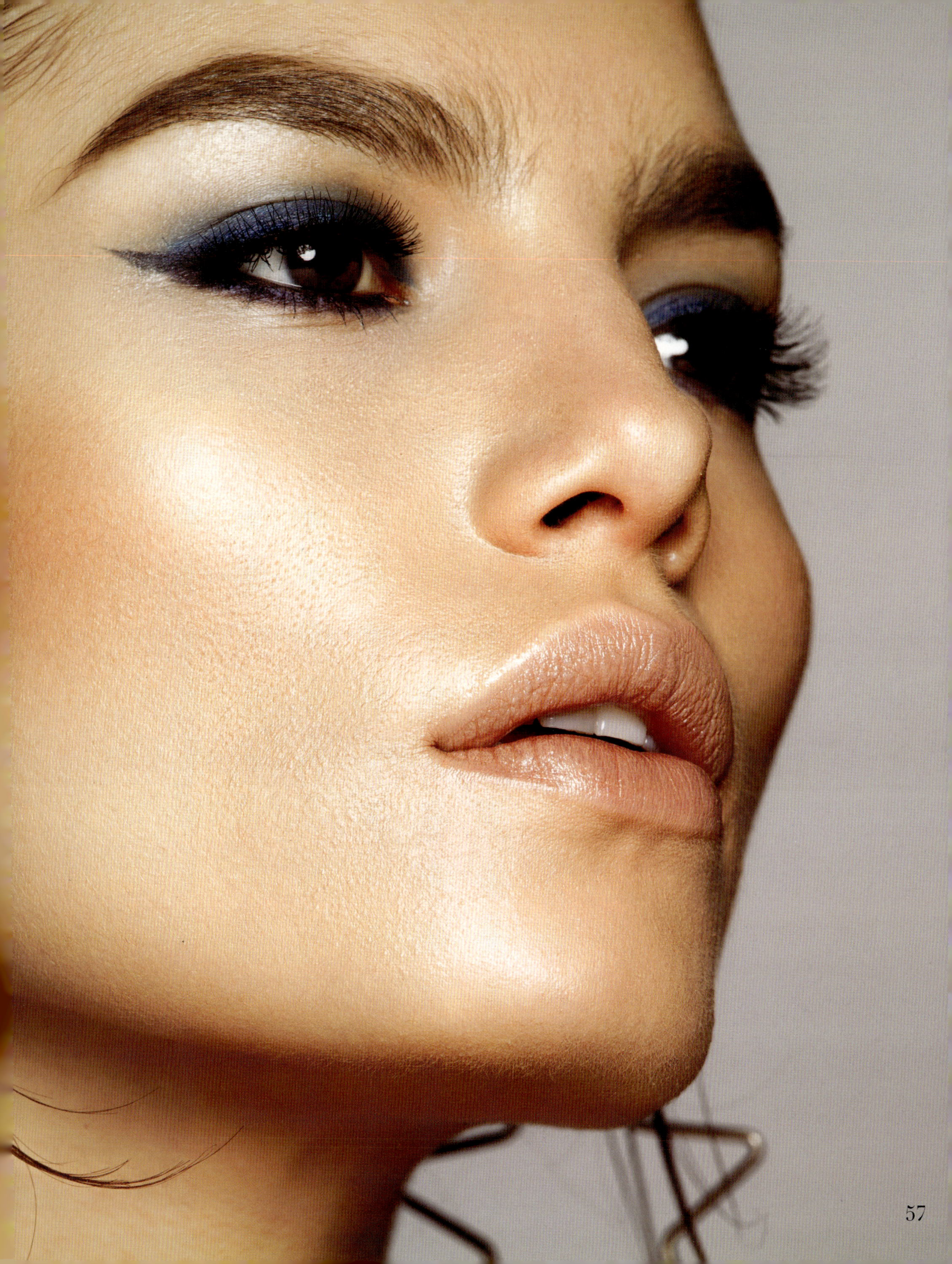

GREEN EYES

I love to highlight green eyes using complementary shades like mauve, lilac, purple, and plum. Analogous shades of brown with green and gold specks will also enhance them.

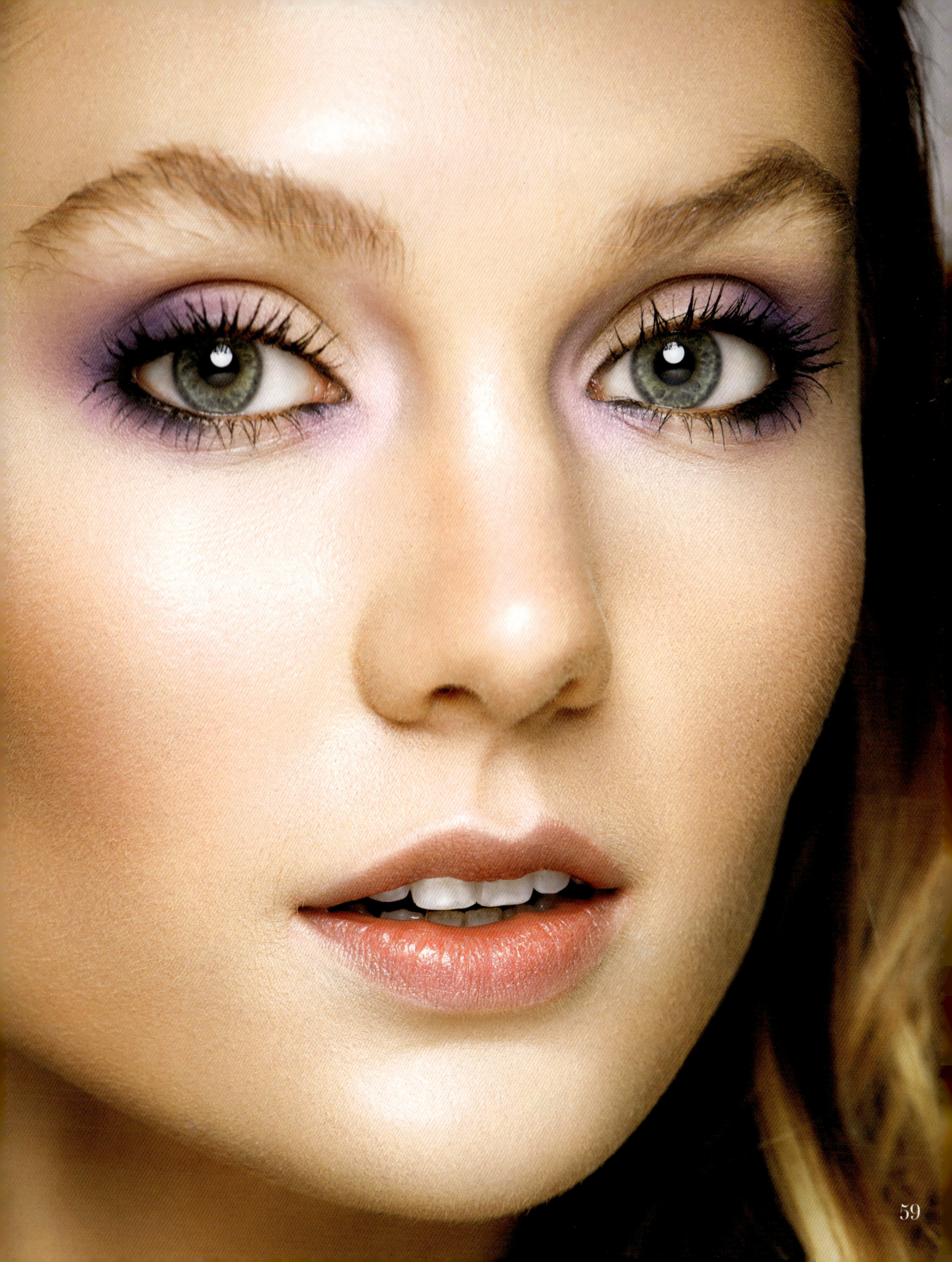

BLUE EYES

Taupe, slate gray, and coral work really well with blue eyes. Rust and terracotta will bring focus to the blues of the eyes. Lilac, amethyst, and purple will create a brightening effect. Avoid pink eyeshadow which will emphasize redness around the eyes.

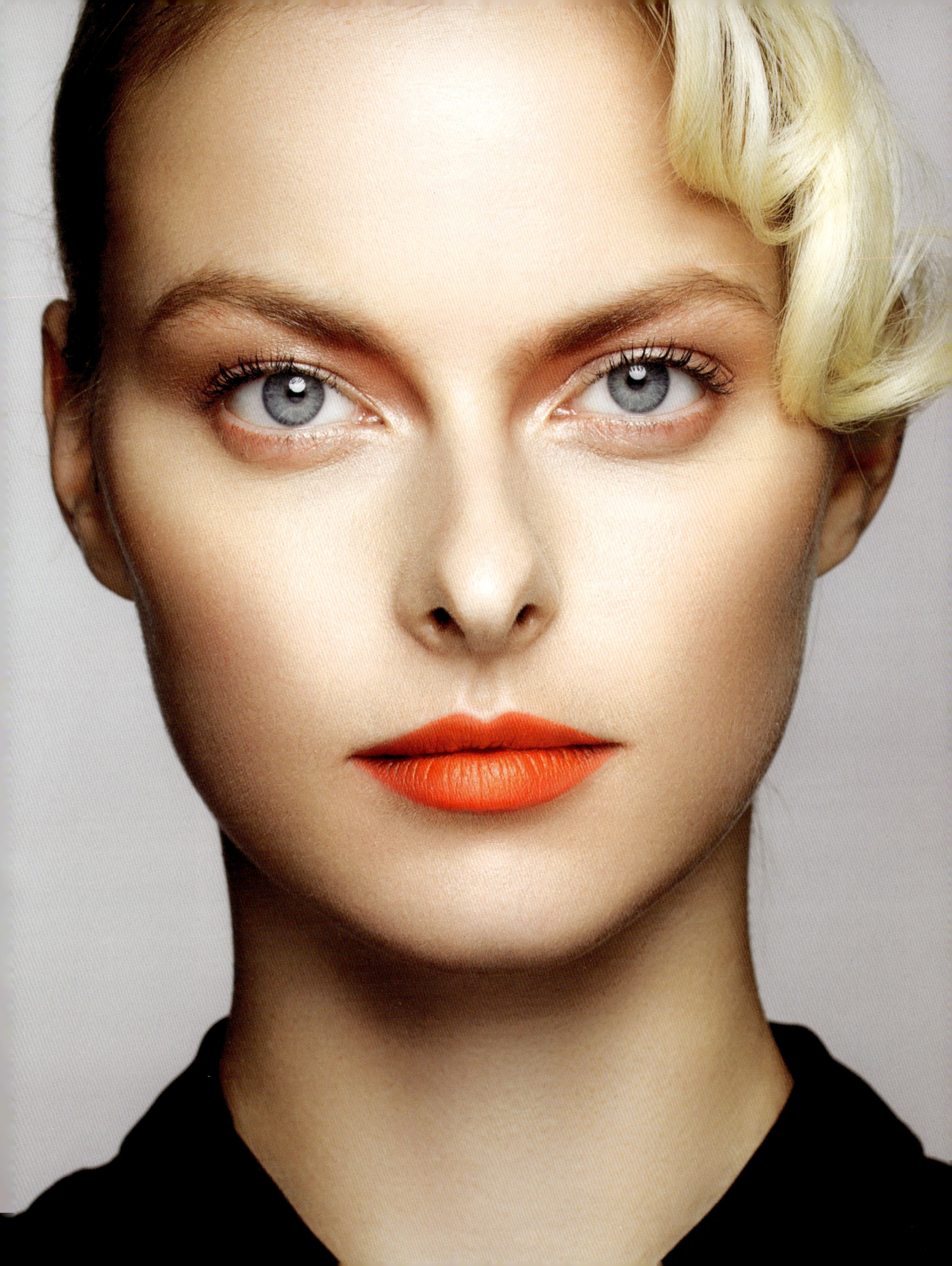

HAZEL EYES

Hazel eyes have that beautiful combination of browns and greens so any eyeshadow shade that has golden and/or green specks will make hazel eyes sparkle. Warm gold, green, and salmon tones located right next to each other in the color wheel will look beautifully in harmony with each other. Complementary shades of purples and rosegold will perfectly accentuate hazel eyes. Avoid pale blues and pinks.

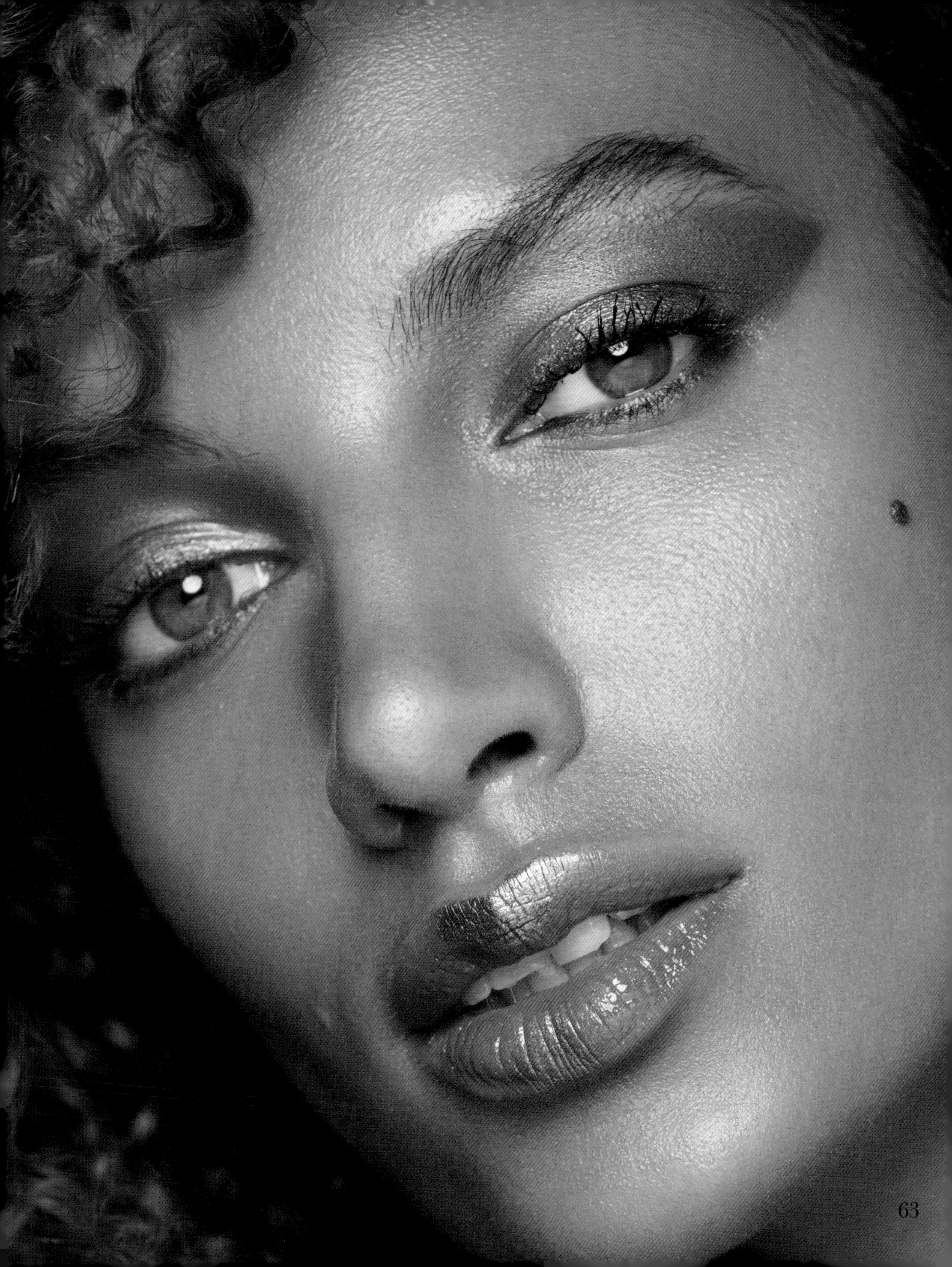

EYESHADOW APPLICATION: WHAT'S YOUR EYE SHAPE?

Almond Eyes

Round Eyes

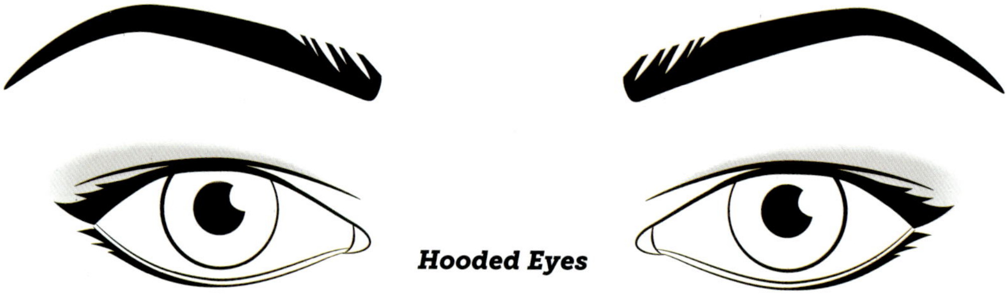

Hooded Eyes

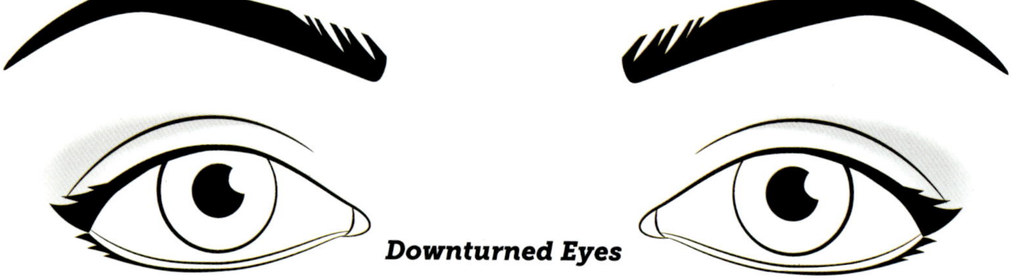

Downturned Eyes

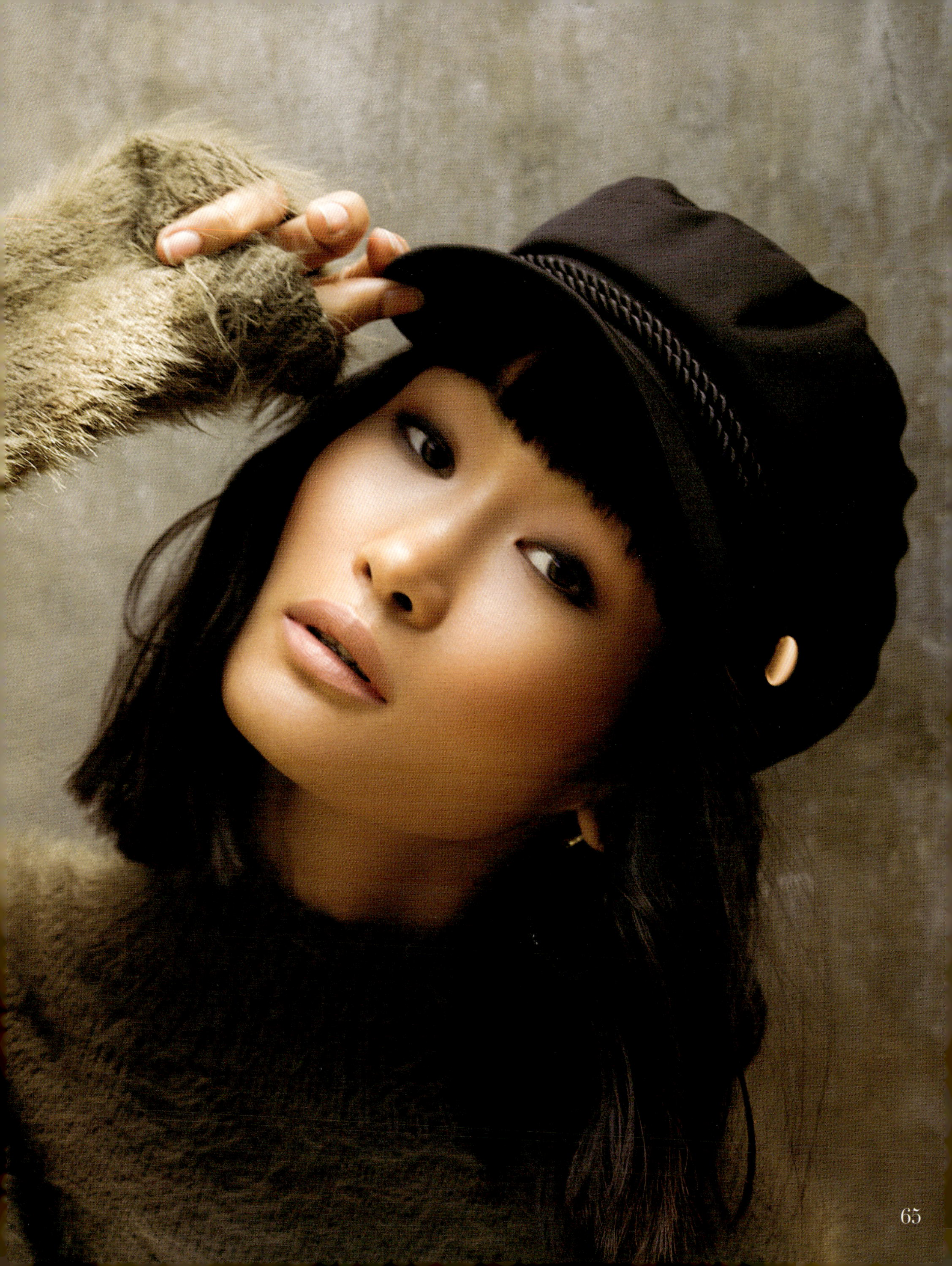

MAKEUP TIPS FOR YOUR *EYE SHAPE*

Downturned Eyes

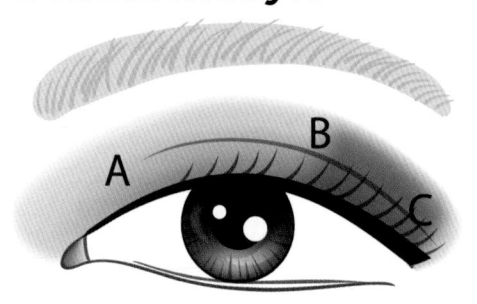

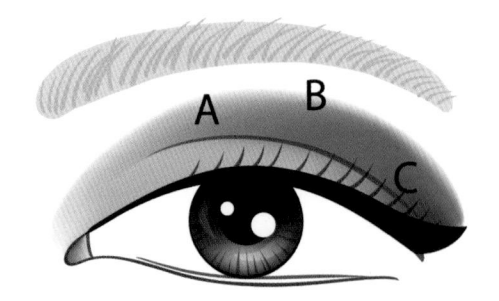

Downturned eyes drop down at the outer corners.
Top Tip! Winged and cat-eye liner looks give this eye type a lift.

Day Look
A. Dust a light flesh-toned eyeshadow all over the lids.
B. Apply a medium, matte shade to the outer corners of each crease to lift the outer third of the eye.
C. Starting at the inner corner of each eye, apply a very thin line of eyeliner, extending up from the middle of the eye to the outer corners to lift and accentuate.

Night Look
A. Dust a light and shimmery flesh-toned eyeshadow all over the lids.
B. Define the crease with a medium shade shadow, concentrating on blending upwards using a fluffy eye crease brush and concentrating at the outer corners.
C. Line the outer corners of each eye and with a smudger brush blur the eyeliner upwards into a cat-eye shape.

Round Eyes

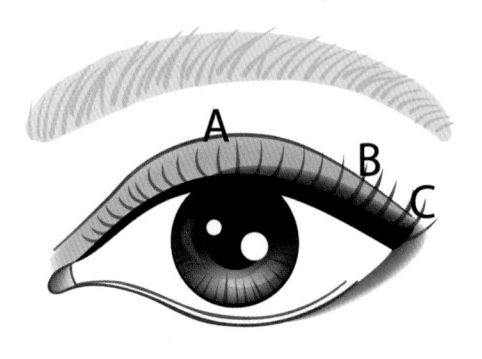

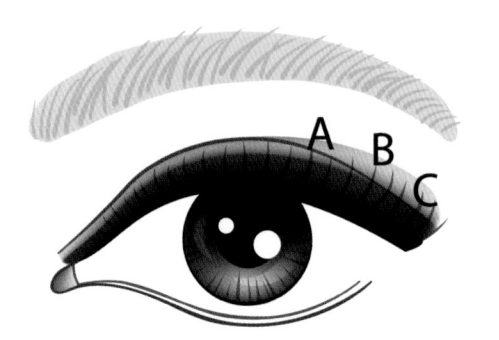

Round eyes are equally curved on the lower and upper lids. When looking straight ahead the whites are visible all the way around the iris.
Top Tip: You can elongate the eyes with eyeliner and eyeshadow to make them appear more almond-shaped.

Day Look
A. With a light flesh-toned eyeshadow, highlight the lids up to the brow bone.
B. Add a medium shade of eyeshadow to the lids and lower lash lines.
C. Use a darker shade of eyeshadow to line the upper and lower lash lines, blending with a tapered brush from the outside to the middle of the eyes.

Night Look
A. Apply a matte medium-to-dark eyeshadow shade close to the upper lash lines and blend upwards.
B. Apply a medium matte eyeshadow shade to each crease to soften the darker shade.
C. Line the upper and lower lashes with eyeliner and smudge with a brush, extending slightly at the outer corners to elongate the eyes.

Hooded Eyes

If you have hooded eyes, the lid is hidden and the natural crease is not visible due to excess skin above the eye. Eyeliner and/or eyeshadow tends to rub off easily.

Top Tip: After you've applied eye color- look straight into a mirror to check your work. If you can't see it then you might want to blend up a little higher on the lid.

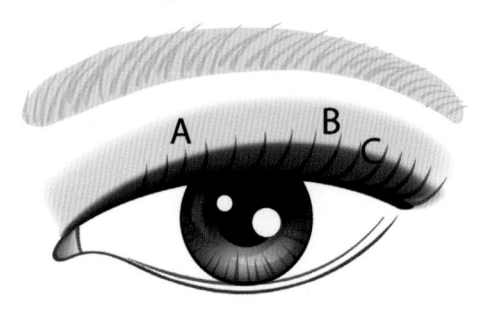

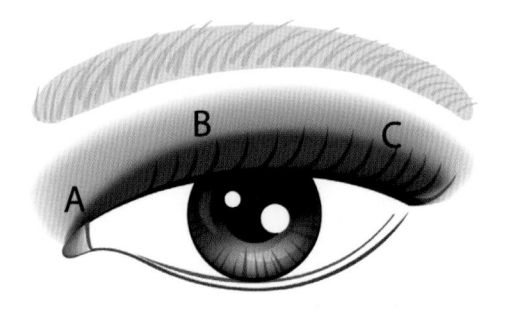

Day Look
A. Sweep a nude eyeshadow shade all over the lids, making sure that the shade is not so light that it highlights the brow bone.
B. Enhance the orbital bone areas with a medium matte eyeshadow. Blend well and carry the color to the lower lash lines.
C. Apply eyeliner to the upper lash lines, creating a very thin line right at the base of the lashes. Use a water-resistant formula.

Night Look
A. Apply a light shimmery eyeshadow shade to the inner corner of the eyes.
B. Apply a darker shade right at the orbital bone areas. Blend up and out.
C. Line the upper lash lines with eyeliner then layer with eyeshadow for a lasting effect.

Almond Eyes

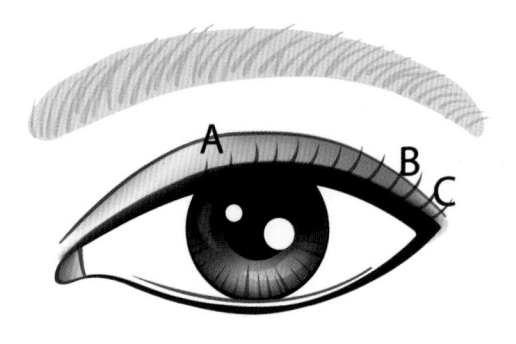

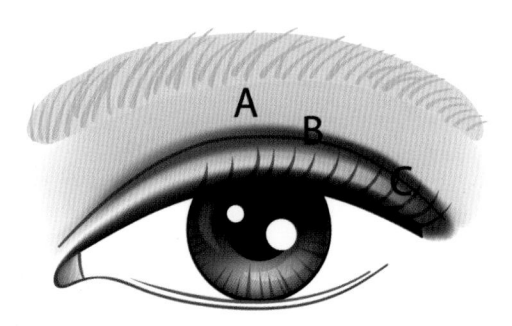

Almond eyes have a symmetrical, almond-like shape, with inner corners that taper.

Top Tip! Almost all eye makeup looks flatter almond eyes.

Day Look
A. Dust a nude eyeshadow shade all over the lids.
B. Starting from the outer corners, apply a medium eyeshadow shade from each lash line to crease.
C. Use a darker eyeshadow shade to line upper and lower lash lines. Use a tapered smudger brush that's small enough to keep the lines thin but fluffy enough to make them look smoky and not so harsh.

Night Look
A. Swipe a nude eyeshadow shade all over the eyelids.
B. Starting from the outer corners, apply a medium eyeshadow shade from each lash line to crease.
C. Define the outer third of each eye by applying a darker shade in a V shape along both the upper and lower lash lines.

HOW TO FIND THE PATHWAY *TO THE PERFECT LINE*

"Apply eyeliner after you've done your mascara to avoid smearing your lids."

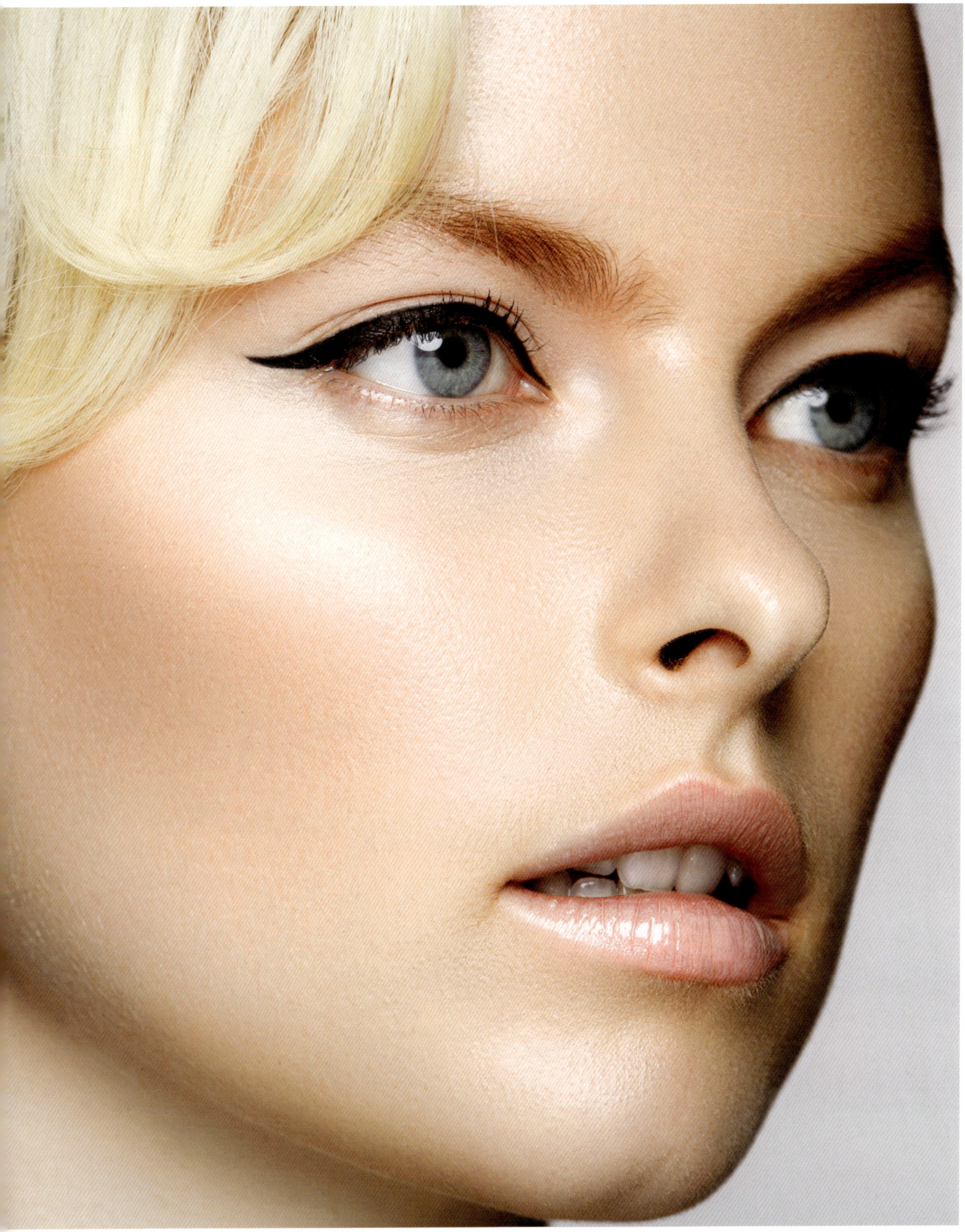

EYELINER TIPS FOR *EVERY EYE SHAPE*

Which Eyeliner is Best?
Selecting your ideal eyeliner (powder, pencil, gel, cream or liquid) comes down to a variety of factors, including how intense or soft you want the look to be and how intricate of a design you're going for. Use this guide to help you narrow down the choices and learn application tips for each.

Downturned Eyes

Use an eyeliner or an angled brush with eyeshadow to line your upper lash lines starting from the outer corners, making the line thinner as you go in. Wing it out and slightly upwards at the outer corners. Bring it in to the outer third of the lower lash line. The goal is to make the eyes look lifted.

Works best with:
Pencil, gel, liquid eyeliner, or eyeshadow.

Hooded Eyes

Apply a very thin line (tightline) to the upper lash lines, winging it slightly at the outer corners. If your hooded eyes cover the line, try creating a winged line that is straight and not as upturned.

Works best with:
Water-resistant liquid or gel eyeliner, or pencil eyeliner with a matte eyeshadow layered over it to seal the makeup in place.

Almond Eyes

Apply eyeliner to the upper and lower lash lines, wing the line if desired. Soften the lower lash line using a Q-tip or a smudger brush.

Works best with:
Gel, pencil or liquid eyeliner, or eyeshadow.

Round Eyes

Line the upper lash line with a thick line and wing it out slightly if desired. Apply liner on the lower lash line and meet the upper lash line at the outer corners.

Works best with:
Pencil, gel, liquid eyeliner, or eyeshadow.

EYELINER TYPES

Pencil Eyeliner
Although pencil eyeliners are considered by many to be the easiest option to apply, they do have a propensity to smudge and smear more easily. Avoid "raccoon eyes" by opting for a pencil that isn't overly creamy or slick, but also isn't so stiff that it tugs at skin.

Tip: To prolong wear, set pencil eyeliner with a similarly-colored powder shadow to prevent smearing.

Gel and Cream Eyeliner
Gel/cream eyeliners (the kind that come in a pot or jar) are a pro makeup artist favorite due to their rich, smooth application, long-lasting wear, and often dramatic color payoff. They are also particularly great for anyone with oily eyelids or for use in humid climates because they're less prone to smearing.

Tip: Keep in mind that pairing your gel/cream eyeliner with the right brush is half the battle.

- If you prefer a tight line, go with a flat, thin brush to distribute the eyeliner between lashes evenly.
- For a slight swoop at the outer corners, a bent liner brush with a narrow tip allows you to control the fluidity for precise application.
- For a dramatic cat-eye, a small angled brush will help you guide the shape of the line. The slanted design allows you to maneuver precise angles as well as thicker edges easily.
- Want one brush to do it all? Opt for a precise, narrow, point-style brush so you have the option of creating a thin line or building color for a thicker line.

Powder/Cake Liner
Using "cake liner" or powder eyeshadow along your lash line produces a softly blurred effect instead of the distinct line of color that other types of eyeliner achieve. Apply wet for a more dramatic effect or dry for a softer look.

Tip: You don't need to buy a special eyeliner powder. Most deeply pigmented powder eye-shadows work well in this regard.

Liquid Eyeliner
Liquid eyeliner is the most dramatic but also tends to be the most difficult to apply. It takes a steady hand but offers a precise, defined line. Liquid liners that come with a thin, fine-point or felt-tip "inkwell" brush offer the most versatility.

Tip: If you want the intricacy of a liquid eyeliner for a cat-eye look, but your hand isn't quite steady enough, use a combination of products. Place liquid eyeliner on the inner and outer corners of eyes, which is where you want the more precise detail, and use a gel or pencil liner in the areas where you want a thicker line.

Liquid formulas can create a beautiful, precise line. I recommend tugging slightly up on your eyelid to draw a sleek and smooth line as close as possible to the base of the lashes.

Cream and gel liners are usually applied with separate brushes. They have a tendency to dry quickly, which makes them a little harder to work with if you are looking for a smudged eyeliner look. Otherwise they're beautiful and usually create a dark opaque look.

Using a damp synthetic eyeliner brush that's been dipped into any eyeshadow (slightly shimmery ones work best), line from the inner corners out. For a more smudged look, use the brush dry and create a thin line along the lashes by pressing and swiping right at the base of the lashes. Can also be used over pencils or creams to set the liner into place or for a fun effect.

Thick or Thin Line?
A good place to start when considering the thickness and intensity of your eyeliner is to keep it in proportion with the size of your eyelid.

For a larger eyelid area, a thicker yet softer line of color can be extremely flattering.

For a smaller eyelid area, a thin, intense line of color defines eyes in a beautiful way.

For hooded eyes, concentrate on lining the upper lash line with a very thin line that also goes in between the eyelashes (tightlining) and follow up with a thicker mascara application to complement eyes.

For drooping eyes, start with a thin line at the inner corner and gradually go thicker towards the outer edge, swooping the eyeliner up ever so slightly. This will help visually reshape the eye, creating the optical illusion of thicker lashes while drawing attention to the high point of your eyeliner.

For any of these techniques, adding highlighter at the inner corners of eyes gives them a fresh, youthful look.

Helpful Hints for Winged Eyeliner
There are hundreds of winged eyeliner tutorials out there because as simple as it seems, this look is harder to get right than you'd think. A trick I've found useful? Use a tapered, fine point liquid eyeliner pen to draw your line (as skinny or as thick as you like) across the lash line, stopping just at th e outer corner. Then place the point of your pen where you want the tip of your wing to be and angle it back to where you want it to connect with your eyeliner. Press firmly against skin to impart the color and make sure it flows into your previously drawn line. *Voila!*

Choosing the Right Eyeliner Color
Picking an eyeliner shade is completely a personal choice and there's no universal rule to it. Different colors complement different skin tones and eye colors and if you want to go a little wild with it, I say more power to you.

Blue eyes can look stunning with a bronze eyeliner, green eyes pop with a purple-toned accent, and brown eyes can even rock a midnight blue. That said, the classics are always going to be flattering! If you want to use eyeliner to add depth to your lashes, making them appear thicker, opt for deeper shades of brown, gray, deep plum, or black.

SOME OF MY FAVORITE EYELINER LOOKS

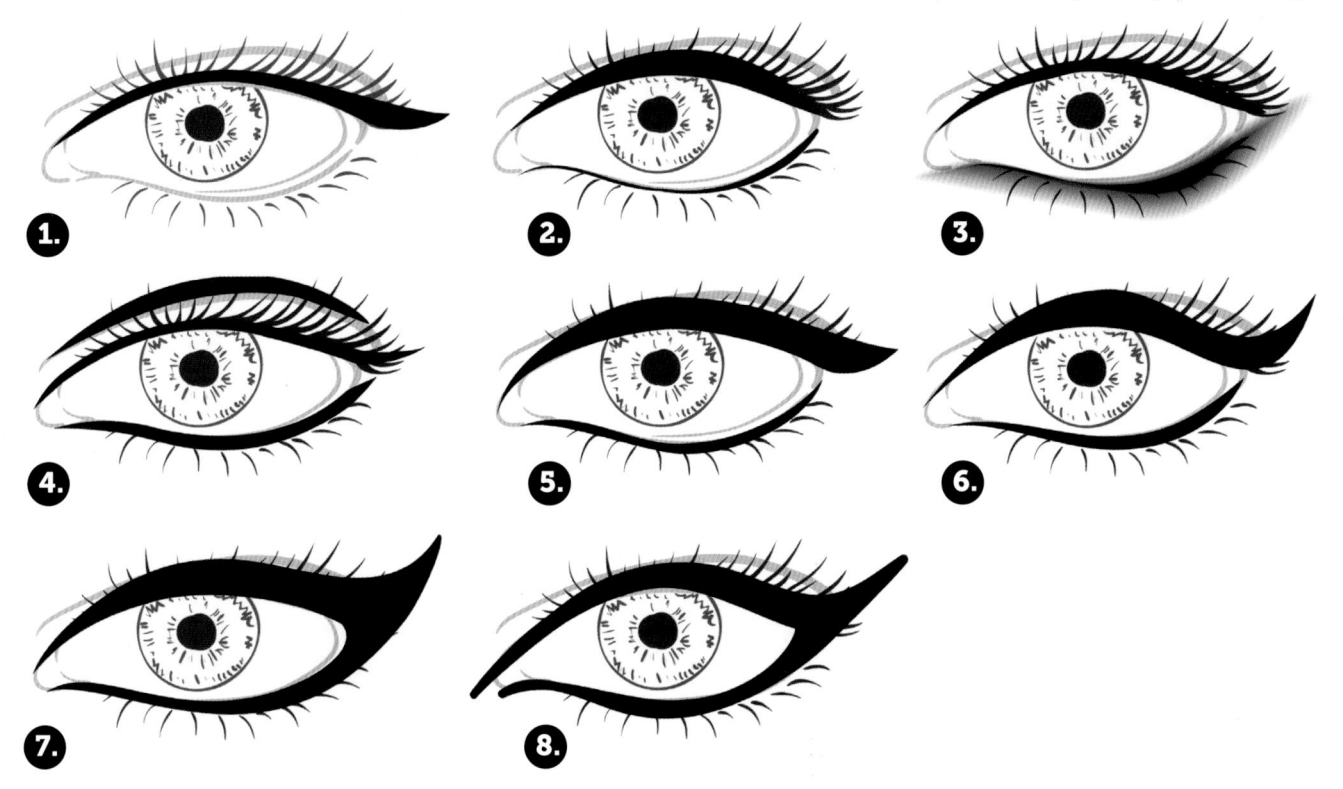

1. An elongated cat-eye works great on monolid or hooded eyes.
2. Tightlining the upper lash line makes the lashes look thicker and the eye color stand out.
3. A tightline and drop-shadow eyeliner makes the eye appear larger, and is also the perfect place to introduce a pop of color.
4. A cut crease that defines the crease area with a tightline all around the eyes has a modern '60s vibe to it. I love to do it with neutral or monochromatic shades.
5. Using gel or liquid eyeliner on the upper lash and pencil or eyeshadow eyeliner on the bottom lash creates a play on textures that gives this look a fun twist.
6. The classic cat-eye. I prefer using cream, gel, or liquid formulas for this look.
7. A full cat eye is dramatic and perfect for almond-shaped eyes, especially if you want to go for a cool, dark eyeliner look. Make sure you don't leave any visible flesh-toned gaps within the liner.
8. Gel or liquid liner that is drawn slightly in at the inner corners creates a fierce feline look. If you've mastered the cat-eye, you might want to try this application. Just make sure that the line is really thin at the inner corners and doesn't go up as far as the sides of your nose.

FIVE STEPS TO THE *PERFECT* SMOKEY EYE

Before

1. On prepped lids (eye primer is optional but strongly recommended!), dust a matte eyeshadow (here I used a matte pink) from lash line to crease and carry it to the lower lash.

2. Swipe a copper brown eyeshadow at the outer corners of the eyes and lower lashline. Next, coat your bottom lash line with a black or brown eyeliner pencil.

3. Then, with an angled eyeliner brush, soften the line and carry it to the upper lash line. Layer a darker (shimmer or matte) eyeshadow over the eyeliner and blend the two shades up and over the lid and along the bottom lash line with an angled eyeliner brush.

4. Rim the inner lash lines with a black or brown pencil for more definition and depth. Finish with two coats of black mascara on both top and bottom lashes.

5. Brush the eyebrows in place and follow with a brow mascara to give them a slight tone and enhance their shape.

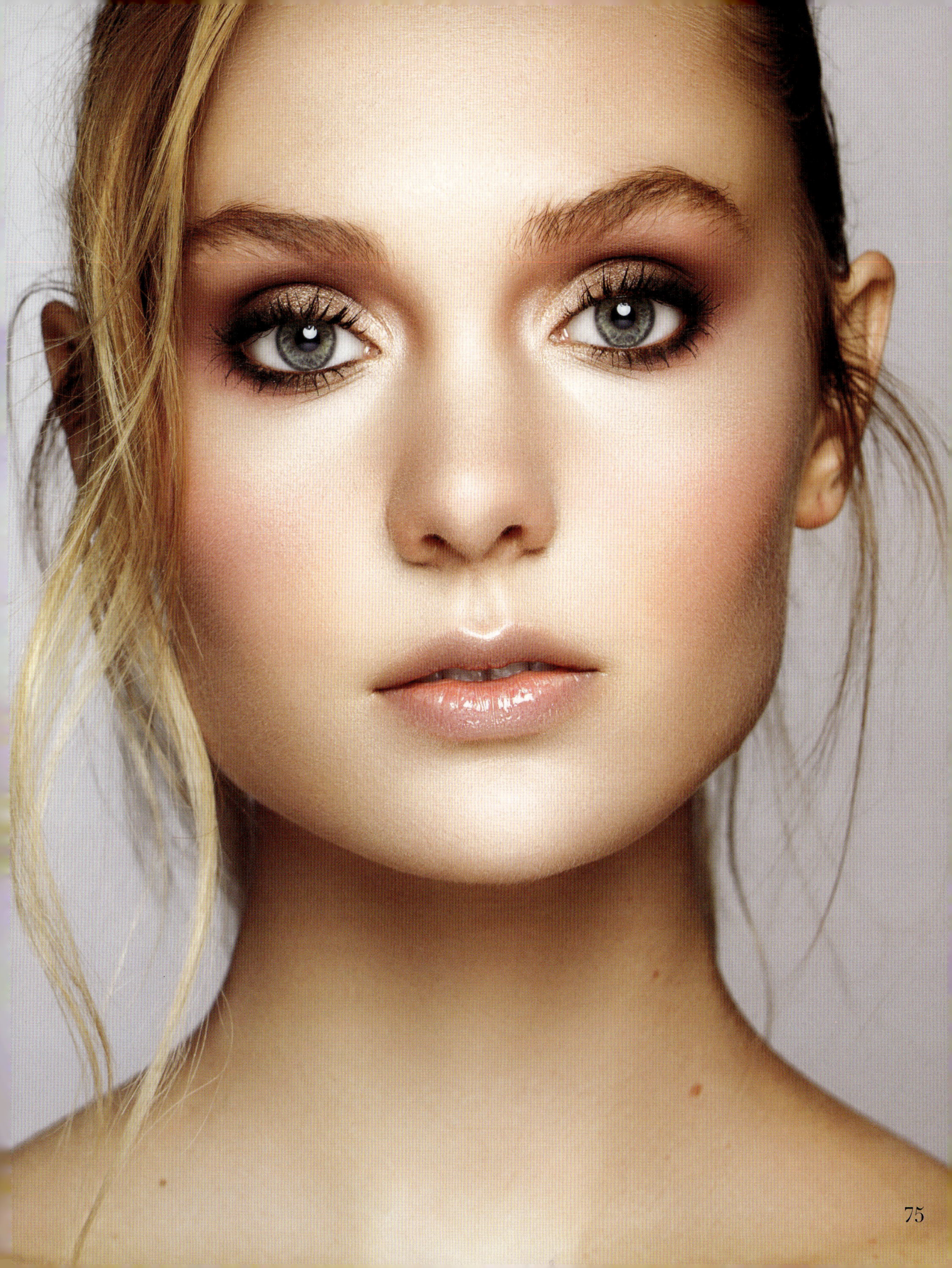

CHAPTER 5

THE PERFECT ARCHITECTURE: *BUILDING BROWS THAT WOW!*

Good eyebrows can perform magic! When shaped correctly, they can take years off your face, as well as make your complexion look brighter and your cheekbones more defined.

They are the perfect face framers when you're not wearing makeup.

77

WOW-WORTHY BROWS

Our faces are not symmetrical!
Sure, a supermodel's features may come close, but for the most part, symmetry is hard to find. It is for this reason that I think most people believe that their eyebrows should look identical. But in real #unfiltered life, eyebrows are not exact matches. So when shaping them, the goal is to make them look close in shape, but not necessarily identical.

Here are some key brow-shaping Dos and Don'ts:

Do
- Leave one eye width of space between eyebrows for a symmetrical look.
- Face directly into a mirror and use natural light when tweezing.
- Brush your brows up, and trim the extra-long hairs that stick up. You'll get a nice full brow without having to fully commit to a certain shape.
- Consider your skin tone. If you have fair skin, your brow shade should have cooler tones. If you have darker skin, you'll want a warmer shade to prevent your brows from looking ashy.

Don't
- Fill eyebrows in a shape that makes them appear too close together or too far apart from each other.
- Over tweeze. Fuller always looks better when it comes to eyebrows.
- Ignore your brows as you age! Filling them in regularly will give you a consistently younger appearance.

Eyebrow Product Types

Type	What?	How?
Precision Liners	Great for adding hair-like strokes.	Fill any sparse areas with a sharpened precision brow liner, working with soft strokes for a natural look.
Gel	These come in color and colorless formulas, and can have a slightly shiny texture. They are great for taming unruly eyebrow hairs.	Use them to brush brow hairs and set them in place after you've filled them in. Many have fibers that help give brow hairs a fuller appearance.
Powder	Usually the most natural options and the best for lighter skin.	Use an angled brush and draw tiny, soft individual hair-like strokes.

Shaping the Brow
While there is a science to shaping the brow, it's not like brain surgery. It's simple. I recommend trying the "pencil test," which is a method I've been using forever. It's ideal for determining where your eyebrows should start, arch, and end. The best thing about this test is that it uses the landmarks of your own face, not a supermodel's, to determine what shape looks best.

All you need are two eyebrow pencils and a mirror.
1. Start by holding one pencil along the side of your nose. The edge of the pencil closest to the nose is where the brow should begin. Use the other pencil to lightly mark the intersection point.
2. Angle the pencil from the side of your nostril to the middle of your pupil. This marks the point where the highest arch of your natural brow should be. Use the other pencil to mark that spot.
3. Finally, take the pencil and angle it from the nostril and across the cheek to the outer corner of your eye. Mark that point. This is where the eyebrow should end.

1

2

3

CHAPTER 6

IN A WINK: *AMAZING EYELASHES*

81

SIX STEPS TO *AMAZING* LASHES

① Curl! Make your eyelash curler a daily must. Start at the base of the lashes and gently squeeze and release the curler.

② Blot! To get rid of product excess before applying, blot your mascara wand on a tissue before applying.

③ Wiggle! Always wiggle your mascara wand while applying to make sure you coat each and every lash. Move the wand side to side as you work outward and up. Repeat on the bottom lashes.

④ Layer! Layer different formulas of mascara quicky, before they dry, to avoid clumps. For instance, start with your favorite lengthening mascara, then add a coat of waterproof on top to make sure it lasts!

⑤ Comb! Always comb through your lashes between coats to prevent clumping and create a natural-looking effect.

⑥ Protect! If your eyelids tend to be oily and/or your mascara tends to transfer onto your lids, dust them with translucent powder first. Then apply mascara and the rest of your eye makeup.

Three Types of Mascara

1. Lengthening
This type of mascara is formulated to make lashes look longer. Some even come with fibers that add amazing length, however they can shed and fall under the eyes (or even in the eyes) during the day. Lengthening mascaras often come with very tightly bristled brushes that are perfect for applying at the tips of the lashes.

2. Volumizing
These mascaras usually come with wands that have evenly spaced bristles to deposit thickening pigments evenly. The formula's technology helps to make your lashes look full. Layer each coat lightly to avoid clumping.

3. Waterproof / Water-Resistant
These formulas stand up to humidity or oily skin around the eyes better than any other mascara type. They can also be used over any other mascara type to boost staying power. Water-resistant formulas are easier to wear and remove.

Dos and Don'ts of Rocking Those Falsies

Do
• *Use* clear glue if you are not going to be wearing eyeliner. Black glue will show at the lash roots.
• *Dab* lash glue onto the base of your fake lashes, then let it dry for about a minute. This helps to keep them from slipping when you apply them.
• *Apply* a coat of mascara after the lashes have dried to make them seem unified with your own.
• *Press* the lashes onto the lash line with fingers or tweezers.

Don't
• *Don't* forget to hide your lash line with eyeliner if the false lashes are not perfectly placed.
• *Don't* curl your lashes until after they've completely dried.
• *Don't* use the same mascara after about three months. Bacteria build quickly in those tubes, so It's time to use a new one!

FAKE 'EM!
When properly fitted and placed, falsies will be your best friends. Different looks offer versatility and boost your lashes.

CHAPTER 7

BLUSH BASICS:
CHEEK & CHIC

The power of blush is undeniable. When applied correctly, a pretty flush on the cheeks creates the healthiest-looking glow.

Figuring out your face shape will let you know what features you would like to amplify and to tone down. Cheek color can help you create an optical illusion and literally sculpt and highlight your face with the right application. Knowing your basic face shape and proper application techniques are essential in order to maximize the awesome effects of blush.

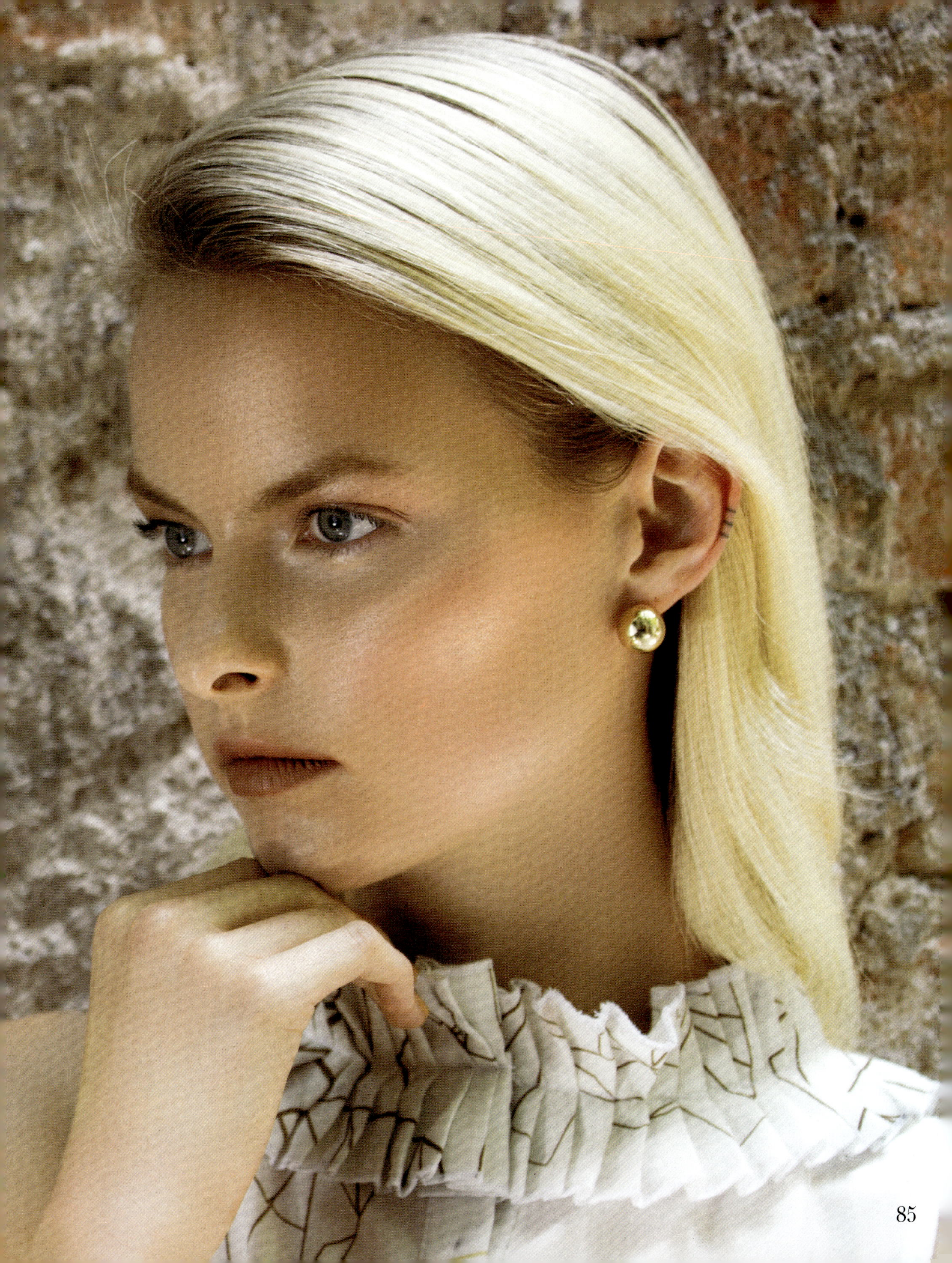

FIND YOUR FORMULA

Powder

Provides sheer to medium coverage and is easy to apply with the correct brush. Avoid formulas that are too sparkly and instead opt for light shimmer. Dust on top of the cheeks and use a clean brush to blend the edges.

Cream

Cream blush should be avoided if you have oily skin or breakout-prone skin. They are best applied with the fingertips, then blended with a synthetic brush. Creams give the skin a naturally flushed look, as long as they are well blended.

Stains & Gels

These formulas can create amazing dewy looks but are often tricky to apply. Avoid streaks by making sure you blend quickly after applying. Use a sponge, your fingertips, or a brush to blend.

7 Blush Tips

1. Sweep blush from the apples of the cheeks toward the ears to give the face a sharper angle.
2. Use a darker shade to contour and recede the hollows of the cheeks.
3. Apply blush to the apples of the cheeks and blend well toward the temples. The ideal face shape.
4. Swirl the blush brush onto the apples of the cheeks using circular motions.
5. Blend well on the hollows of the cheeks and toward the temples.
6. Brush wider horizontal strokes on top of the cheekbones to create balance between a long jaw and high forehead.
7. Contour at the temples and jaw.

Dos and Don'ts of Applying Cheek Color

Do:
- *Dust* color onto the apples of the cheeks, then blend slightly in and up and outward motion toward the temples.
- *Use* circular motions and delicate strokes to blend well. Wait a couple of minutes for your moisturizer and foundation to dry before applying blush. This will ensure the most even application.
- *Apply* blush gradually, in layers, to build intensity and avoid overkill (i.e. a clown look).

Don't:
- *Use* sparkly cheek color to contour. It will emphasize and brighten the area, not define it.
- *Don't* use blush to achieve a tanned look. It will look orange or fake.
- *Skip* moisturizer when wearing blush! Streaks will be much harder to avoid if your skin isn't properly hydrated before you apply.

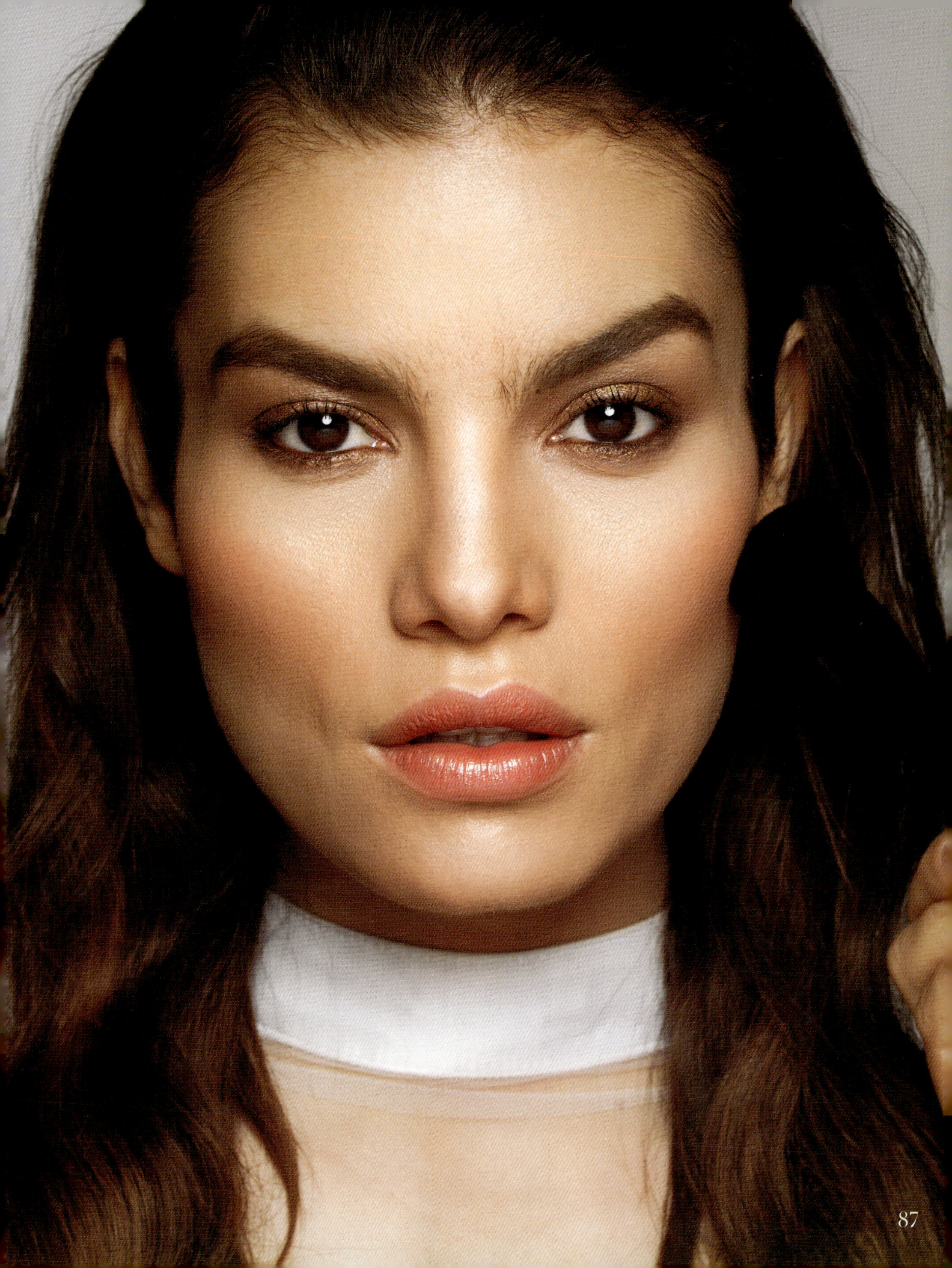

KNOWING YOUR FACE SHAPE *AND MAPPING YOUR BLUSH ZONES*

Knowing your face shape will help you understand which features you should amplify and which you should tone down, and is essential to maximize the awesome effects of blush. With the right application, cheek color can create an optical illusion that literally sculpts and highlights your entire face.

Cheek color shades for your skin tone:

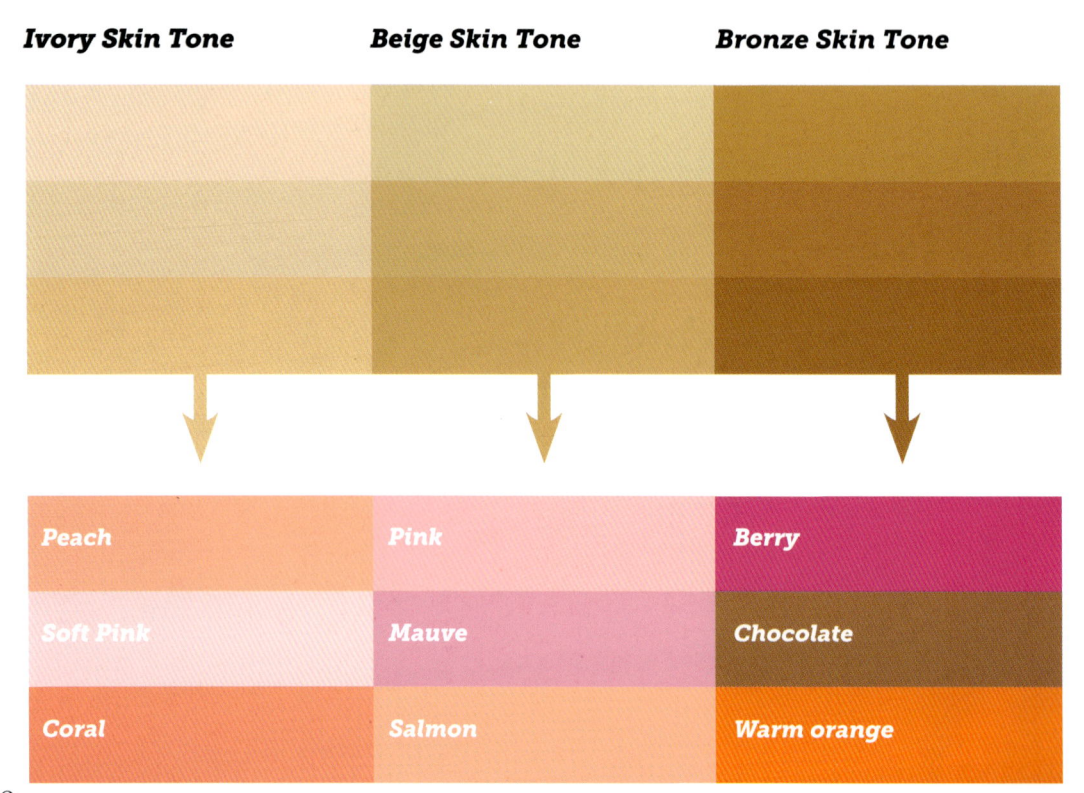

Ivory Skin Tone — Peach, Soft Pink, Coral

Beige Skin Tone — Pink, Mauve, Salmon

Bronze Skin Tone — Berry, Chocolate, Warm orange

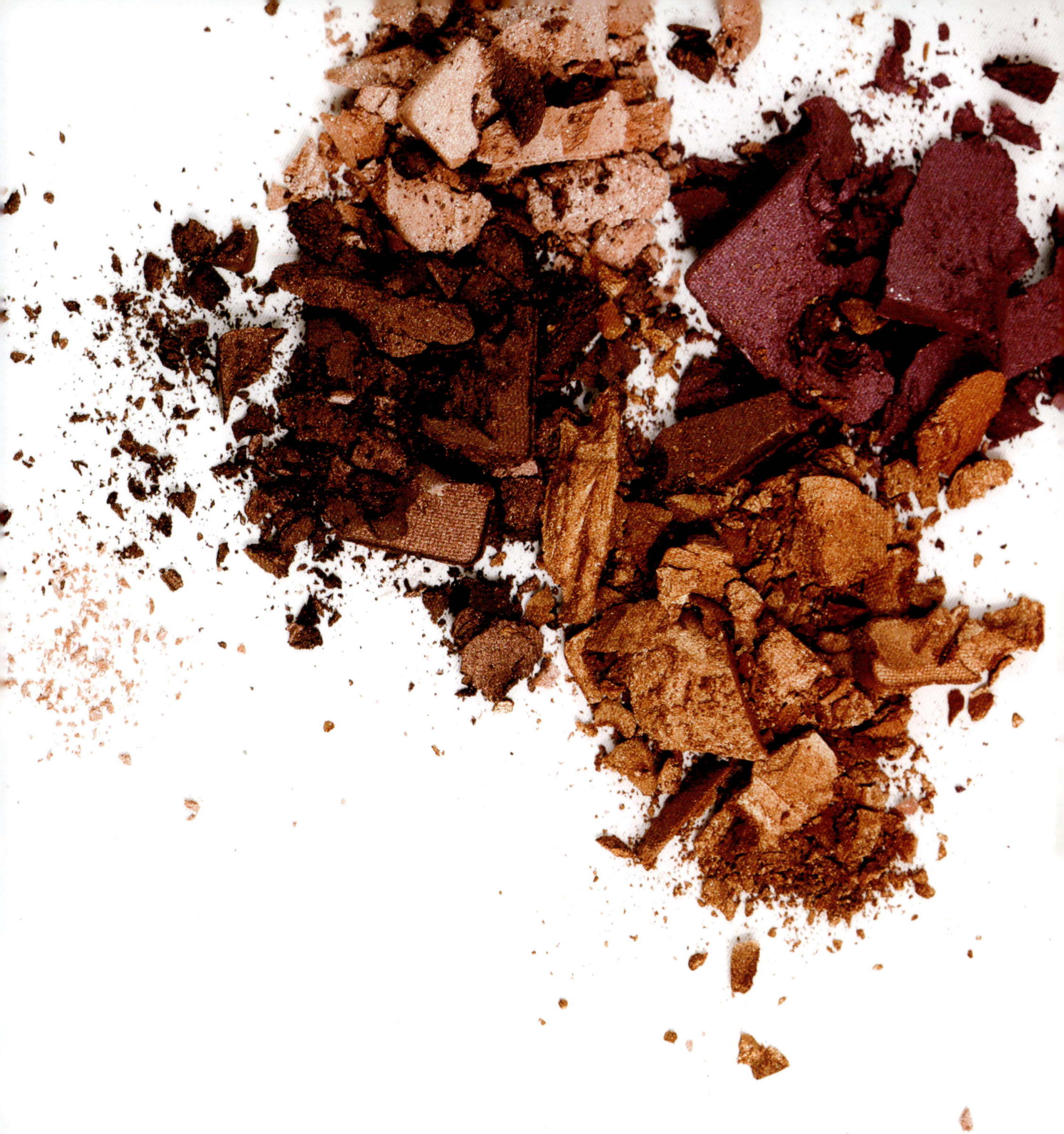

CHAPTER 8

CHISELED CHEEKBONES: #CONTOURING & HIGHLIGHTING

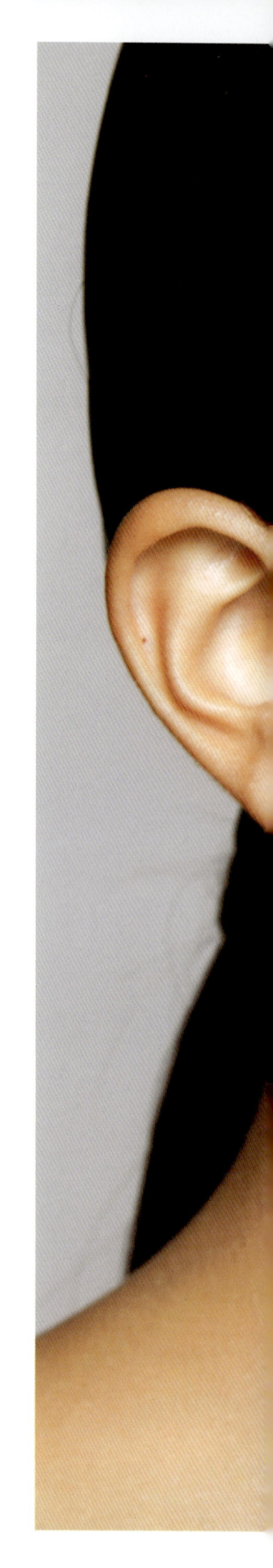

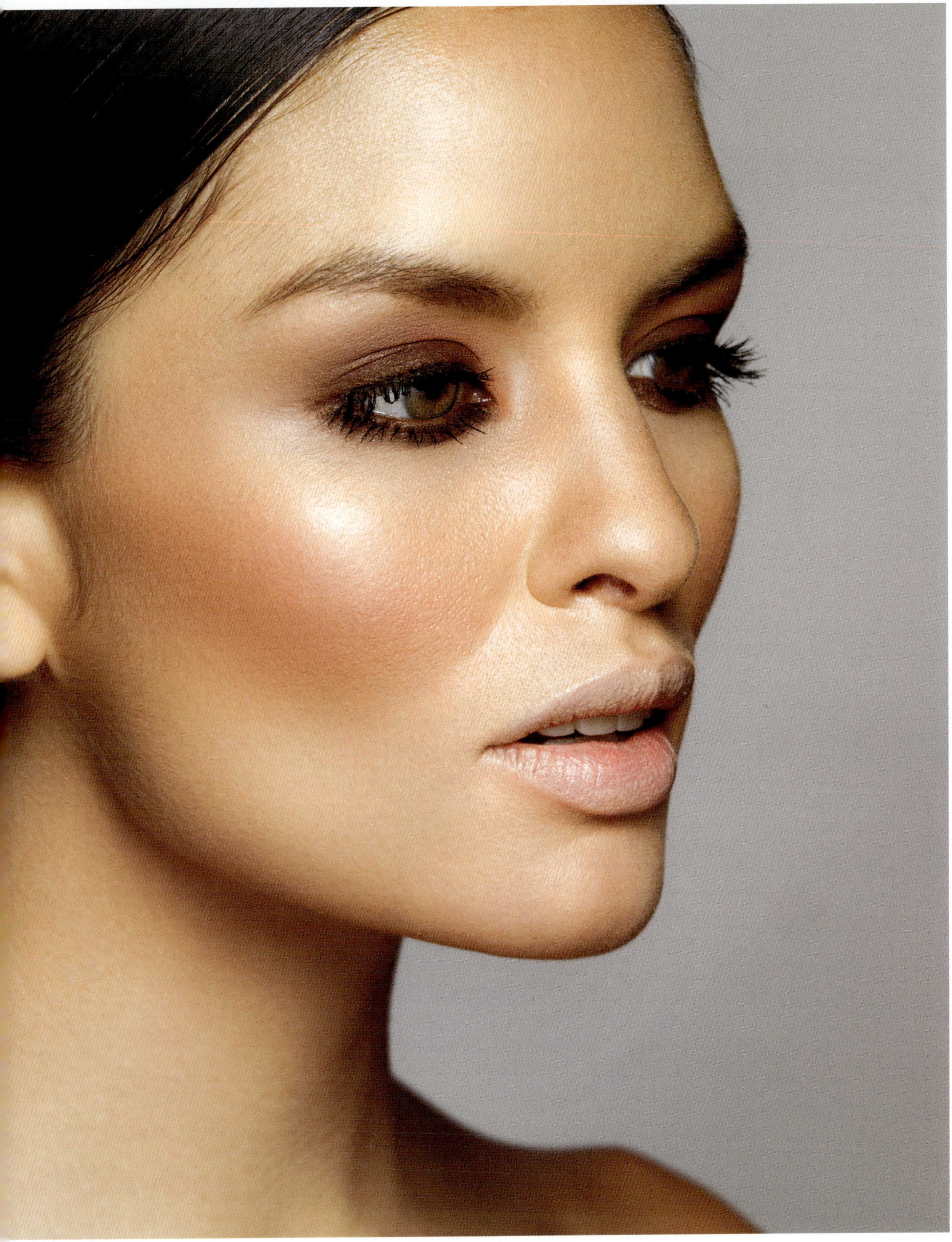

HIGHLIGHTERS & STROBING

Strobing is a technique that, when used correctly, brings forward certain areas on the face, making them appear fuller and more pronounced. These areas include the top of the cheekbones, under the arches of the brows, and on the bridge of nose. The technique also works well on bare arms, shoulders, and décolletage. Skip the forehead, though, as skin can appear greasy.

It's worth mentioning that lighting is very important when it comes to strobing (which means that it may not be the best look for real life[ay]). Strobing can look amazing indoor or by candle light, but can look way too bright when out in the sunlight. So consider your surroundings carefully and adjust it if you are shifting from a day to a night look. And remember that the bigger the sparkle particles in whatever product you are using, the shinier they will look on mature or less-than-perfect skin. I'd advise using small particles that create a glow rather than a sparkly mess!

Contouring for your face shape

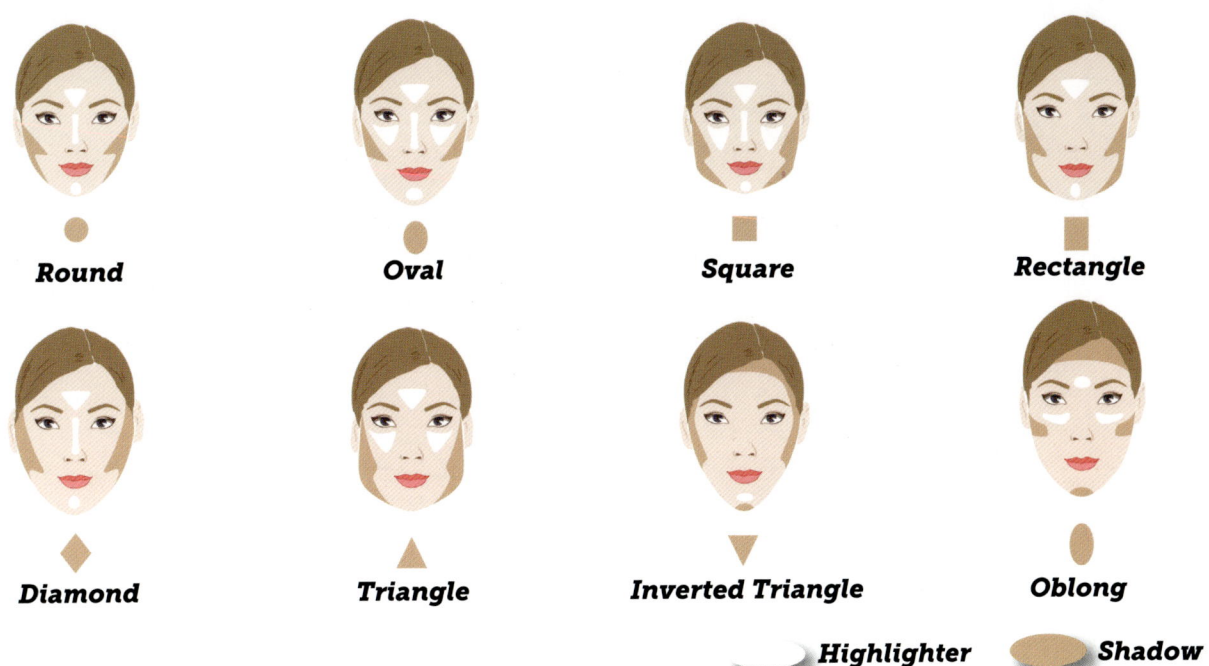

Round | **Oval** | **Square** | **Rectangle**

Diamond | **Triangle** | **Inverted Triangle** | **Oblong**

Highlighter   Shadow

Contouring & Sculpting

Contouring is another trend that's very popular on social media. Basically, it involves using shades that are a bit lighter and a bit darker than your skin tone to sculpt and define certain features. As a makeup artist, it is a technique that I use everyday on my clients. And the key word when it comes to good contouring? Blending!

Undetectable contouring is the goal. It's all about creating shadows that to areas of the face appear narrower. In my opinion, contouring darker skin is much easier than light skin. But regardless of skin tone it can be tricky to do, and you always want to make sure that the product you use looks like your skin, only darker. If you need to correct darker areas, see the "Ace the Base" chapter.

You can contour using:

Powder or powder foundation — Apply over moisturizer and foundation that has had time to dry. Use two brushes—use one to deposit the product and another to blend—and always make sure that your brushes are clean.

Foundation — Foundation is good for contouring because there are so many shades to choose from. Apply with a foundation brush and blend with fingers or a sponge. Remember to look for shades that look like your skin, only darker.

Cream-to-Powder Foundations — These also can work but remember that they dry to a powdery finish, which means that you have to blend them fast. Best when used over properly moisturized skin.

Concealer — Remember that concealers have more pigment than regular foundation, so use sparingly. And never use it over powder as this will create a muddy effect. Use fingertips or a wet sponge to apply and blend.

DARE TO *BAKE*?

Here's How to Pull it Off

Baking is a technique that's been used in the entertainment industry for a long time. It involves using powders (translucent or specific "baking" ones) to both highlight and recede areas of the face. Powder is applied generously to specific areas of the face (under the eyes, on the bridge of nose, chin, and jawline, etc.) and then left to sit — or "bake" — for at least a few minutes. When you wipe the powder away, it leaves behind a marked highlight that chisels out your facial features. I do not recommend this technique for dry skin, unless you use the powder sparingly. See details on how to do it below!

Baking to Highlight/Contour

Apply foundation: After skincare application, apply a matte finish, medium-to-full coverage foundation to the face. Use a foundation brush to stipple the product onto the places where the most coverage is needed, then use feathering strokes to blend out. An oval padded brush is also great for a full-coverage look as it has hundreds of tightly packed bristles that easily add layers and coverage.

Highlight: Identify the areas you want to highlight and bring forward. Using a cheek brush, apply a generous amount of a very light or translucent powder to your chin and jawline, under your eyes, in the center of your forehead, and onto the bridge of your nose.

Tip: Hold the bristles tight with your fingers to ensure a precise application.

Contour: Brush a darker matte contour powder under your cheekbones, around the hairline, and under the jawline. Leave the powders on the face and allow them to "bake" while you apply the rest of your makeup.

Tip: When "baking," I prefer to apply concealer first and then use the powders to create the added brightening effect. Applying concealer afterward might create a "muddy" look.

Clean up: Once you're done with the rest of your makeup, use a clean brush to swipe away the traces of powder. On the cheeks, follow with your chosen cheek color and if need be, use a contour powder or bronzer to warm up any areas of the face that might seem too light. The goal is to illuminate the areas that you want to highlight so that the face has a more chiseled look.

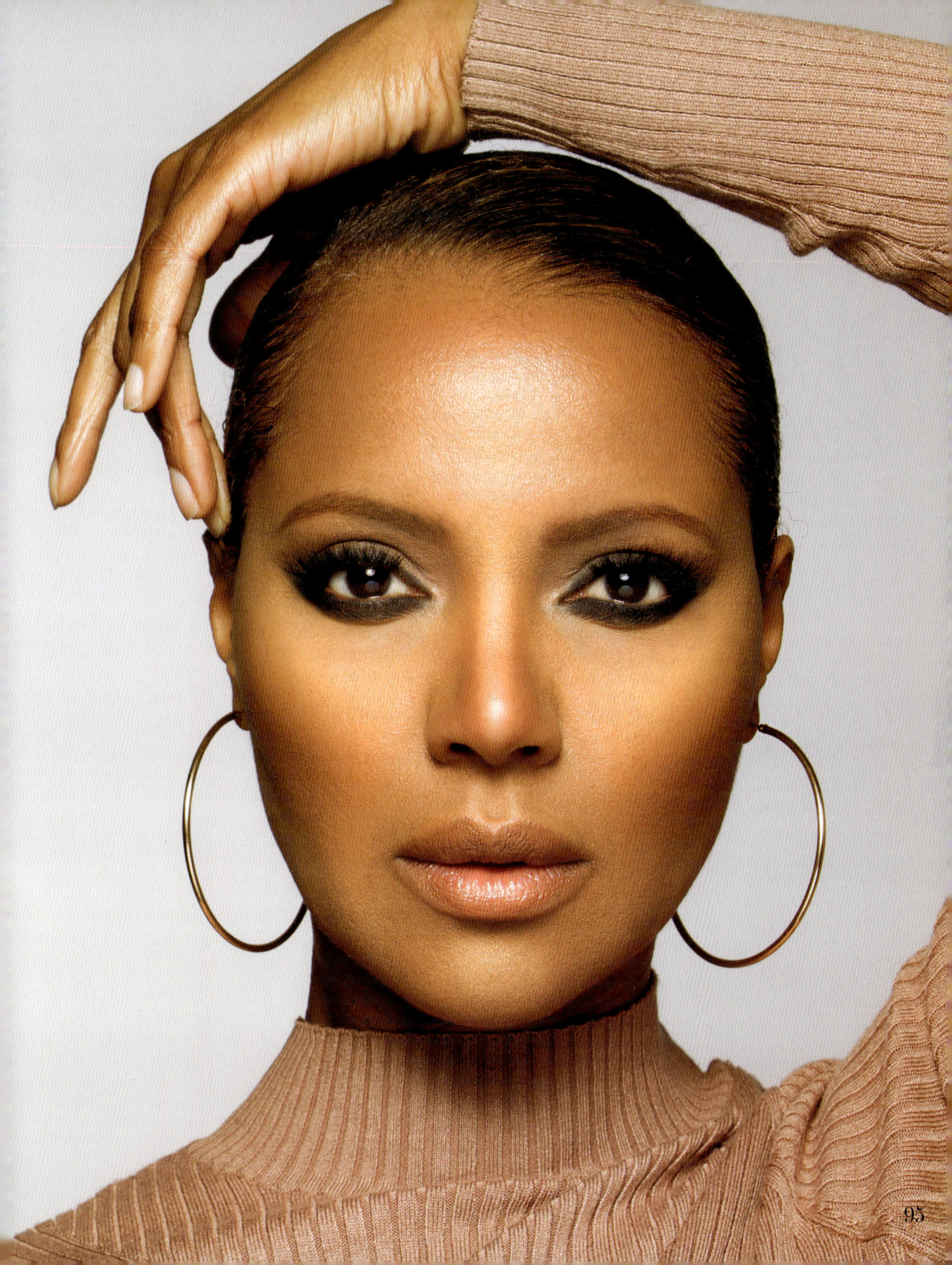

CHAPTER 9
GIMME SOME LIP: *PERFECTING YOUR POUT*

According to a poll conducted by Mintel, 81% of women say they use lipstick, while only 64% use foundation and 59% use blush. This makes lipstick the MOST popular cosmetic product sold worldwide!

The best lip color for your skin tone

Skin Tone	Lip Color	
Light	Light Pink	Light Peach
	Beige	Maroon/Gold
Medium	Medium Pink	Red
	Coral	Orange
Medium Dark	Dark Pink	Dark Red
	Magenta	Dark Orange
Dark	Dark Maroon	Dark Fuchsia
	Dark Magenta	Beige/Gold

97

LIP CARE

"At times, it's easy to feel like you can't avoid dry lips. But chapping can be easily treated in a few simple steps."

Having to combat the look of dry lips is one of my pet peeves when doing makeup. Did you know that the lips lack sweat glands? It's true — the natural oils that hydrate and protect the rest of your skin are not helping out your pout. Which is why lips become chapped and dry so easily, and why it's important to exfoliate and moisturize them regularly.

Don't forget — your lips need just as much protection from the harmful rays of the sun as the rest of your face. Be sure to use a lip product that contains SPF, and to reapply when you're outdoors. You can wear a sheer SPF under your favorite lipstick or lip gloss.

You also need to drink a lot of water. Dehydration is a major cause of dry skin, especially in the lips. Remember to gulp down those eight glasses a day, and don't wait until you feel thirsty — that's a sign of dehydration!

During the cooler, drier seasons, the sun, the wind, and even licking your lips will dehydrate this sensitive area and cause it to flake. Using an exfoliating lip scrub is essential, and an absolute must before wearing a matte or long-lasting lipstick formula.

Lip scrubs can be used at night and in the morning, and should be followed with a lip moisturizer that contains ingredients such as vitamin E, shea butter, and coconut oil.

Correcting Lip Shapes

The best way to redefine the lips is to find a neutral lip liner that is close to or just a touch darker than the true color of your lips. Draw the corrections as needed, and depending on the look you are going for, fill in the whole lip area or just create an outline. If you have a problem with lipstick running or feathering, or if you'd like to create a base for your lipstick to stay on longer, make sure to fill the entire area.

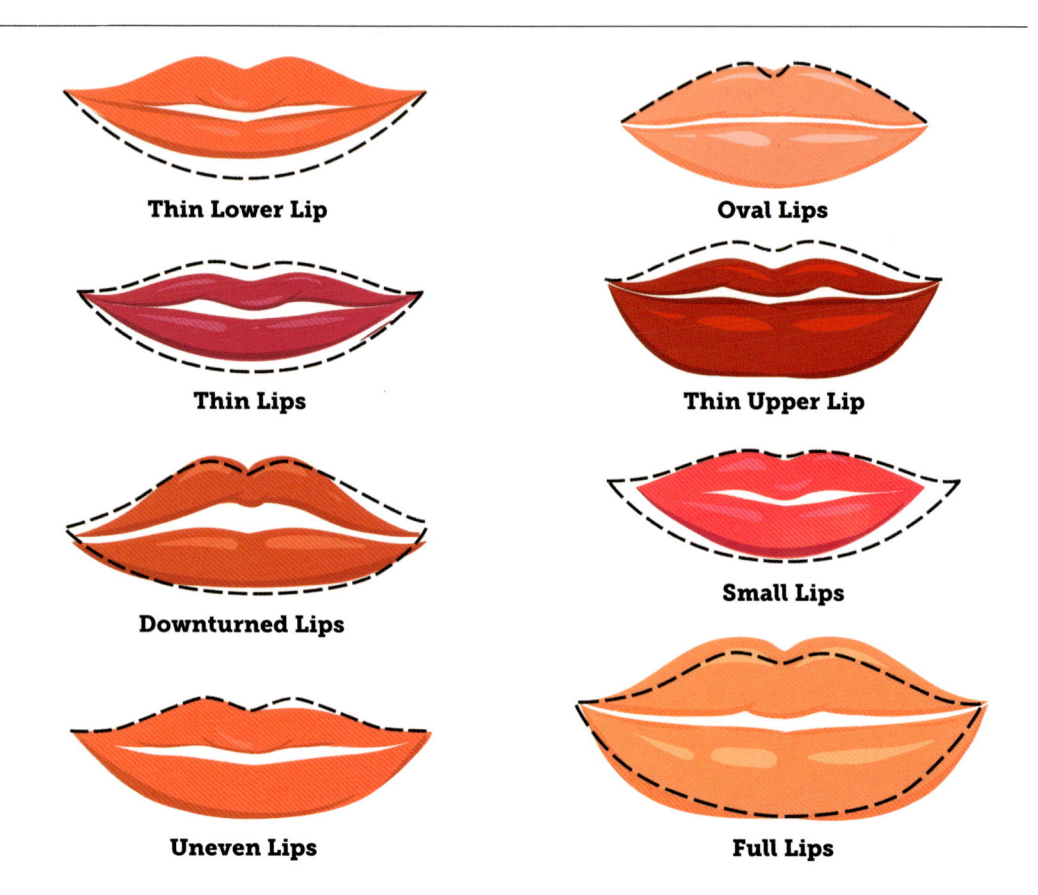

Thin Lower Lip

Thin Lips

Downturned Lips

Uneven Lips

Oval Lips

Thin Upper Lip

Small Lips

Full Lips

99

CHAPTER 10
TOOLS OF THE TRADE: #UNFILTERED APPLICATION

Using the right tools will really bring your makeup game to the next level. When used properly, they not only create flawless looks but also save you time and money — and who doesn't want that? Here are some of my whats-and-whys for using different tools.

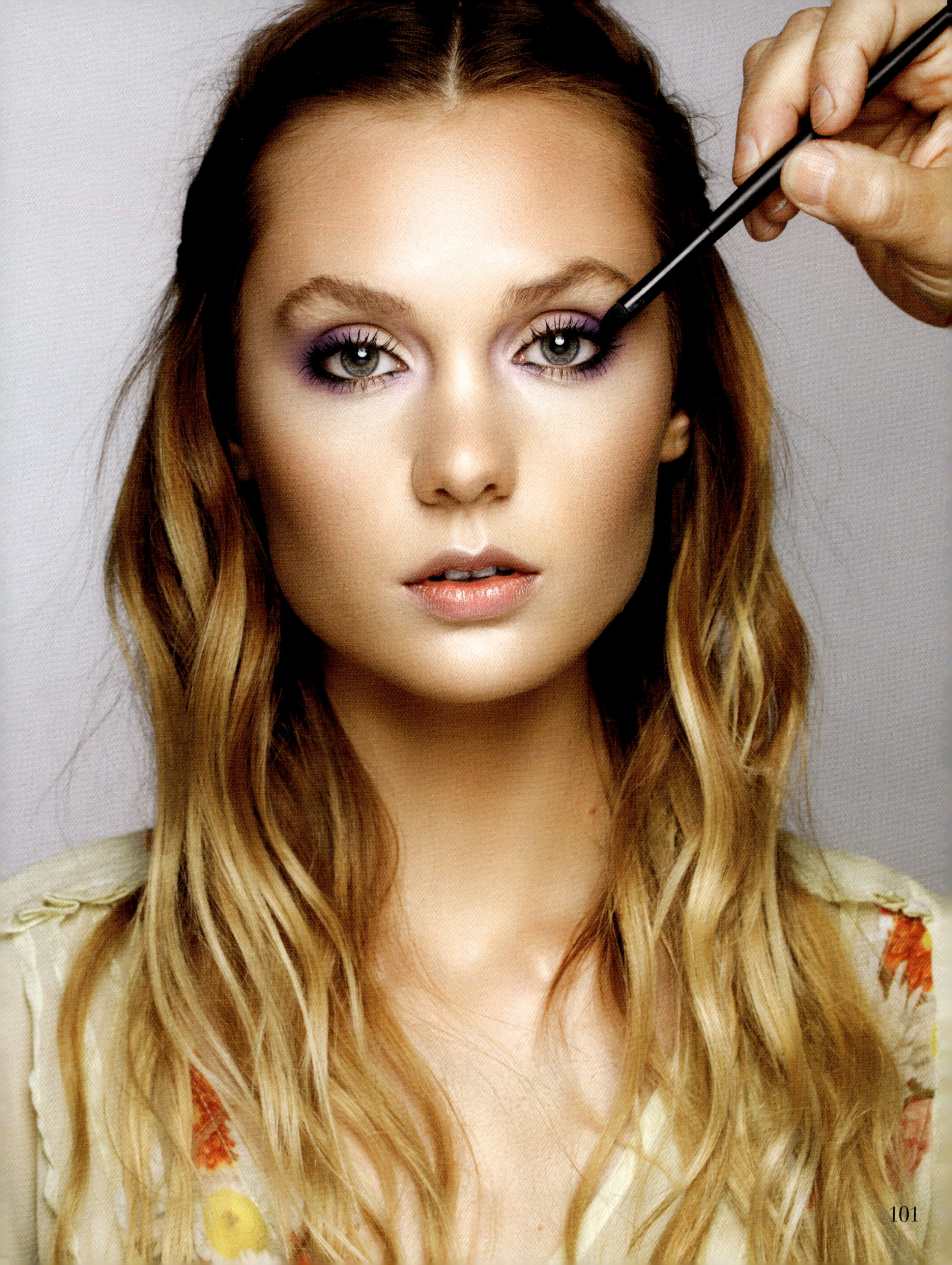

THE FILTERING TOOLS

Brushes:

Synthetic vs. Natural Bristles: What's the Difference?
Synthetic bristles consist of manmade materials and work best with creams or liquid forms of makeup, such as foundation, lipstick, concealer, and cream eyeshadows. They are easy to clean, maintain their shape longer than natural bristles, and don't absorb too much product so there's less waste. Synthetic fibers allow for great flexibility that help to easily blend any makeup product and feel very soft.

Natural brushes are usually made from animal hair sheddings. They are very soft and allow for more precise application. Natural bristles pick up a lot more product and can deliver a strong punch of pigment, which is why some makeup artists and makeup lovers prefer them. They can also make blending easier (but messier!) because the bristle hairs are so soft. You do have to take good care of them and clean them carefully. They do not work well with liquids or creams.

Synthetic brushes offer the most flexibility and ease of use, which, in my opinion, makes them the better candidate for the average makeup wearer. But it's your choice, and all the shapes below can be found in both synthetic and natural bristle brushes.

Flat Fluffy Brush: Can be used as an all over eyeshadow brush. Perfect for blending creases.

Double-Sided Angle Brush: This side is for combing your brows and can also be used to separate lashes after applying mascara. The other side is for cutting the crease on the eyelid and to blend brow pencil and make the application look more natural.

Angle Fluffy Brush: This brush can be used on the brow bone and the nose contour, as well as on the eyelid to accentuate the crease.

Flat Thin Brush: Perfect for applying and blending concealer, as well as sweeping eye color all over the lids. It's also awesome for applying concealer to hard-to-reach areas like around the nose.

Blending Brush: The bristles of these oval brushes, which look a bit like hair brushes, are usually made up of a ton of tightly packed fibers. This makes them soft and perfect for applying cream and lotion type products like foundation.

Fan Brush: This brush is great for dusting off loose powder and sweeping away excess powder under the eye area. It is also the perfect strobing and highlighter tool.

My Favorite Brush Shapes & Styles

Brush Type

Liquid Foundation Brush: Perfect for applying liquid foundation or CC cream. It can also be used to apply blush, and can help set your powder when you want to bake under the eyes or jawline. It's also great for blending.

Cheek Brush: This brush can be used to blend contouring on your neck, forehead, cheeks, and jawline. Used for foundation, powder, contouring, and blush application. It can also be used to apply blush, and can help set your powder when you want to bake under the eyes or jawline. It's also great for blending.

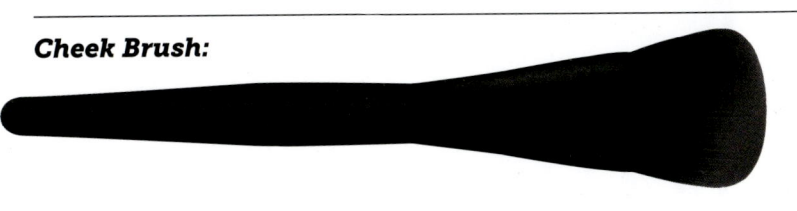

Big Fluffy Powder Brush: Good for applying powders and blending away harsh lines. It can also be used as a bronzer brush to give your neck and shoulders some glow.

Pointed Blending Brush: Great for creating creases on hooded eyes. It also works perfectly to soften and blur eyeliner for a soft, smoky look. The pointed tip makes adding a highlight to the inner corner of the eyes easy. It also makes a great lip brush.

But the key word here is CLEAN. It might seem obvious, but it's so important — before you touch your face or eyes, always wash your hands to avoid unwanted skin irritation and reactions.

Makeup Sponges: Ideal for buffing foundation on and blending out harsh edges. The ones with flat, diagonal edges are great for blending concealer and/or applying powder under the eyes. If you are a fan of "baking" your powder on, this is also the tool to use because it helps to precisely apply powders and creams.

Fingers: Don't forget these terrific tools that don't cost a thing! Using your fingers gives you the most control when applying a product, and is the best way to feel a product's true texture. And because your skin is warm, your fingers help products blend seamlessly into the skin. Too much foundation? Blend it away with clean fingers. Want a soft, stained look on the lips? Tap the product on your pout with your fingers. Your digits are also divine for applying skincare and giving yourself a facial massage.

Powder Puffs: Use them to apply powder and create a matte effect, then blend with a powder brush to make the look appear natural. Powder puffs are also great for setting looks by pressing them onto your skin right after your makeup is applied. They are also ideal for touch ups as they won't don't disturb the perfected look of the skin.

Applicators: These little disposable tools can really come in handy when brushes are not around. They're great for tapping on eyeshadow and letting texture show. The narrow ends are also perfect for softening eyeliner.

CHAPTER 11

A MAN FOR ALL SEASONS: *EASY GROOMING TIPS THAT MAKE ALL THE DIFFERENCE*

This is the look that will take your grooming to the next level. The key to makeup looks for men, especially when it comes to special occasions and photographs, is to make sure that any product used is undetectable to the naked eye.

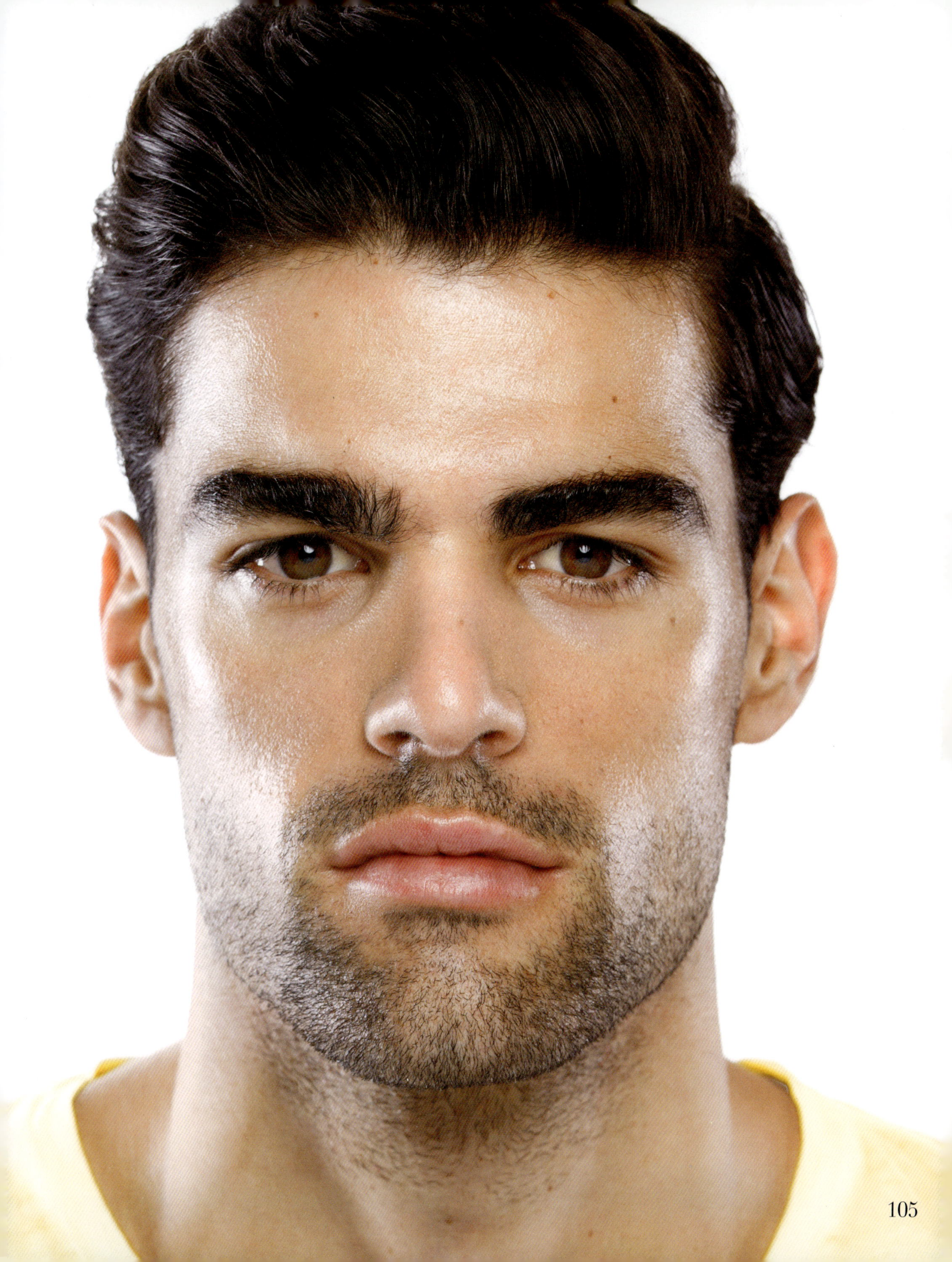

PHOTO-READY *LOOK*

The Basics: Showering at night might give you extra time to shave, but if you have stubborn beard hair, you should wait until the morning. When washing your face, look for a product specific to your skin type so that it gets your face clean without leaving it feeling too tight or too slick. (For example, dry skin can benefit from a cleanser with extra moisturizing ingredients, while oily skin can benefit from cleansers that prevent extra oil production yet keep the skin fresh and moisturized).

Tip: Wash your hair first, then your face. You want the cleanser — not a fragranced shampoo! — to be the last product that goes on your face when you're in the shower. Use a regular face cleanser daily and apply a scrub a couple of times a week to exfoliate your skin.

Shave as soon as you are out of the shower and keep rinsing the blade and using warm water. I personally shave my head in the shower and it works great for me. It's the best way to prevent ingrown hair and irritation.

Moisturize, moisturize, moisturize! I can't stress this enough. The process only takes a few seconds and it makes a huge difference in the look of your skin. Dry, dull skin can cause flakiness, redness, and other annoying skin issues. Moisturizing daily provides your face with the much needed hydration that will keep it smooth and supple. For best results, always apply moisturizer right after the shower when your pores are still open, and use a moisturizer with SPF coverage. On days when you are shaving, apply moisturizer after you've shaved. Pay extra attention to the just-shaved areas, as they will be more sensitive post-shaving.

For a special occasion or a picture, you can take things to the next level by adding the following makeup to your daily skincare routine.

1. Use a CC cream or a tinted moisturizer. If needed, you can mix both products together to dilute. The point is to even out tone and eliminate any redness or ruddiness while keeping the skin looking natural.
2. Use concealer under the eyes or over blemishes if you need the extra coverage. Make sure to use a tiny amount and to apply after you've smoothed on your CC cream and/or tinted moisturizer.
3. Use a translucent (colorless) setting powder to minimize shine.
4. If needed, use a lip scrub to slough off any dead skin cells on the lips, then apply a moisturizing lip balm. Blot away any excess shine, but make sure the lips still look supple and hydrated.
5. Groom unruly brows. If they are too long, brush them in an upward motion and trim them slightly. You are not looking to create perfectly shaped eyebrows; you just want them to look even and not distracting. A clear brow gel or a toothbrush with a tiny bit of hairspray will keep them in place.

Before

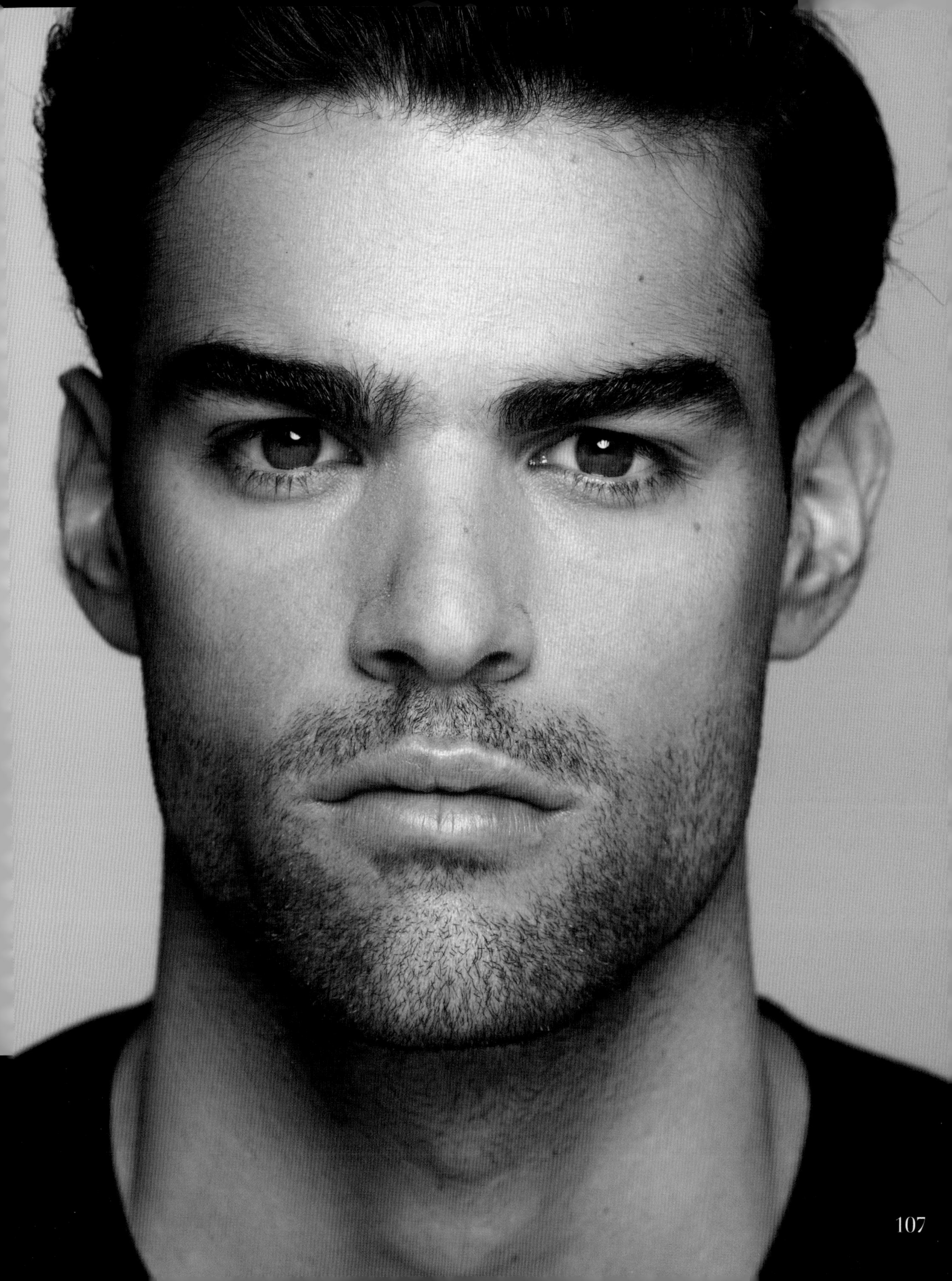

CHAPTER 12

TURN BACK THE CLOCK: *TOP TIPS FOR A YOUNGER LOOK*

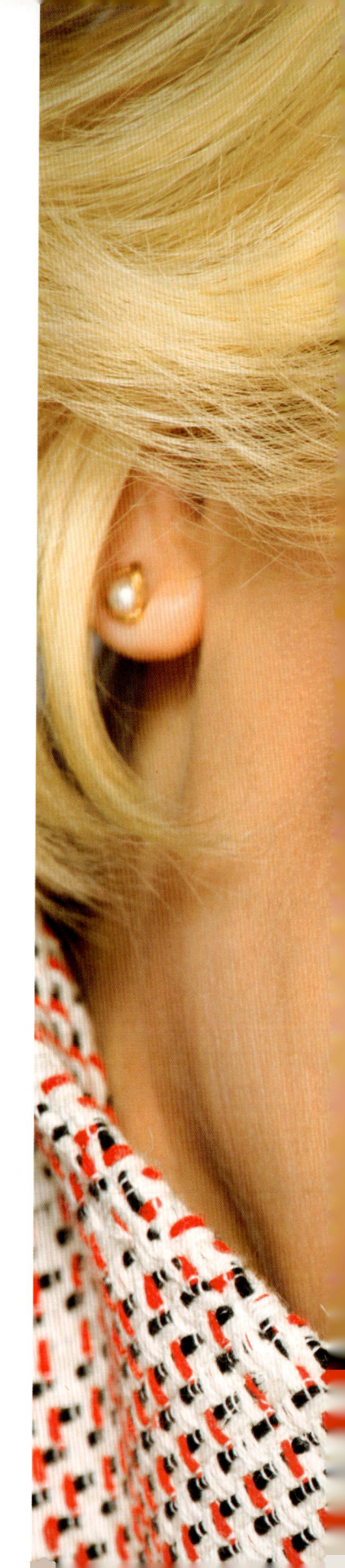

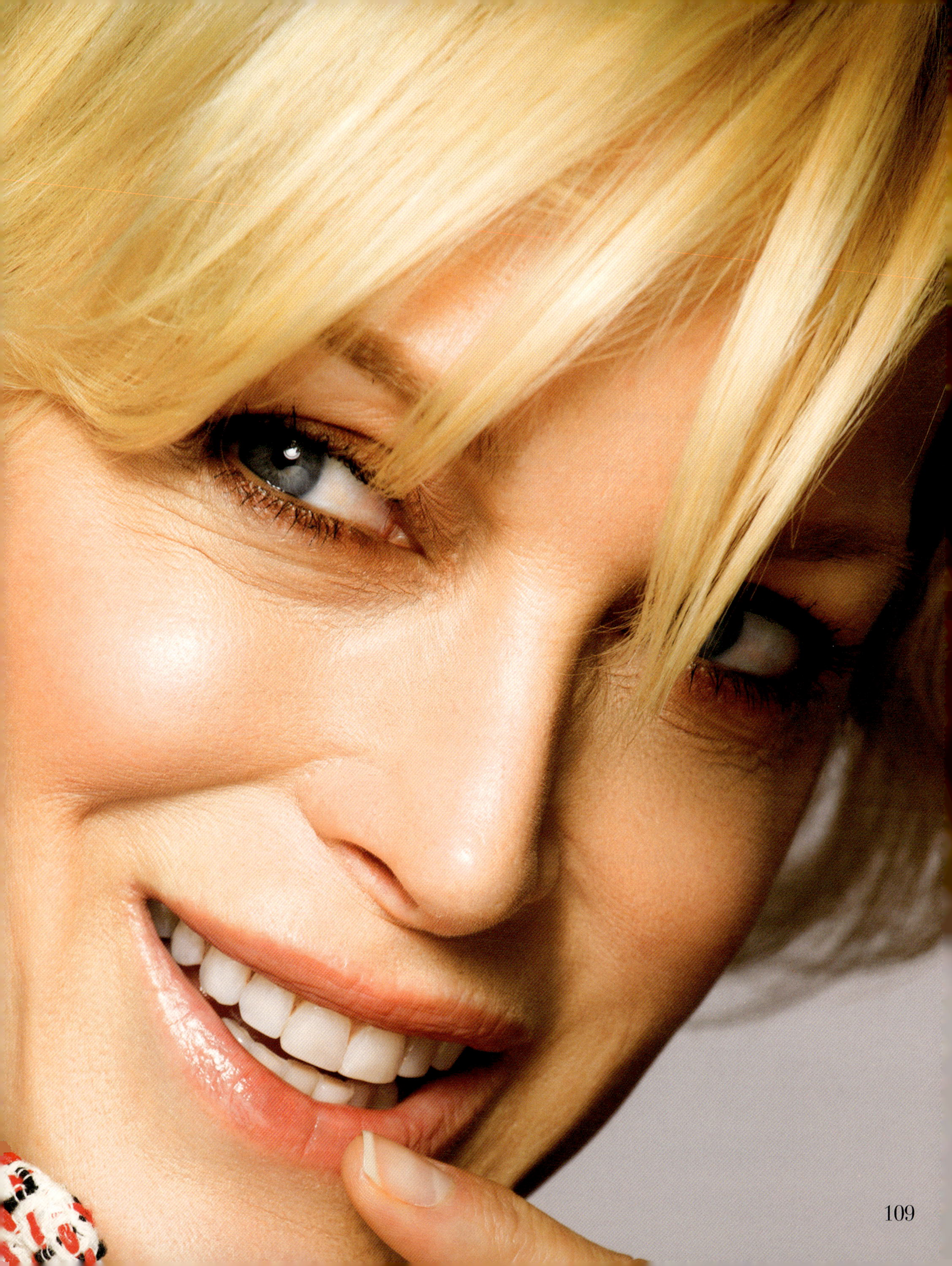

IN A BEAUTY RUT?

Here are some Dos and Don'ts to help you improve your makeup game *at any age!*

DO — **Go easy on the powder.**
Using too much powder to set your makeup can magnify lines and accentuate dry spots. Instead, apply a translucent powder only to areas where it's needed, such as the t-zone, around the nostrils, and on the forehead and/or chin.

DO — **Try gray or brown eyeliner instead of black.**
Black eyeliner can look harsh if overdone and applied too thick. It can also make hooded eyes appear heavier. Opt for a lighter eyeliner shade instead, or smudge black eyeliner into a softer hue.

DO — **Use blush.**
Blush can be the best tool to lift and give the face a very youthful look. Try sheer formulas that do not have a lot of shimmer.

DO — **Pick the right foundation.**
The key to choosing the right foundation is to avoid formulas that are too dry or thick, as they can settle into fine lines and emphasizes dry areas. Make sure you always prep your skin with moisturizer and use a foundation formula that's light but still corrects imperfections. CC creams or luminous foundations are great for this.

DO — **Go easy on the eyeshadow.**
Eye color that's too bright or too dark can make your eyes look severe and accentuate droopiness. Opt for soft washes of color. A little bit of shimmer is okay, as long as it's well-blended and worn with mattes.

DON'T — **Don't ignore your eyebrows.**
Shaped eyebrows give the face an instant lift, so always fill them in softly. Because our natural brow hairs tend to disappear as we age, ignoring them can add years to your face. But they can be your best friend if you take the time to groom and fill them in!

DON'T — **Don't overdo the concealer.**
Use foundation sparingly as it can accentuate fine lines. Find a creamy formula and use a tiny amount under eyes or to conceal imperfections. Use your fingertips to blend it seamlessly.

DON'T — **Don't skip primers.**
Face primers, eye primers, lash primer, and lip primers are all key for long-lasting and better-wearing makeup. When used on the face, they can also help blur imperfections. So use them! (But always remember that less is more when it comes to this type of product.)

DON'T — **Don't overdo the lip liner.**
If you have fine lines around your mouth, using a lip liner that's too dark or dry can accentuate them. Instead, use a nude liner or a liner that closely matches your natural tone. And don't overline — this will also make imperfections stand out.

DON'T — **Don't skip lipstick.**
Hands down, a pretty shade of lipstick can instantly brighten your face. Pinks, mauves, and corals are great shades to try. Avoid heavy berry and dark brown.

110

111

CHAPTER 13

#UNFILTERED LOOKS 54+

113

GORGEOUS AT ANY AGE: 3 LOOKS FOR A YOUNGER YOU

"Neutral shades are perfect for those who are new at makeup or are not sure about what colors to wear. When applied subtly, they can be virtually foolproof. That's their hidden power!"

❶ SOFT NEUTRAL

❷ WORKING OVERTIME

❸ PAINTING THE TOWN

115

❶ SOFT NEUTRAL

"Soft and neutral, that's just what I wanted this look to convey. It's a look that works each and every time."

Eyes
Mature or hooded eyes benefit from a primer applied all over the eyelid and lower lash lines (the areas where you will apply eyeshadow). The primer will act as a base for eyeshadow and allow it to look smoother and stay on longer. Begin by using an eyeshadow brush to dust a matte ivory/bone eyeshadow all over the eyelid. Using a clean eyeshadow brush, follow with a rosy brown eyeshadow applied to the eyelids and lower lash line.
Tip: If you have hooded eyes, you want to make sure you still see the eyeshadow when your eyes are open. To do this, apply the shadow while looking straight ahead into a mirror. It might mean that you need to apply the shadow higher than you normally would. With a clean eyeshadow brush, blend the shade into a soft hue that gently surrounds your eyes. Swipe eyeliner or a darker matte eyeshadow at the lash line to amplify the look of your eyelashes. Finish by curling the lashes and applying a coat of lengthening mascara.

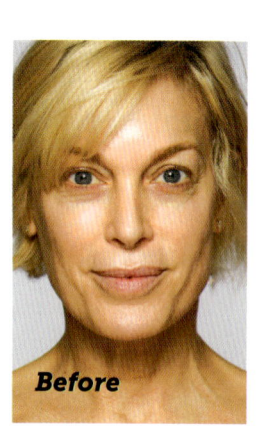

Cheeks
Cheek color applied on the tops of the cheeks creates a lifting effect. Using a cheek brush, swipe the blush right over the apples of the cheeks in a circular motion, then blend. Cream blush is another great alternative as it adds a pretty glow to mature skin. Apply it with your fingertips and blend to a soft hue.

Skin
Dust a little translucent or pressed powder onto the t-zone to give the face a perfected look. Use a finishing spray at the end of makeup application to seal in the look.
Tip: Spritz the finishing spray in the air in front of you and "walk" into the mist to get very light, yet thorough, coverage.

Before

Lips
Line and fill the lips with a nude lip liner, then use your fingers to tap a bit of lip balm on top. Repeat the process for a longer-lasting effect.

❷ *WORKING OVERTIME*

"This is a build-up from the Soft Neutral look. It will showcase your features enough to get you noticed, but only in the right way!"

Eyes
Use a firm eyeshadow brush to dust copper eyeshadow all over the lids and lower lash lines. Use a cream color brush or your fingers to tap a gold eyeshadow onto the middle of the lids and just above the irises for a brightening, doe-eyed effect. Curl eyelashes and apply a volumizing mascara.

Tip: Avoid using eyeliner in a look like this to create a background for your eyelashes to stand out against. Use a waterproof mascara if you will be out in hot weather.

Skin
With a large powder brush, dust a matte bronzer or contour powder onto the cheeks and temples to create a bronzed, tanned look. Take whatever makeup is left on your brush and dust it over the tip of the nose for an overall sun-kissed look.

Lips
Exfoliate and moisturize your lips. Follow by applying a creamy lipstick in a beige-mauve shade.

3 PAINTING THE TOWN

"Girls just wanna have fun! So why shouldn't you? Here's THE perfect festive look that you need to try."

Eyeliner
Starting at the outer corners of the upper lashes, use an angled brush to draw small, short strokes with a liquid or gel eyeliner pencil.
Tip: For an easier application of liquid eyeliner, you can use the angled brush to gently swipe away the product. Applying it with a brush as opposed to the pen applicator gives you another application choice that can make it easier to master. Stay as close to the lash line as possible and end at the inner corners of the eyes, making the line thinner as you bring it in. Use a pointy smudge brush to soften the line if you desire, but make sure that the look stays dark at the base of the lashes.
Tip: On hooded eyes, you might want to start at the outer corners and only line about three quarters of the way in, creating a line that's as thin as possible. This will make the eyes appear larger by leaving a highlighted area in the inner corners.

Eyelashes
Curl the top lashes and coat them with a layer of black mascara. You might want to use a different formula than the lengthening one we used before. For instance, add waterproof over the lengthening formula. Comb through lashes to avoid any clumps.

Fake Lashes
Falsies really help to lift and open the eyes. A strip is usually easier to apply than individual lashes. Start by measuring the strip on your eyes and trimming it to fit.
Tip: Trim from the outer corners, as the inner corners are usually already trimmed shorter to fit more naturally. Swipe a thin layer of glue to the base of the lashes and let it dry for about a minute. Then "drop" and place the strip of lashes right on top of your natural lashes. The mascara you've already applied will create the perfect "shelf" to hold them in place.

Skin
Powder the skin with a dusting of translucent powder.
Tip: Use a large powder brush and press and roll it onto the areas you would like to mattify. Apply sparingly everywhere else and follow with a finishing spray to make the look last and stay fresh.

120

121

ONE GIRL FOUR LOOKS

"I designed these four looks on the same model and photographed them in sequential order. I started with a soft, monochromatic look, then built up the looks by adding and intensifying different shades. It's the perfect way to take a look from daytime to nighttime and everything in between!"

④ *NATURAL BEAUTY*

⑤ *SOFT CHIC*

⑥ SMOKEY

⑦ SULTRY GLAM

123

④ *NATURAL BEAUTY*

Lips
Prep and moisturize the mouth with a lip mask, then follow with a lip balm. Take a nude lip liner (it should be about one shade lighter than your actual lip color) and apply all over the lips, on top of the balm. Blend with your fingers for the most natural effect.

Tip:
Use your fingers to blend away any visible lip lines for a diffused, natural effect.

Before

This look is based on a wash of color. You can use different variations of pink or brown, but I opted to use a rosy matte shade on the eyes. Nothing is too overdone, but the contour on the cheeks and the simplicity of the look makes it work for any occasion.

Eyes
Apply a matte primer all over the eyelids and lower lash lines. Dust a matte, light nude eyeshadow all over eyelids, starting at the base of the lashes. Follow with a matte rose eyeshadow applied from the lids to each crease and lower lash line. Finish with a coat of natural mascara in dark brown or black. Fill in any sparse areas in the brows using a brow pencil, then blend with a brush to a natural finish.

Cheeks
Use a cheek brush to lightly contour the cheeks with a matte bronzer or contour powder. Follow with a warm champagne, slightly rose blush. Apply the darker shade first to avoid a "muddy" effect. Blend well.

⑤ SOFT CHIC

*"**For this look, I dialed up the intensity on the eyes and lips** while still keeping things neutral. I think of this woman as going out to meet her girlfriends for lunch or a day of shopping. It's a basic go-to look!"*

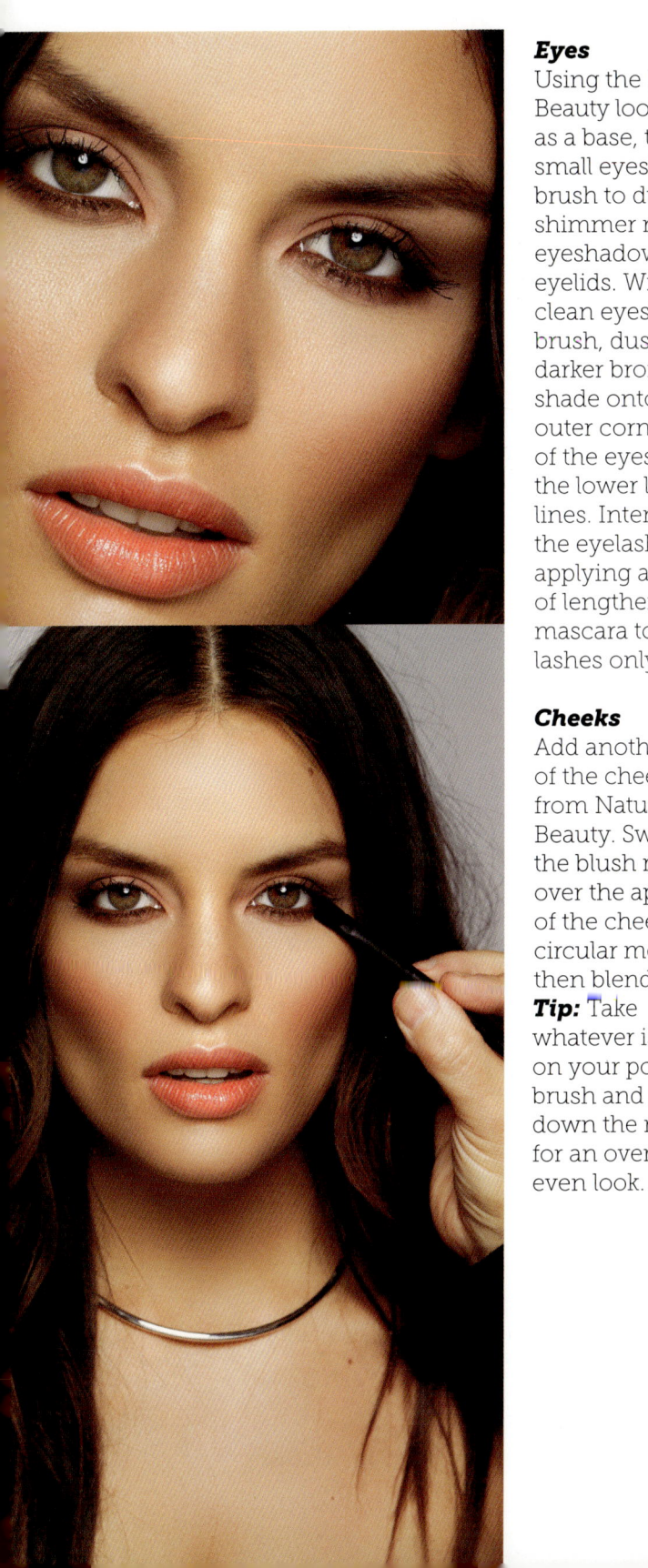

Eyes
Using the Natural Beauty look *(p. 124)* as a base, take a small eyeshadow brush to dust a shimmer rose eyeshadow to the eyelids. With a clean eyeshadow brush, dust a darker bronze shade onto the outer corners of the eyes and the lower lash lines. Intensify the eyelashes by applying a coat of lengthening mascara to the top lashes only.

Cheeks
Add another layer of the cheek color from Natural Beauty. Swipe the blush right over the apples of the cheeks in a circular motion, then blend.
Tip: Take whatever is left on your powder brush and run it down the neck for an overall even look.

Lips
Cover the lips with a coral lip liner and finish off with more lip balm, if desired. Repeat the process for a longer-lasting effect.

Skin
Dust a little translucent or pressed powder onto the t-zone to give the face a perfected look.

⑥ SMOKEY

Eyeliner
Starting at the outer corners of the upper lashes, draw small, short strokes with a brown or black eyeliner pencil. Stay as close to the lash line as possible and end at the inner corners of the eyes, making the line thinner as you bring it in. Use a pointy smudge brush to soften the line. Continue with short strokes and draw the liner just at the lower lash line. Smudge.

Tip: On smaller eyes, you might want to start at the outer corners and only line about three quarters of the way in. This will make the eyes appear larger by leaving a highlighted area in the inner corners.

"This smokey eye look adapts itself to all eye shapes by accentuating both the lower lash lines and the outer corners of the eyes. Anyone can use it to add length and drama to their eye makeup depending on their own taste. You can make it as soft or as glam as you'd like!"

Eyeshadow
With an eyeshadow brush or your fingers, apply a brown/wine color matte eyeshadow to the lids. Smudge just below the crease and on the lower lash line.

Eyelashes
Curl the top lashes and coat them with a layer of black mascara. You might want to use a different formula than the lengthening one we used before. For instance, add waterproof over the lengthening formula. Comb through lashes to avoid any clumps. This gives you double benefits, length and longer staying power.

… # ⓖ *SULTRY GLAM*

"**Strong eyes and lips** can seem scary but the key is knowing how to pair them with a glowing, natural complexion."

Eyes
Add two layers of rusty brown eyeshadow to the lids, as well as a heavy eyeliner line to create a sultry effect. Use matte rose eyeshadow to blend out any edges.
Tip: Protect the under-eye area from makeup fallout by holding a folded tissue under the eyes while applying dark eyeshadow.

Cheeks
Use a round, medium size powder brush and swirl highlighting powder onto tops of the cheeks, the tip of the nose, and any other area you'd like to emphasize. Clean the brush and blend away any hard edges.

Lips
To match the intensity of the eyes, use your fingers to dab a wine/dark shade of lipstick to the lips. Line the lips with a berry or deep red lip liner (or fill them in all the way for a longer-lasting effect). Then, starting at the middle of the lips, dab on a blackberry lipstick and feather out with your fingers. Repeat the process.

THE NEUTRALS

"Neutral shades are perfect for those who are new at makeup or are not sure about what colors to wear. When applied subtly, they are virtually foolproof. That's the hidden power of neutrals!"

8 *GLOWING BEIGE*

9 *SWEET MATTES*

10 *SHEER NEUTRAL*

11 *SLATE NEUTRAL*

12 *RADIANT!*

13 *SHEER BRONZE*

14 *SUMMERTIME*

"Neutral shades are hues that are unsaturated with color. Beige, brown, gray, and black are amazing shades to master in your makeup wardrobe. They can create the perfect canvas on which to add pops of color. What you get is a no-distraction type of beauty. The focus is on you and your features, not on the makeup."

⓼ GLOWING BEIGE

"This look gives you that post-gym glow without the workout!"

Skin
For skin that glows naturally, begin by using a moisturizing sheet mask either the night before or the day of your makeup application. After smoothing on your foundation, apply a bit of moisturizer on top. Think of what you look like after working out or after a hot yoga session. It's a natural glow and not a shimmer.

Eyes
With an all-over eyeshadow brush, apply a flesh-toned shimmery eyeshadow to the eyelids. To add a playful touch, use a clear sparkly lip gloss and tap it over the lids with your fingers. Try not to carry the gloss above the crease. It will crease at some point, but don't worry, you are not after perfection! Finish the eyes with a coat of mascara.

Cheeks
Using a shade of cheek color that's a little bit deeper than what you'd normally wear, apply blush over your foundation and right on top of the cheeks with a sponge, then blend with your finger. This technique makes the cheeks look flushed, creamy, and naturally pink. Avoid adding power to that area if possible.

Before

Lips
On the back of your hand, mix a soft beige lipstick with lip balm. Then use your fingers to tap it onto your lips, creating a soft lip stain. Repeat for added intensity.

❾ SWEET MATTES

"Here's a very modern makeup look that pairs all-matte color products with fresh, glowing skin."

Eyes
Three eyeshadows give this all-matte look a beautiful effect. Begin by dusting a matte light taupe shadow onto the lids with an eyeshadow brush, then blend up to the crease. Use an eye crease brush to blend the color up and above the crease. Apply a soft hazelnut shade to the bottom lash lines using a smudger brush. At the inner corner of the eyes, apply a pink-apricot matte shade to brighten up the eyes.

Tip: As an alternative, you can apply blush to the inner corners of the eyes. Finish the eyes with a light coat of mascara on the upper lashes only.

Tip: Create the most natural look for your lashes by using a tissue to remove any excess mascara from the brush before applying it.

Cheeks
Use a slightly angled cheek brush to apply a salmon blush to the hollows of the cheeks, then blend up to avoid any harsh lines.

Lips
Apply a nude lipstick that's one shade lighter than your own lips, which will accentuate your lips without stealing the show.

Before

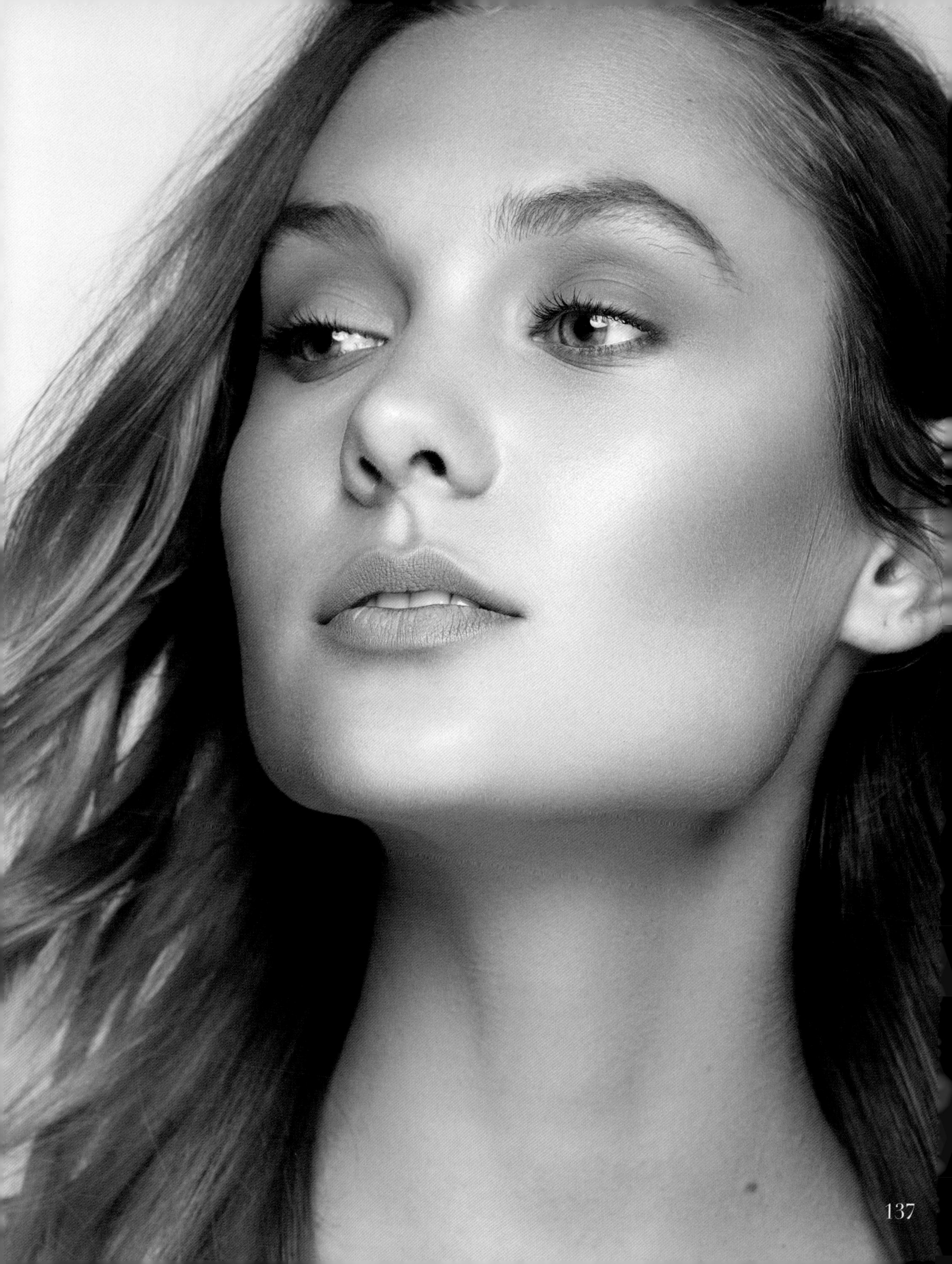

10 SHEER NEUTRAL

"This is the perfect out-the-door look. It requires very little effort and is excellent for every day."

Eyes
Apply eye primer to both eyelids and lower lash lines. This will help the color stay put longer and will intensify the sheen of the eyeshadow. Use an eye crease brush to define the crease and the lower lash line with a brown/mauve sheer shadow. Then use a fluffy eyeshadow brush to dust a lighter beige eyeshadow onto both lids starting at the base of the lashes, blending the crease shade softly. Continue by curling the eyelashes and applying a coat of mascara.

Tip: To curl your lashes for a maximum effect, curl first at the base, then at mid-section, and finish off by curling the little baby lashes on the outer corners of the eye — those make all the difference! Use a brow gel to brush eyebrows into place.

Skin
Apply a light dusting of translucent powder over the face to avoid shine and help set the makeup in place.

Cheeks
Dip a cheek brush into a peachy/pink blush then blow off excess from the brush and dust gently onto cheekbones and above the outer corners of eyes to the temples.

Lips
For a natural yet polished look, apply lip pencil all over the lips. Smudge the color with your fingertips, then apply a nude or flesh-toned lip gloss.

Tip: Using a large powder brush, press the powder onto your skin, then roll the brush to blend. Repeat the process. This will set your foundation without leaving behind any residue. Concentrate on the forehead, nose, and chin.

SLATE NEUTRAL 11

"Simple yet sophisticated, gray is the perfect alternative to black or brown on the eyes."

Eyes
Cover lids with an eye primer and also apply to the lower lash lines. Use an eyeshadow brush to apply a matte flesh-toned eyeshadow all over the lids. Follow by adding a shimmery powder eyeshadow in a similar shade to the lids, from each lash line to crease, and on the lower lash lines. Next, use a gunmetal gray eyeliner pencil and line the upper lash line, making sure you rim the base of the lashes. Follow by applying a slate gray eyeshadow over the pencil liner. Finish by lining the outer third of each lower lash line with the slate gray eyeshadow only. Apply two coats of mascara.

Lips
To slough away dry skin and smooth the texture of the lips, apply a coat of a lip scrub, leave on for a few seconds, then wipe off with a warm cloth. Follow with lip balm. Dot a shimmery pink gloss on the center of the lower lips and press the lips together for a sheer, natural look.

Cheeks
Use a matte bronze powder to contour and enhance the cheeks. Suck in your cheeks, then use a cheek brush to apply a taupe bronze powder that's a shade darker than your skin tone to the hollows of the cheeks. Make sure the contour line ends below the apples of the cheeks. Blend, blend, blend! Follow with a luminizing pink blush on the apples of the cheeks.

⑫ *RADIANT!*

"Radiant skin is key to this neutral look. Incorporating a brightening serum into your skincare routine and using a facial mask regularly will help strengthen and repair the skin, bringing back its luminosity for a beautiful glow."

Before

Eyes
Apply a champagne shade eyeshadow to the inner corners of the eyes using a pointy smudger brush in soft, circular motions. Follow by dusting a rose gold eyeshadow from the lash line to crease using a clean eyeshadow brush. Then use small, circular strokes to apply a soft brown matte eyeshadow to the outside of the crease with an eye crease brush.
Tip: This helps to add depth to a hooded eye. Blend really well to avoid leaving behind any visible lines. Finish with a coat of mascara.

Cheeks
Using a shade of blush that's a couple of tones darker than your skin tone, define the cheek bones with a cheek brush. Blend up onto the apples of the cheeks for a lifted effect.

Lips
Use a lip liner that's a shade darker than your own skin tone and line all over the lips. Follow with a swipe of a creamy peach/brown lipstick.
Tip: The idea here is to give your eyes the dimensional look of eyeliner without actually using eyeliner for a softer, more natural effect.

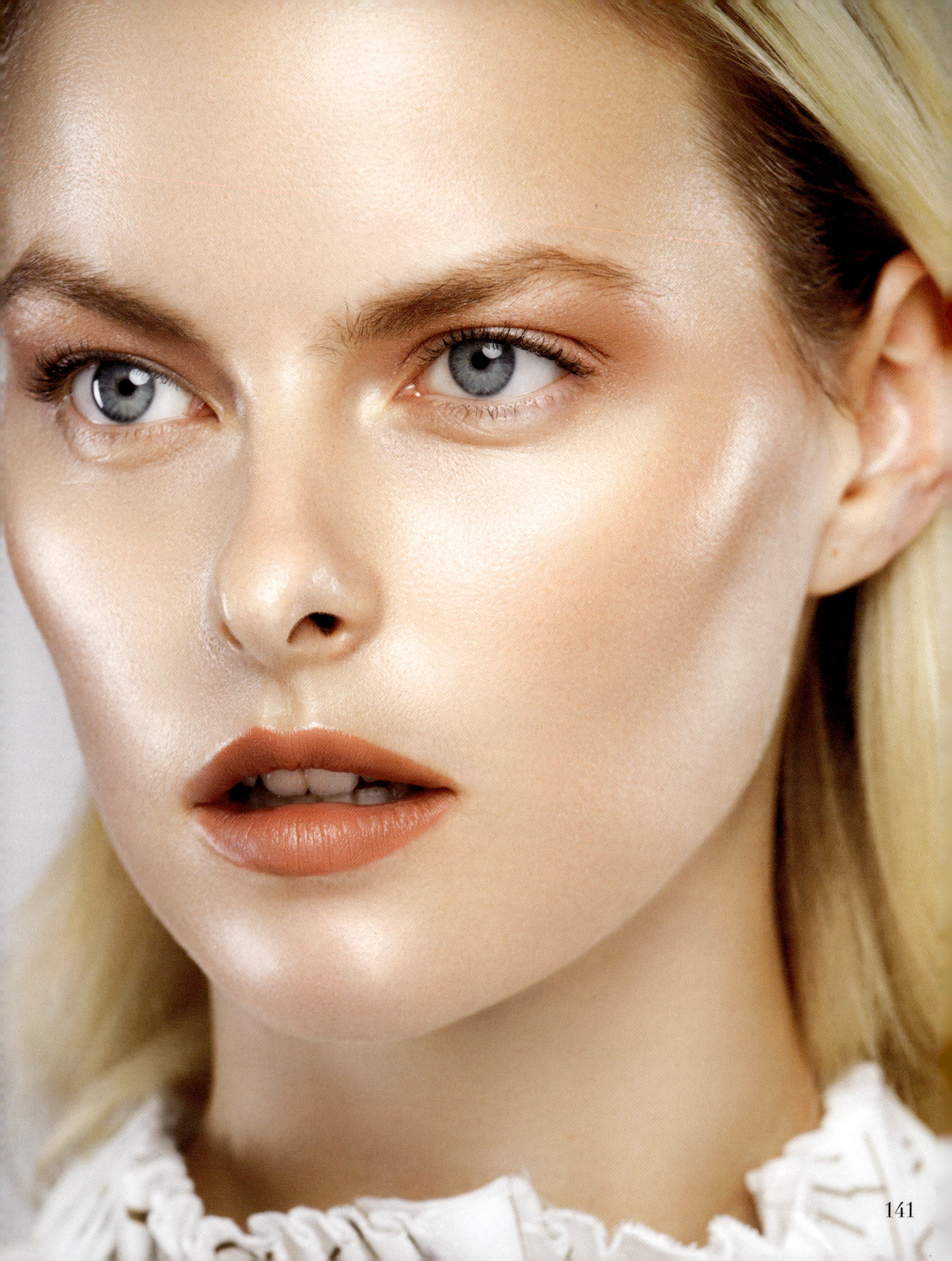

13. SHEER BRONZE

"Using metallic textures is my favorite way to add an interesting sheen to any neutral makeup look."

Eyes
With your fingers or a small fluffy brush, apply a gold shimmery eyeshadow all over the eyes. Using a crease brush, define the area right above the crease and extend it up and out slightly to create an elongated effect. Then use a dark brown pencil eyeliner to softly define the lash lines all around the eyes. Use a smudger brush to blend the liner. For added intensity, create a thick smudged line. Curl and apply a coat of mascara to both lashes.

Lips
For a fun look, apply a creamy nude lipstick to the lips, then use your fingertips to dab a little bit of a gold eyeshadow to the cupid's bow area. You can also do this with a metallic gold liquid lip. It's an easy version of an ombré lip that works really well with neutral shades.

Cheeks
Mix a sparkling berry blush with a bronzer and apply to the cheeks. The best way to do this is to use a cheek brush and first apply the bronzer to the top of your hand, then swirl the same brush onto the blush to combine the shades. This will create a warm berry tone that looks very natural and really pretty.

SUMMERTIME 14

"Here's a very modern makeup look that pairs all-matte color products with fresh, glowing skin."

Eyes
Use a firm eyeshadow brush to dust copper eyeshadow all over the lids and lower lash lines. Use a cream color brush or your fingers to tap a gold eyeshadow onto the middle of the lids and just above the irises for a brightening, doe-eyed effect. Curl eyelashes and apply a volumizing mascara.

Tip: Avoid using eyeliner in a look like this to create a background for your eyelashes to stand out against. Use a waterproof mascara if you will be out in hot weather.

Skin
With a large powder brush, dust a matte bronzer or contour powder onto the cheeks and temples to create a bronzed, tanned look. Take whatever makeup is left on your brush and dust it over the tip of the nose for an overall sun-kissed look.

Lips
Exfoliate and moisturize lips. Follow by applying a creamy lipstick in a beige-mauve shade.

BEAUTY SCHOOL: #UNFILTERED LOOKS

"Your teenage years are a great time to find your identity, discover your own style, and use makeup to experiment and express your attitude. Try different colors and textures depending on your mood."

15 COMING UP ROSY

16 YOU GLOW, GIRL

17 CHARMING

18 SOFT METALS

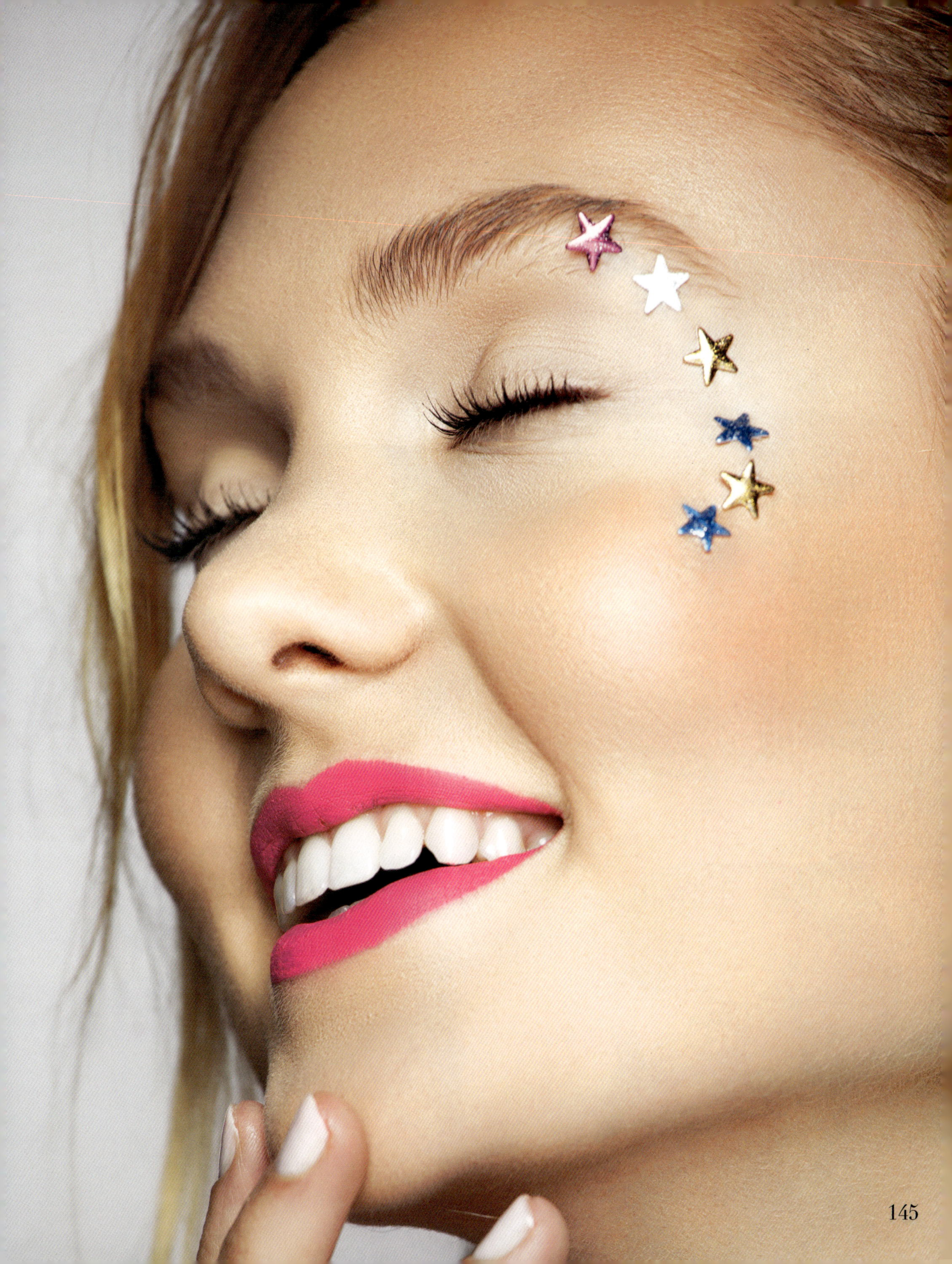

15 COMING UP ROSY

"This look was created using soft, warm pastels on the eyes, cheeks, and lips. Light and feminine, pastel shades are a great way to add depth to any makeup look without making it look overdone."

Eyes
Define the brows by filling them in with an eyebrow pencil, then dust a matte, flesh-toned eyeshadow onto the lids. Use an eyeliner brush to apply a soft peach matte eyeshadow all around the eyes. Next, use a smudger brush to diffuse the line, concentrating on the outer corners of the eyes. Curl lashes and apply a coat of mascara.

Cheeks
Give the apples of the cheeks a natural-looking flush by swirling a rosy champagne blush using a tight round kabuki or mineral powder brush to the apples of the cheeks. Blend with a larger cheek brush.

Tip: If the cheek color looks too strong, sweep a tiny bit of translucent powder on top to tone it down.

Lips
Moisturize and protect the lips, which is key for any matte lipstick application. Then follow by applying a coral lip liner all over the lips for a natural rosy effect.

Before

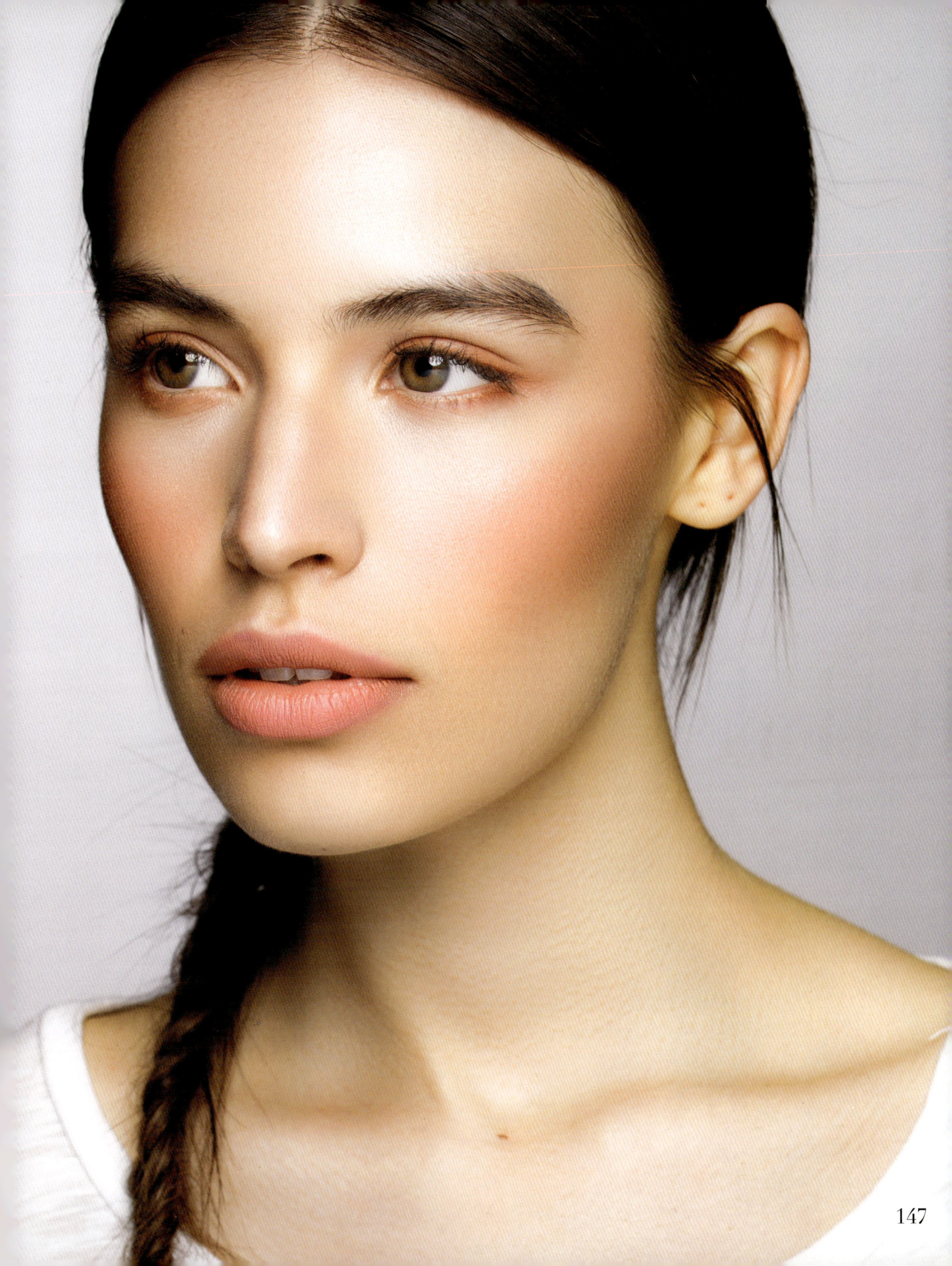

16 YOU GLOW, GIRL

"Put away the bubble-gum pinks and opt for a blush pink which gives this look a fresh, young sophistication. This look can be created in five minutes with only a few products."

Eyes
Take the same sparkling pink blush used on the cheeks and use your fingers to tap it onto the eyelids. Use a crease brush to blend up and out to the crease. Soften and blend well to create a wash of color on the eyes. Finish with a volumizing mascara.

Lips
Apply a dab of sparkly peach-pink lip gloss to the middle of the lips, then press the lips together and distribute the product using the lip gloss wand or your fingers.

Skin
Prime and moisturize the skin, then follow with a light veil of CC cream or light liquid foundation. Add concealer where necessary. Apply translucent powder to the t-zone area, and dust whatever product is left on your brush over the rest of the face.

Cheeks
With a cheek brush, dust a sparkling pink blush over the cheeks and blend toward the ears and the temples. Add highlighting powder to the tops of the cheeks and if desired, on the tip of the nose, the cupid's bow, and the chin.

Before

149

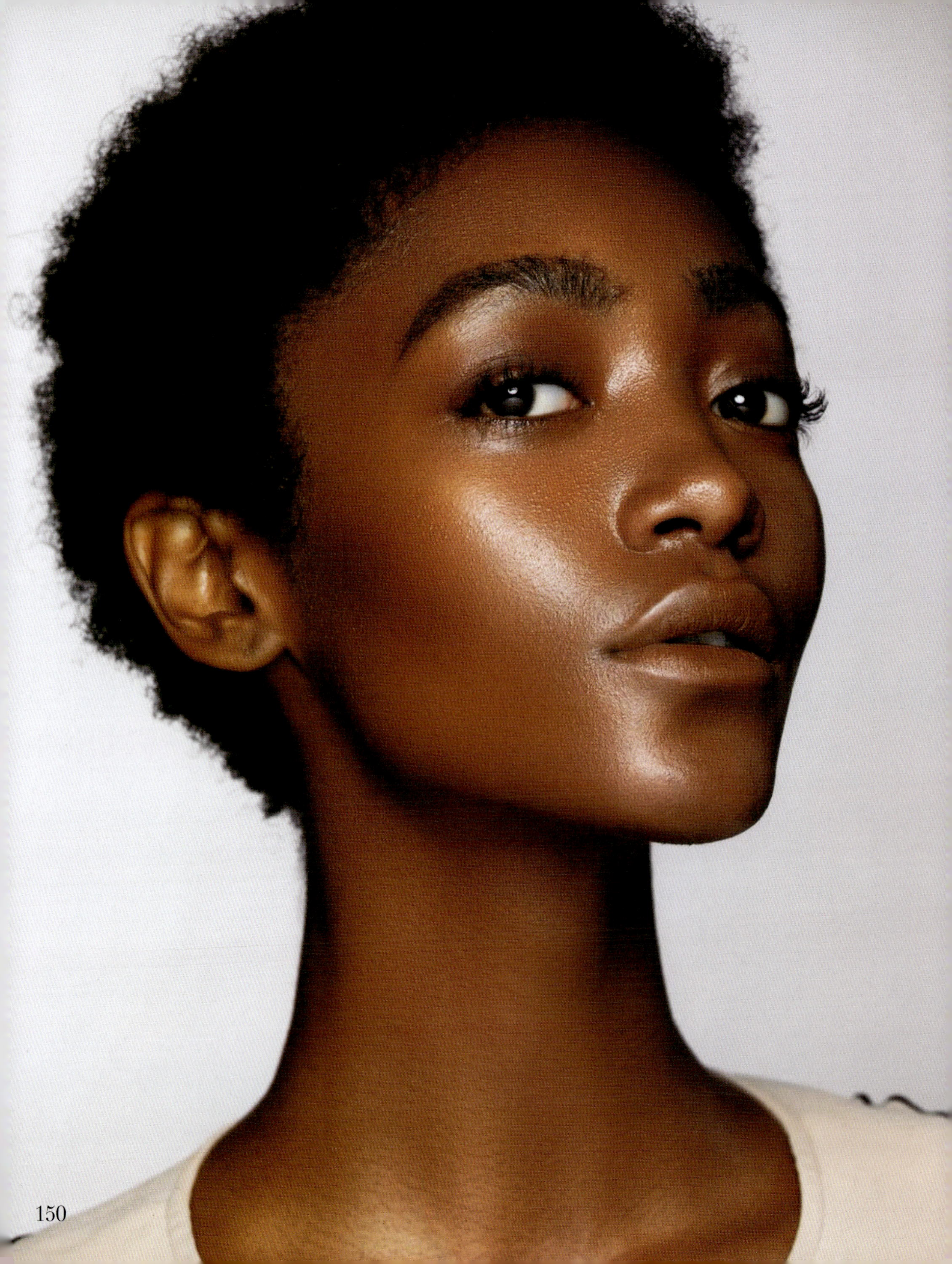

CHARMING 17

"Soft, simple to achieve, and full of benefits! This look makes the most of your own features while creating the perfect canvas to build on when you want to have fun."

Skin

Good skincare for deep skin tones is essential. Cleanse skin in water at least once a day using a mild cleanser. Exfoliate manually no more than a couple of times per week. You want to lift dead skin cells away, but not over-dry the skin or aggravate it if it's acne-prone. Moisturize daily with an oil-free lotion, and no matter what your age or skin tone, always wear sunscreen, even on a cloudy day.

Dark skin can have red undertones; if that's the case, you want to find a foundation that has more of a blue base. If you have a more golden complexion, look for warm, rich shades of foundation. If you're not sure, your best best is to seek out a professional that can help you or at least let you try out the foundation in natural light before you buy it.

Be sure to test any face powder on your skin, as well, and make sure that it is warm, deep, and does not look ashy. Opt for yellow to orange shades of powder, or use oil-blotting sheets that have no color to them.

Before

Eyes

Keep things simple by using the following three staple eyeshadow shades based on your skin tone.

1. A shade that's slightly lighter than your skin tone. Make sure it's not too light or frosty, however it's okay if it's a little shimmery.
2. A matte shade that's about two shades darker than your skin tone.
3. A dark brown to black matte eyeshadow.

Apply shade 1 to the eyelids with an all-over eyeshadow brush. If your lids are oily, you might want to dust a tiny bit of powder on them first, or use an oil-controlling eyeshadow primer. Follow by applying shade 2 from the lash lines to the crease with an eyeshadow brush, starting at the outer corners and working in until it disappears. If desired, carry shade 2 under the lash line toward the inner corners of the eyes. Use shade 3 as an eyeliner right at the base of the lashes. Curl your lashes and apply a coat of lengthening mascara. Use shade 2 to fill in your eyebrows and brush them in shape with brow gel.

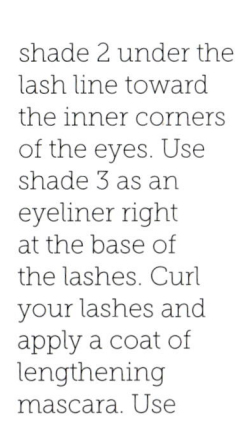

Lips

Finish the look with a warm golden blush and a nude lip gloss.

151

18 SOFT METALS

"By using just the right combination of glimmer and matte around the eyes, this look creates a fun, trompe l'oeil-like optical illusion!"

Eyes

Begin by applying an eye primer to the lids. With an eyeshadow brush, lightly tap a silver eyeshadow onto the lid so that the color is barely visible when the eyes are open. Repeat for impact. Then, using a silver/black eyeliner, define the base of the lashes all around the eyes. Soften with a smudger brush so the liner blends into the eyeshadow and there are no visible lines.

Using a crease brush, define the area right at the orbital bone with a matte taupe-brown eyeshadow. For added 3D impact, use the tip of a smudger brush to apply a dot of light pearl eyeshadow to the inner corners of the eyes and right above the irises. Blend into the silver shade to create a foiled look. Create a visible contrast between the matte and shimmer textures, then blend upward until the crease shade disappears under the eyebrows. Apply a couple of coats of mascara to the top and bottom lashes.

Lips

Using your fingertips, dab a tiny bit of berry lipstick onto the center of the lips and feather out all over the lips. Apply a second coat if desired.

Before

153

EYELINER LOOKS

19 *PERFECT LINE*

20 *CHARCOAL LINE*

21 *COLORFUL LINE*

22 *PRECISE LINE*

23 *GRAPHIC LINE*

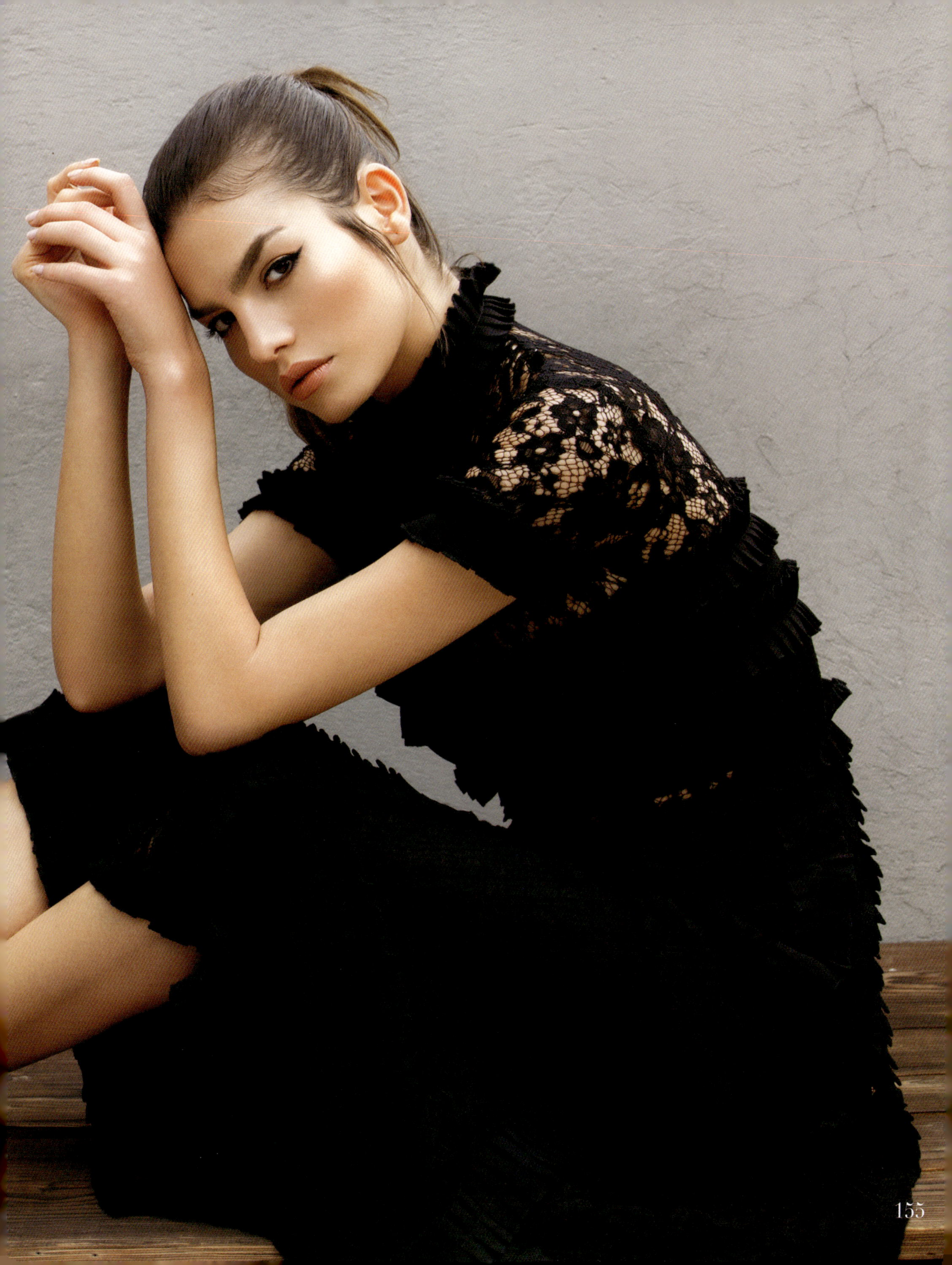

⑲ PERFECT LINE

"Who says hooded eyes can't have fun? Here's a perfect cat-eye that works on eyes that are smaller or have heavy lids."

Eyes
Begin by dusting a flesh-toned matte eyeshadow all over the lids. Apply a liquid or gel eyeliner, following the contour or curves of the eyes, hugging it right at the lash lines. The thinnest point of the line should be at the inner corners; it should begin to thicken slightly at the center of the lid to the outer corner. Follow with a coat of water-resistant mascara on the upper lashes and a second coat at the tips of the lashes.

Tip: Tap the brush on both sides while dipping it into the eyeshadow for even distribution.

Tip: The heavy fold of hooded eyes might not allow you to give this cat-eye a sharp lift; instead, opt to pull the eyeliner in a straight line from the outer corners. This will give the eye a dramatic, elongated effect without getting lost in the eye fold. Don't forget to check your work while looking straight ahead as much as possible.

Cheeks
Use a cheek brush to apply a light apricot blush, giving the cheeks a natural glow. Apply a very light coat to the apples of the cheeks, then blend in small circular motions toward the ears and the temples. Make sure you blend all edges well.

Lips
Use a lip primer to help prevent any lip product from bleeding or creeping into fine lines around the lips. Follow with a nude lip liner if preferred, then apply a natural rose lip gloss.

Tip: Use a blotter sheet to dab the lips if the gloss looks too shiny and/or you want to add additional layers.

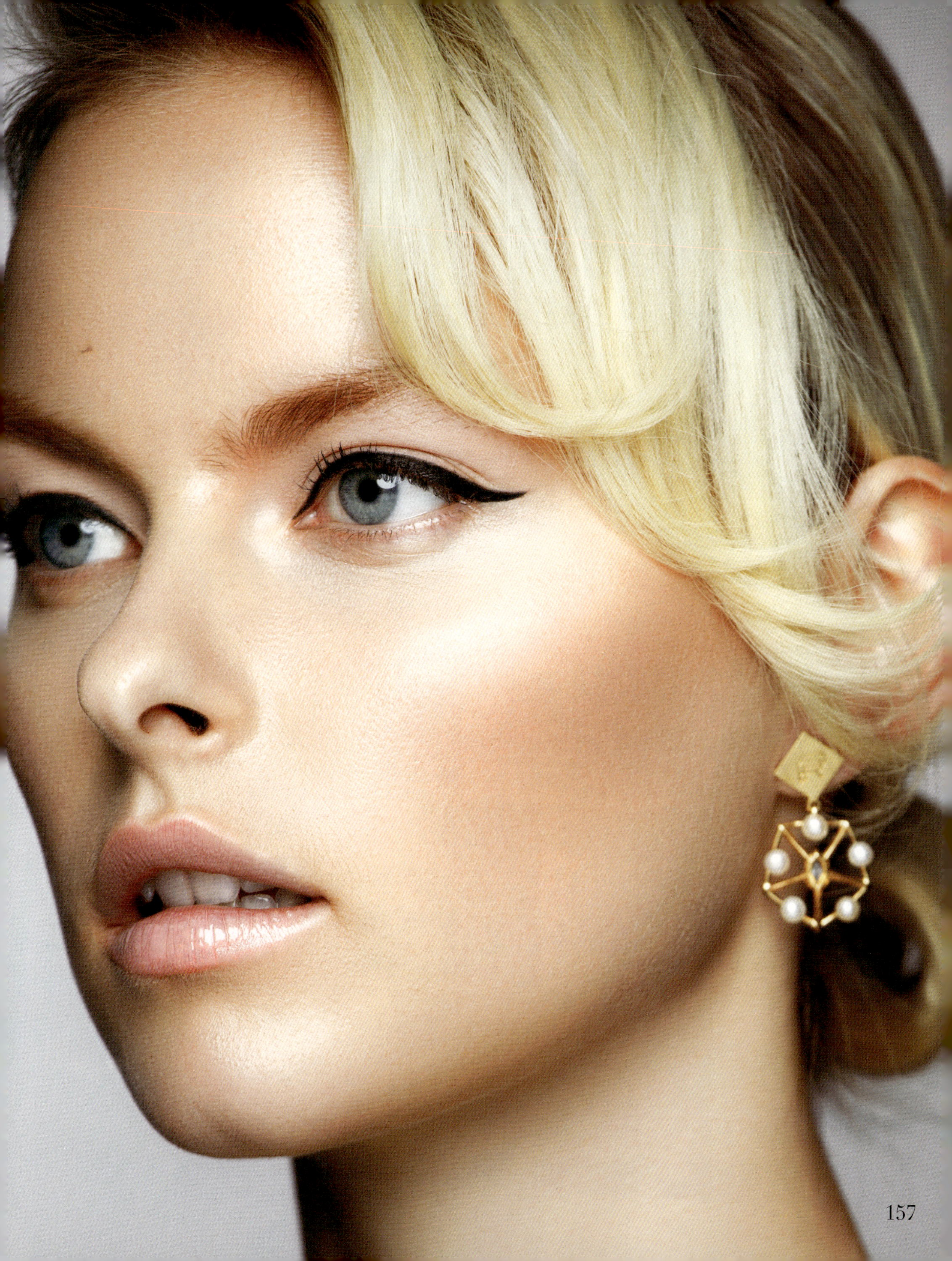

⓴ CHARCOAL LINE

"Here's another cyeliner option which is great for hooded or Asian-shaped eyes. It actually involves using no eyeliner at all!"

Eyes

For this look, make sure you apply primer to both the eyelids and the lower lash lines. Apply a rose gold eyeshadow from the inner corner of the eyes out to the whole lid using a cream or eye color brush. Add a darker brown shade right at the orbital bone to give the eyes more definition using the angled side of a crease brush, then blend the color out using the longer bristled side. Spritz an angled eyeliner brush with water and while slightly damp, coat both sides of the brush with a silver granite eyeshadow to distribute the product evenly. Outline around the eyes to create a bright eyeliner effect. Drag the brush right at the lash lines and out to the outer corners. Lift the line slightly at the outer corners and carry down to the lower lash line.

Tip: If you like the look of bold eyeliner, apply a thin tightline right at the base of the lashes using a gel or liquid eyeliner. Fill in sparse eyebrow areas and use a spoolie brush to shape them into place. Curl the eyelashes and apply two coats of water-resistant mascara.

Cheeks

Use a cheek brush to define your cheekbones with a coral blush, then using the same brush, grab the bristles tightly and pick up some highlighting powder. Dust highlighter onto the tops of the cheeks, then blend with a new, clean brush. If your face is longer, place the blush on the apples of your cheeks. If round, apply all along your cheekbones.

Before

Lips
Apply a sheer pink lipstick with slight shine. Build up the color using layers, if necessary.

㉑ COLORFUL LINE

"Adding a pop of color to your eyes using a lively, bright shade is a great way to cheer up any makeup look. It will transform your eyes and give off a hint of your personality. Using eyeliner is a great way to achieve this — mix it with an eyeshadow and you can create endless combinations!"

Before

Eyes
Use a fluffy eyeshadow brush to apply a neutral shadow all over the lids from inner to outer corners, slowly building to just above your natural crease. With an eye crease brush, softly blend the shadow around the outer edges so the color gradually disappears. Use a black eyeliner to create a very thin line at the base of the lashes, around the entire eye. Make sure that the line encircles the eyes with the darkest color closest to the lash line.

Tip: Tightlining round, dark eyes will create a beautiful contrast and make your eye color stand out. Line the upper lash line with an aqua blue eyeliner, then use an angled eyeliner brush to tap a teal blue eyeshadow as close to the lashes as possible. Extend the line slightly past the corner of your eye.

Tip: Layering an eyeshadow over a pencil eyeliner will help set the shade into place for longer lasting wear. Highlight the inner corners of the eyes with a champagne eyeshadow. The contrast of the lighter color will make the teal shade pop even more. Apply an eyelash primer to add length and volume, then add one or two coats of mascara.

Eyebrows
Use the tip of an eyebrow gel applicator to saturate stubborn brow hairs. Brush with the full wand to set them all into place.

Skin
Use a foundation brush to blend a creme-to-powder foundation in a darker shade than your skin tone onto the sides of the nose, under the cheekbones, and at the jawline and temples. Then apply a foundation that matches your skin tone everywhere else to seamlessly highlight and contour.

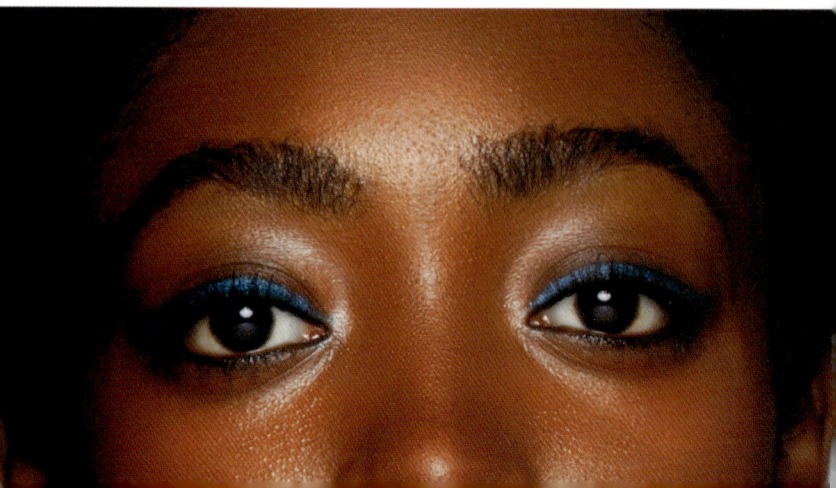

160

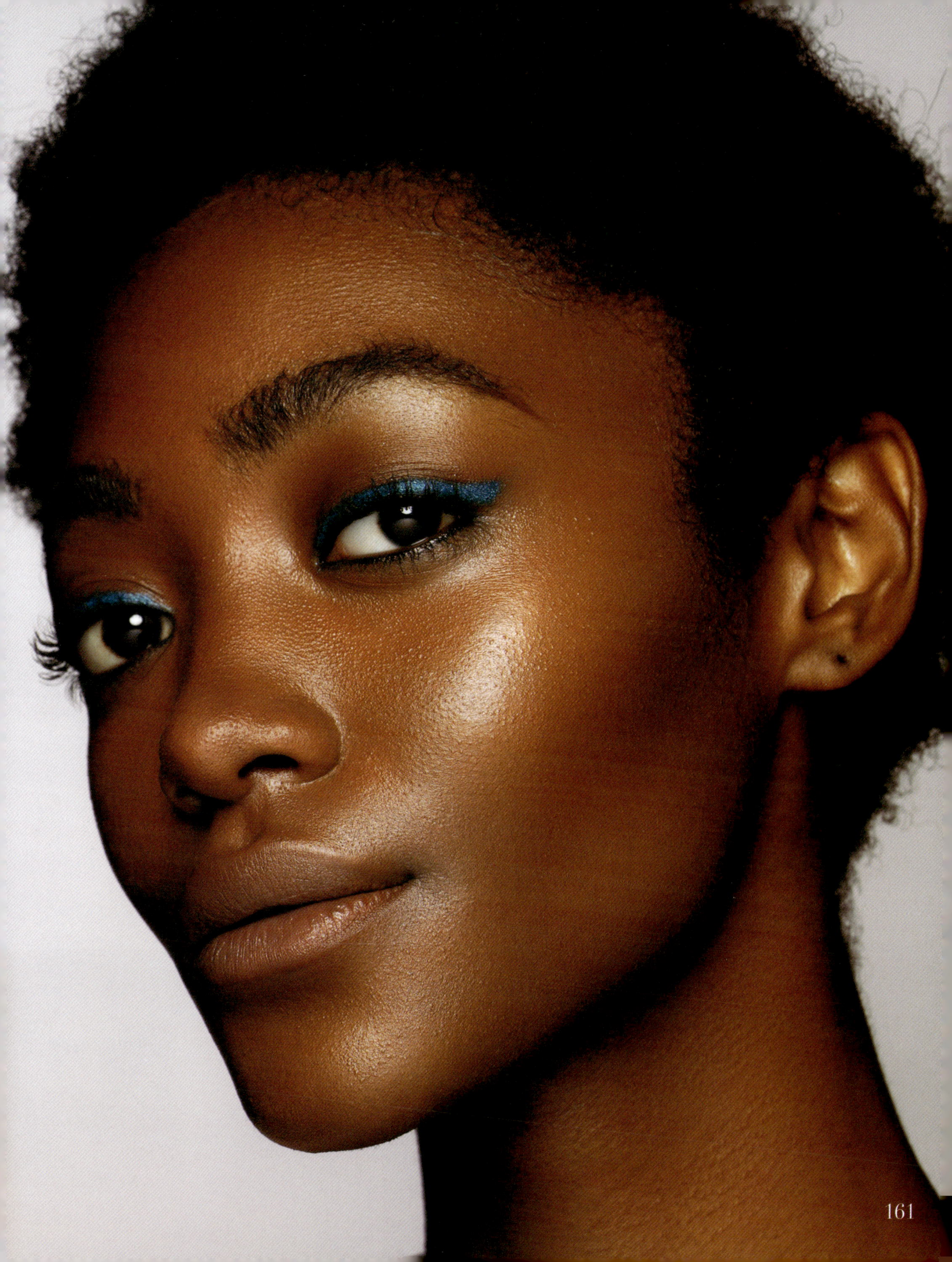

㉒ PRECISE LINE

"It takes practice and precision, but the benefits of nailing a perfect cat-eye way outweigh the efforts. This geometric eyeliner look can be intensified or played down depending on your mood."

Eyes
Priming the eyelids is a must for this look. Apply the primer with a synthetic brush so you can get close to the lash lines and the inner corners of the eyes. With an eyeshadow brush, dust a bronze eyeshadow onto your eyelid and up to the crease. Blend well at the outer edges for a seamless look. Then, starting at the inner corners of the eyes, draw a thin line of liquid or gel liner and stop right when you reach the outer corners.

To elongate your eyes, draw a line at the outer lash lines that goes slightly up and follows the line of your lower lid. Go up as much as you'd like, then create a V shape by taking the line to the upper lash line. Fill in any sparse areas and make sure there are no light spot that show up. Line the lower lash line.

Brows
Apply a tinted brow gel that's a shade lighter than your natural brow color. This will help tone down heavy brows and keep the focus on your eyes. If you have brown to dark brown hair, use a medium-brown tinted gel.

Lips
Line the lips with the tip of a rose champagne metallic liquid lipstick, then fill in the whole lip area.

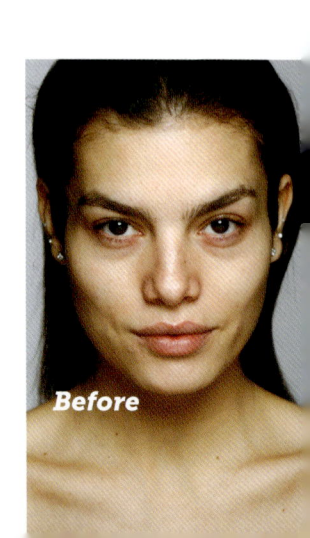

Before

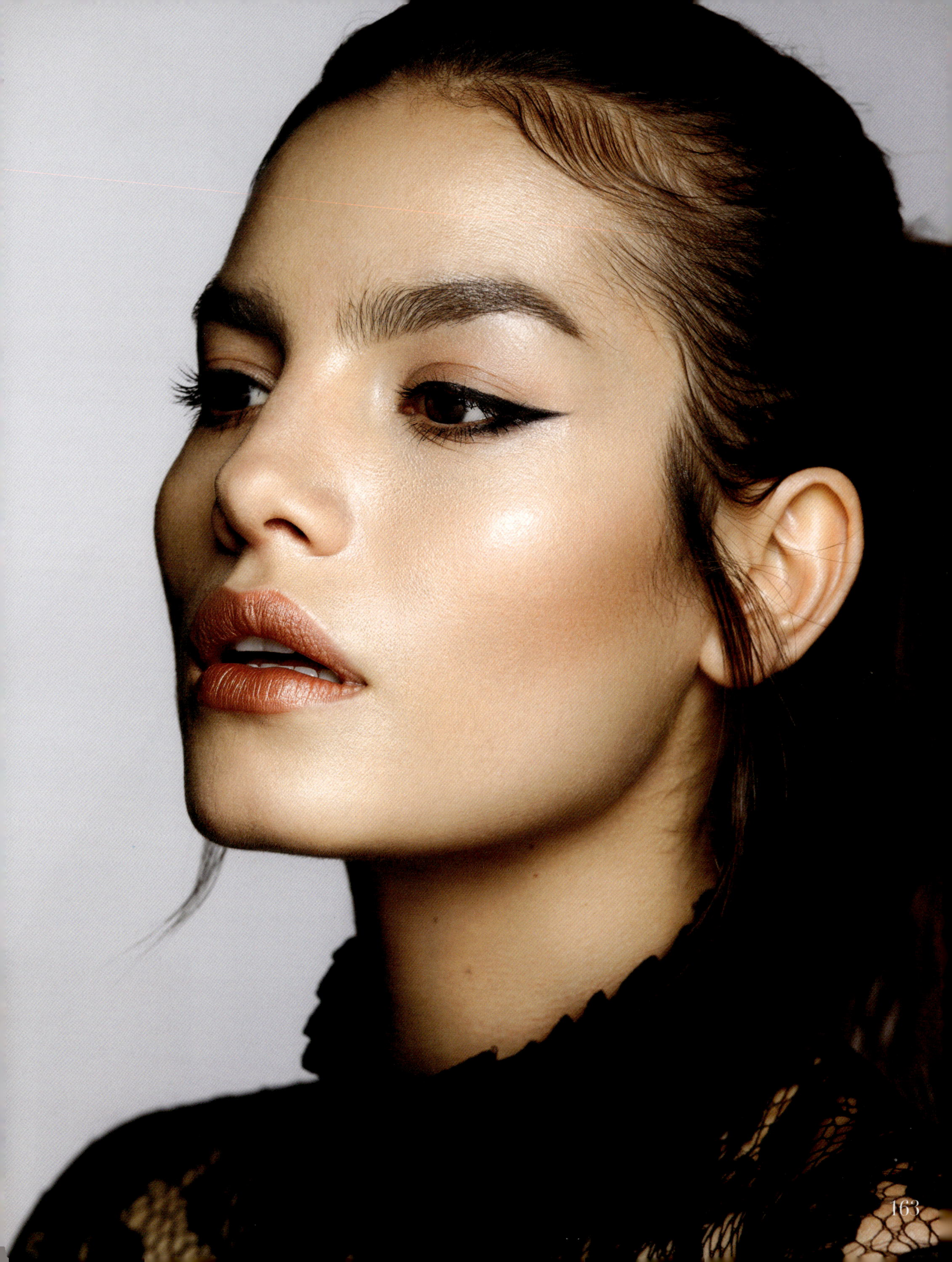

㉓ GRAPHIC LINE

"This is a bold, negative-space eyeliner look that's totally customizable. Stop at a slight wing or go for the drama of a '60s-inspired shape."

Eyes

Apply an eye primer to the lids, then rim the eyes with a slightly shimmery gold eyeshadow.

Look down and relax your eyelids. Steady your hand by placing the inside of your wrist just above the side of your jaw. Begin sketching your desired shape with a pencil eyeliner, starting from the outer corners and tracing a line from the outer to the inner corners of the eyes. Use short, light, and feathery strokes, and leave as much skin showing between the lash line and the eyeliner, which will give the eyeliner a floating effect. The negative space you are creating will make the eyes look larger and create a cool look. Apply a gel or liquid liner over the pencil to obtain the desired shape.

Lips

Starting at the center of the lips, swipe a matte hot pink liquid lipstick right on the lips. Repeat the process as many times as desired.

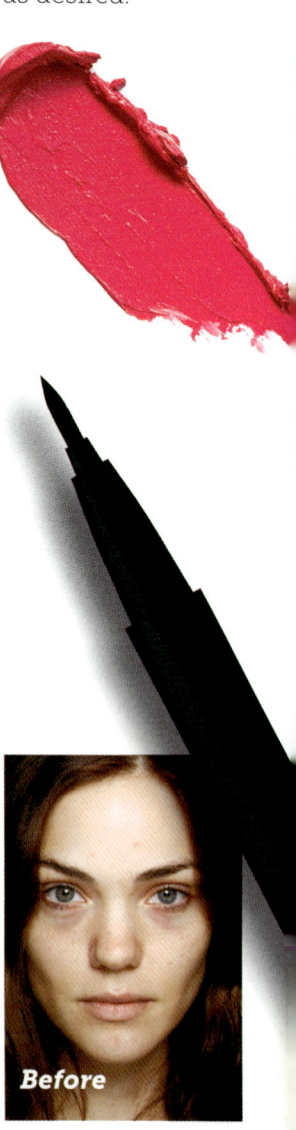

Before

165

A POP *OF* COLOR

㉔ *OMBRÉ*

㉕ *TEAL GAZE*

㉖ *HOT PINK*

㉗ *BURNT CORAL*

㉘ *SPARKLING VIOLET*

㉙ *BOLD RED*

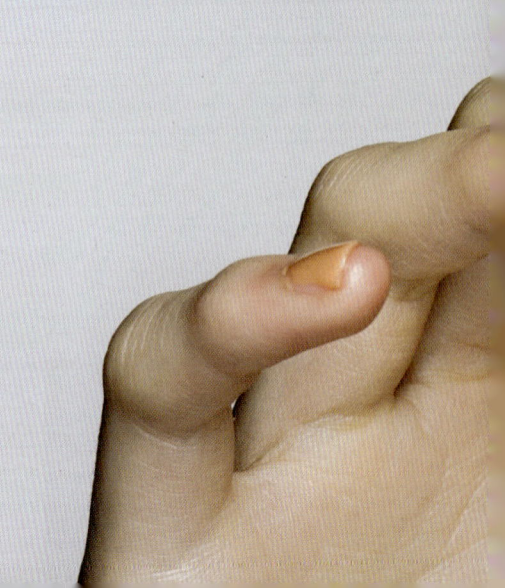

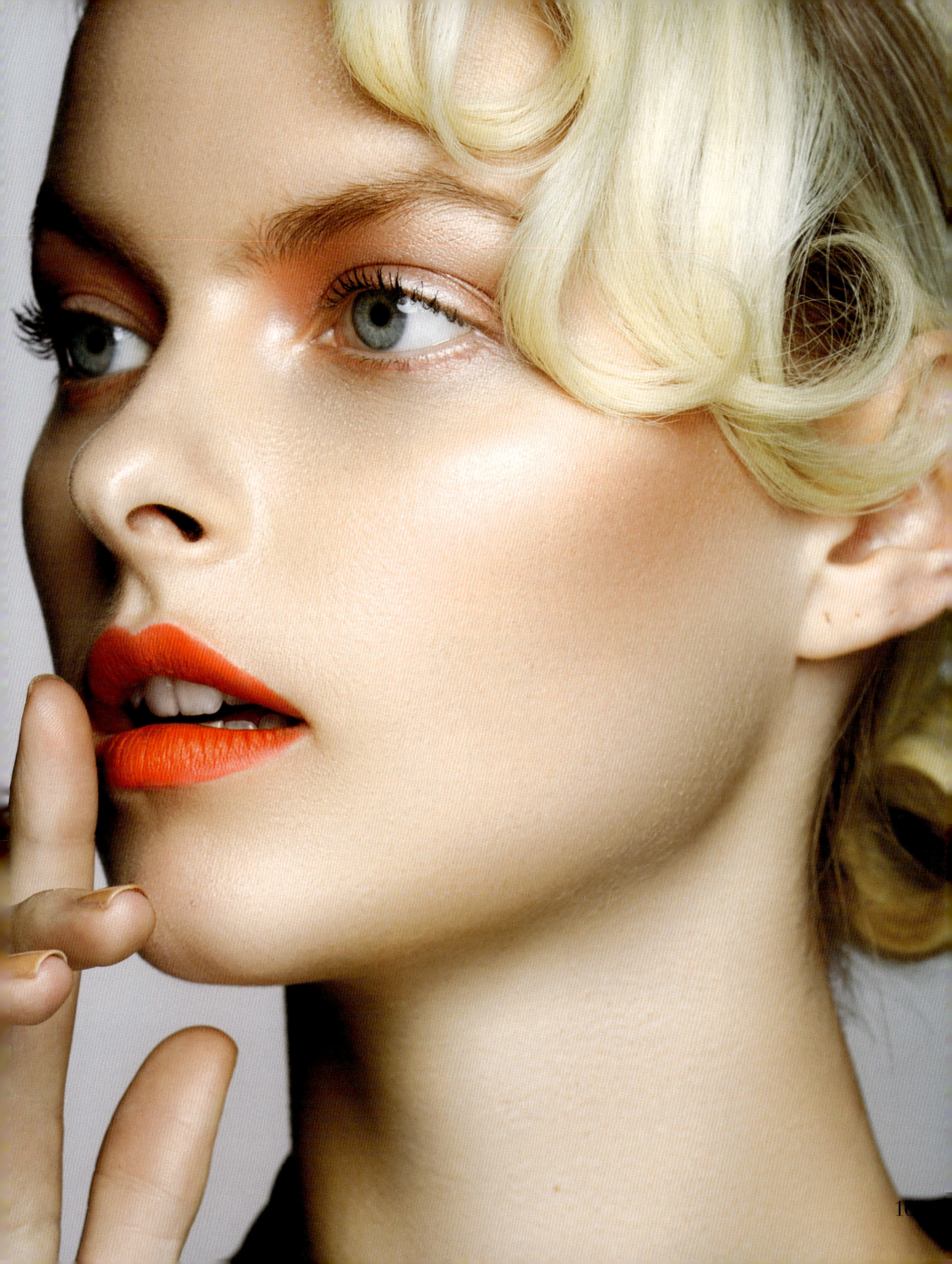

24 OMBRÉ

"Derived from the French word for 'shadow,' ombré can be achieved using color tones that are shaded or graduated from dark to light. It is one of the easiest ways to create a cool lip look that features as many shades as you want!"

Skin
Luminous fresh skin is key for a matte lip look like this. Even out the skin tone by applying a foundation that has skin-brightening effects. You can also add a tiny bit of glow lotion or highlighter to the tops of the cheeks to add shape that's subtle and doesn't compete with the lip color.

Using a soft cheek brush dipped in a nude/pink shade, apply a hint of color to the apples of the cheeks, then blend upwards and downwards.

Tip: When using more than one shade on the lips, it's much easier if you use lip products with the same texture (all creamy, all matte, etc). You can also tap a small amount of translucent powder over the lips to set them and help the look last.

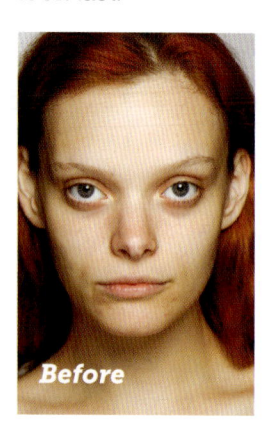

Before

Lips
This look is all about the lips, so start by exfoliating and hydrating them. You can also apply a lip primer to make the effect last longer. Precision is required to create a look like this one, so I'd recommend using an angled brush with synthetic bristles to apply the lipsticks. Begin by dabbing a pink lipstick onto the middle of the lips. Press your lips together to distribute the product (don't worry about it looking perfect yet). Then, use an angled brush to line the outer right side of the lips with an orange lipstick. Clean the brush or use a fresh one to apply a berry shade lipstick onto the other corner of the lips. Press your lips softly to blend, then use your fingers or the brush to blend all the shades together. You can use two, three, or as many shades as you want, as long as they look well-shaded into an ombré effect. Finish by sharpening the outline using the same angled brush dipped into concealer or foundation. This will highlight the lips' shape and prevent the lip color from running.

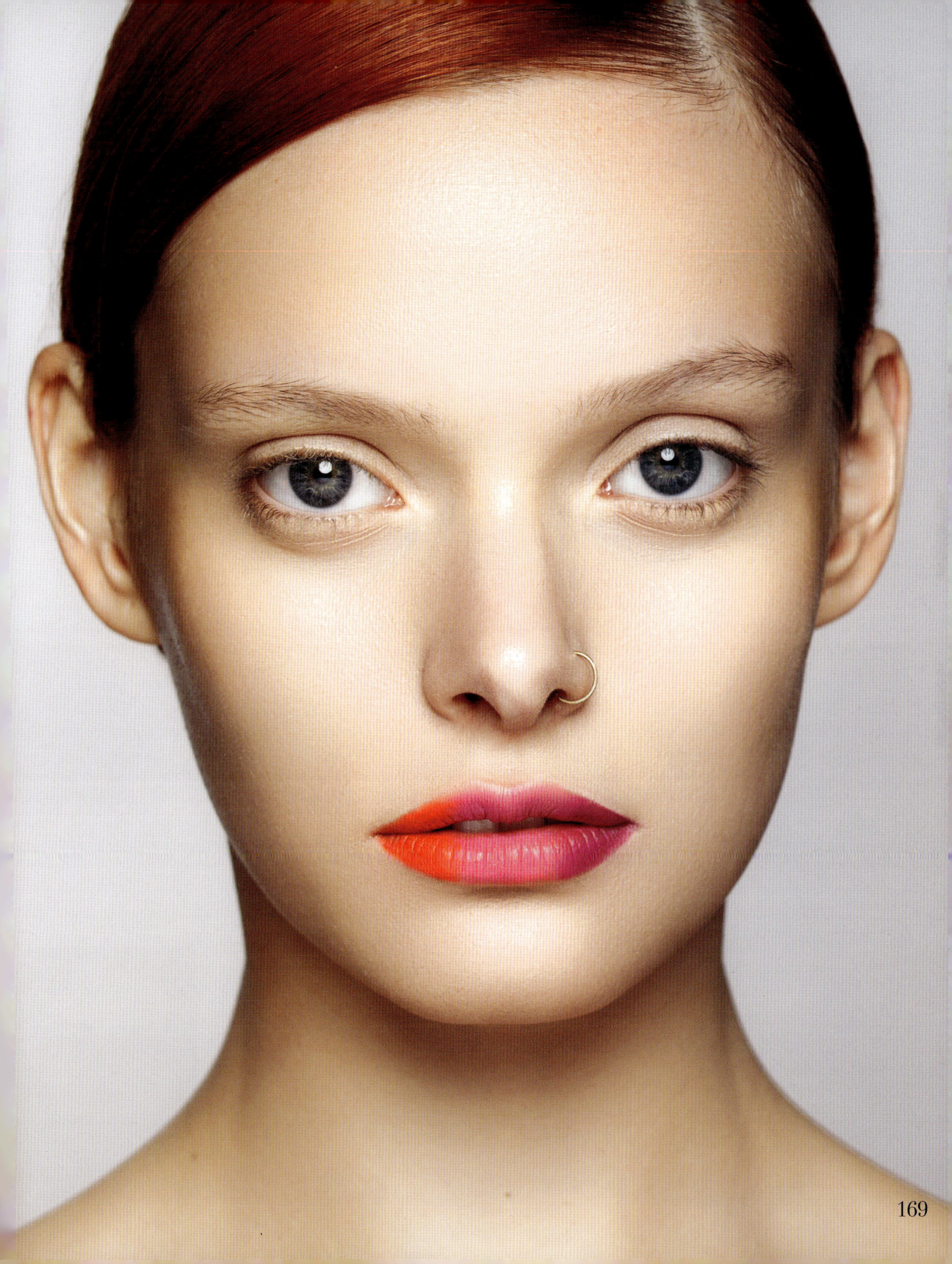

25 TEAL GAZE

"This look is perfect for brown eyes. The blue is a beautiful contrast shade, while the green intensifies the hazel specks and makes the eyes look brighter. I call it a win-win."

Eyes

Base: With an eyeshadow brush, dust a matte, flesh-toned eyeshadow all over the lid. This shade will look almost invisible on the eye, however it will serve as the perfect base for the other eyeshadows.

Enhance: Using the flat side of an eyeshadow brush, tap a deep blue matte eyeshadow onto the lid, following the shape of the eye contour and the lower lash line. Blend softly up to the crease, keeping the color's intensity close to the lash lines.

Line: Use a mossy green shimmer eyeshadow to line all the way around the eye with a slightly damp smudger brush, pulling the line up and out at the outer corners to elongate the eyes. Once dry, use the side of a crease brush to blend.

Highlight: With a light shimmery eyeshadow that reflects the whites of the eyes, use a pointy smudger brush to apply to the inner corners of the eye. Curl the lashes and apply a black lash-lengthening mascara.

Lips

Use a rosy, semi-shine lip color to enhance the lips' natural shade, as well as make them look full and slightly shiny.

Before

170

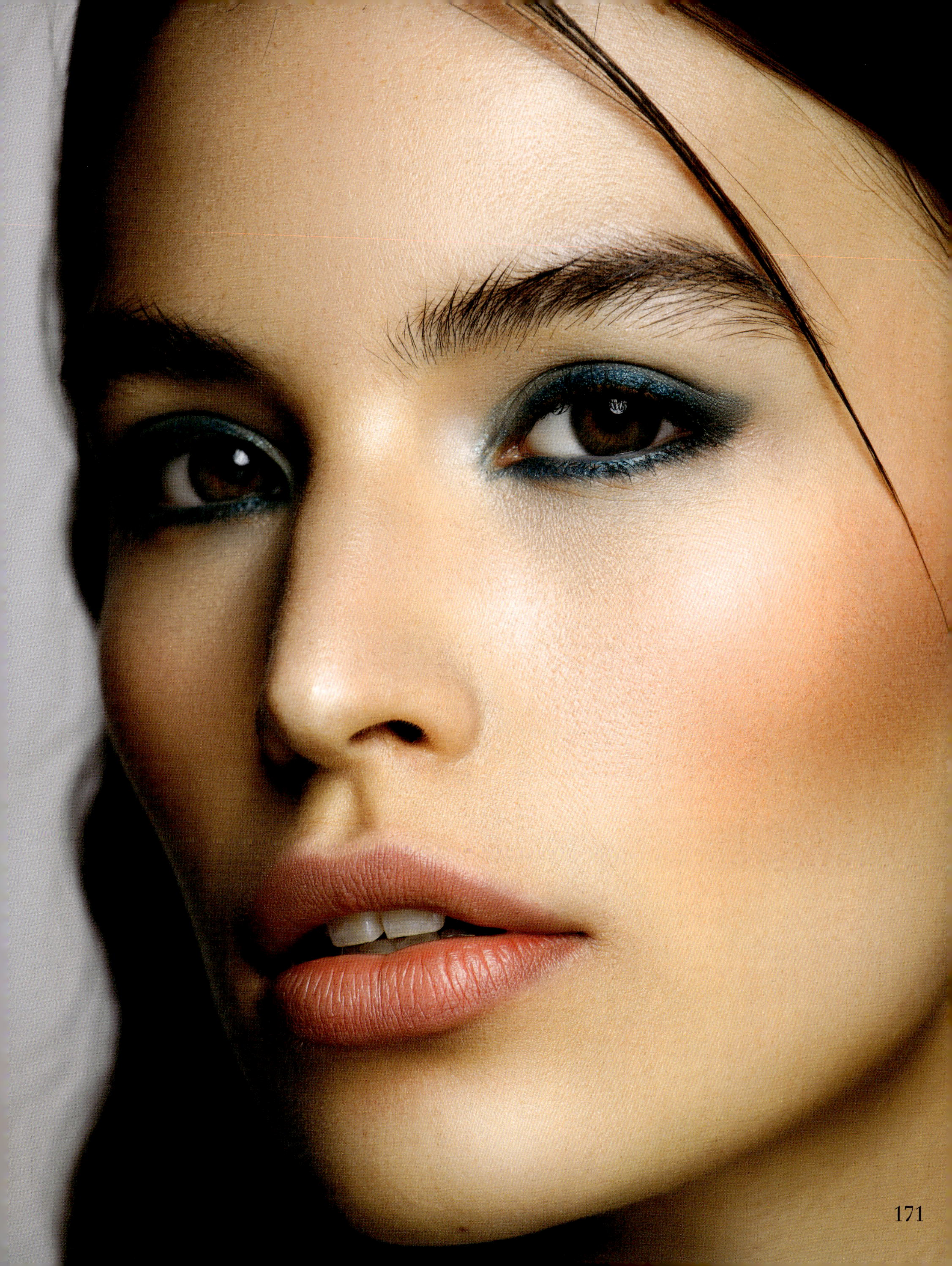

26 HOT PINK

"Whether the look is fun or sophisticated, a bright lipstick is the easiest way to add a pop of color to any face. It takes five seconds, try it!"

Eyes

Base: Apply eye primer to the eyelids and lower lash lines. Follow by applying a light concealer to the inner corners and underneath the eyes. Blend with your fingertips or a cream color brush. Dust a flesh-toned eyeshadow all over the lids with an eyeshadow brush.

Crease: Using a crease brush, sweep a light taupe eyeshadow onto the crease and lower lash lines. Blend well to create a slight shadow.

Lashes: Curl lashes twice and apply a volumizing mascara to the upper and lower lashes for a wide, doe-eye effect.

Cheeks

To create perfect harmony with bright lips, use a champagne/berry cheek color. Start by applying it under your cheekbones, then blend well using a cheek brush. You should base your blush's intensity on the strength of your lipstick tone—the brighter the lips, the brighter the blush. Make sure your eyes are always played down.

Lips

Use a pink lip liner to outline the shape of the lips.

Tip: Rest your hand on your chin to give you a steady hold while applying lip liner. With a bright pink liquid or matte lipstick, carefully fill the lips starting from the middle and blending outward. Press your lips together and repeat the process. Use an angled brush dipped in a tiny bit of concealer to clean up the edge of the lips.

Before

173

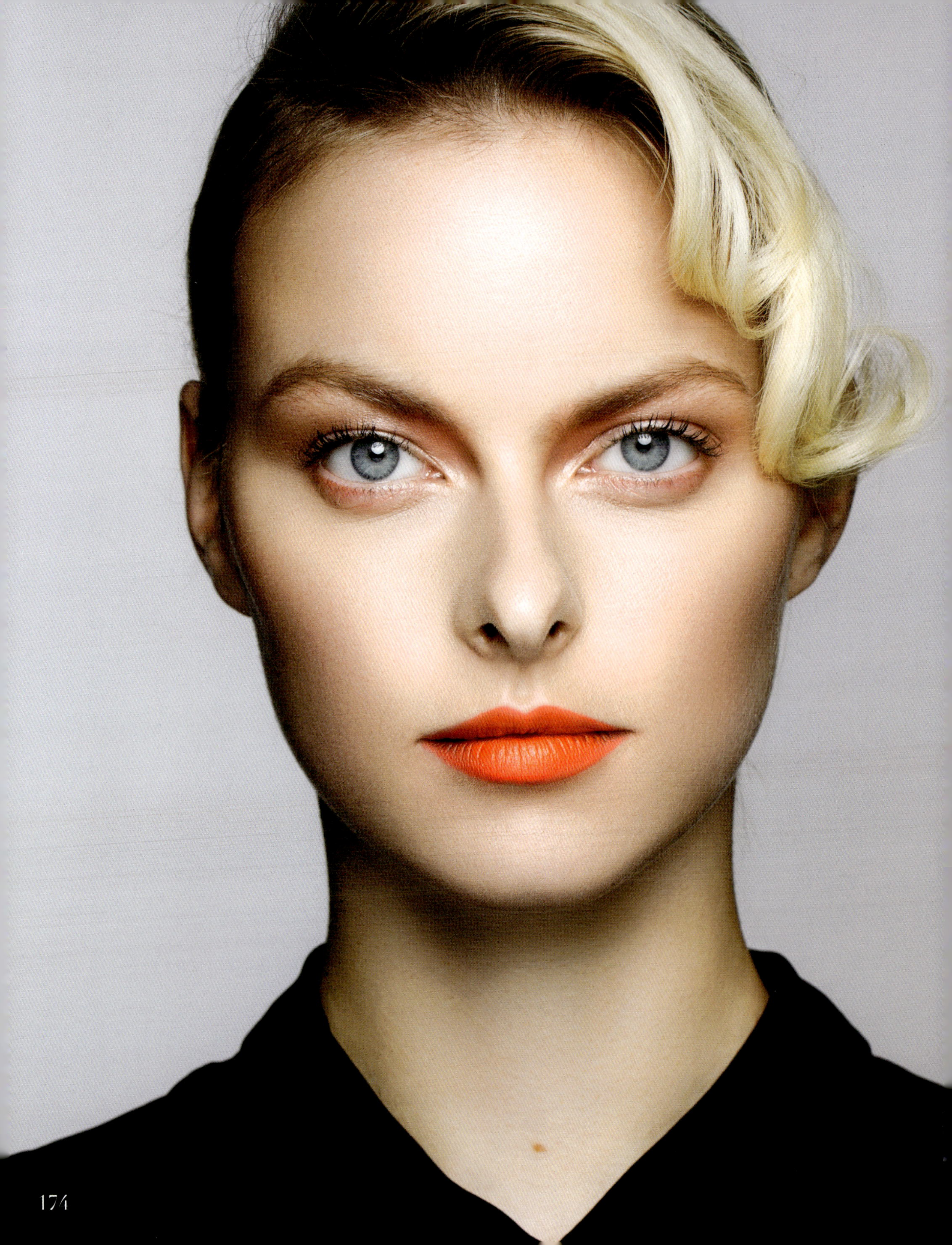

BURNT CORAL 27

"This is a sophisticated, modern way to wear a pop of color. The shades work harmoniously throughout the face, but the fun belongs to the mixture of textures. Shimmery eyes, luminous skin, and matte lips. Trés chic!"

Skin

Give the skin a luxurious feel the night before by applying a brightening and lifting facial mask. The ingredients will work throughout the night and you will wake up with better-looking skin. That translates to better and longer-lasting makeup.

Cheeks

Contour the face softly using a cheek brush and a warm contour powder. Start at the hollows of the cheeks and blend well under the jawline, making sure there are no lines of demarcation. Follow by applying a coral cheek color to the tops of the cheeks. It's fine if the blush has a little bit of shimmer to it, as it will bring your eyes up and create an overall lifting effect.

Eyes

Base: Use a fluffy eyeshadow brush to dust a slightly shimmery, flesh-toned eyeshadow to the lids.

Tip: You want to achieve a brightening effect, so the shade shouldn't be too light or dark. Ideally, it should match your skin tone. You can also use a matte version if you don't want shimmer, however I always recommend using eyeshadow primer to give the eyeshadow something to adhere to.

Highlight: Apply a champagne-gold eyeshadow from the lash line to right under the crease. Begin by using the wider side of an eyeshadow brush and tapping it right on the lid in the area above the iris. Blend until it disappears right under the crease.

Enhance: Using an angled crease brush, define the crease with a matte, dusty rose shade. Concentrate on the inner two thirds of the upper crease, the outer corners, and lower lash line. Curl lashes and brush on a waterproof mascara.

Lips

Prime the lips for a smooth lip application by sloughing off dead skin cells using a lip mask. Follow with a clear lip balm and leave it on while doing the rest of your makeup. Blot off any excess product, then line the lips with a nude lip liner. Fill in the lips with the liner, then swipe on a couple of layers of an orange/red matte or semi-matte lipstick.

Before

175

28 SPARKLING VIOLET

"One of the easiest ways to add a pop of color to your makeup wardrobe is to pick an unexpected shade of eyeshadow. The effect doesn't have to be drastic, you can totally control how strong the effect is by gradually building the shade to your comfort level. It's one of the easiest ways to revamp your makeup look!"

Brows:
Use a precision brow liner in a blonde shade that allows you to draw thin, hair-like strokes that will look like your own brows. Use an angled brush to softly blend the lines, then brush the brows into place with a spoolie brush.

Eyes:
Apply a matte ivory shade all over the lid with an eyeshadow brush. Using a cream eyeshadow brush, tap a shimmery, light violet shade onto the lid right at the crease and under the lash line. With a crease brush, apply a tan shade at the crease as a transition, making sure there are no visible hard edges and that the violet shade is seamlessly blended. Finish by curling the eyelashes and adding a coat of volumizing mascara.

Cheeks and Lips:
Before you powder the cheek area, use a beauty sponge to apply a light berry color to the cheeks. Then, use the flat side of a damp sponge to deposit the product onto the tops of the cheeks. Tap and stipple until the color is well-blended. This trick will give you the look of a cream blush without being too shiny. Line the lips with a nude lip liner, then apply a soft pink semi-shine lipstick on top.

Before

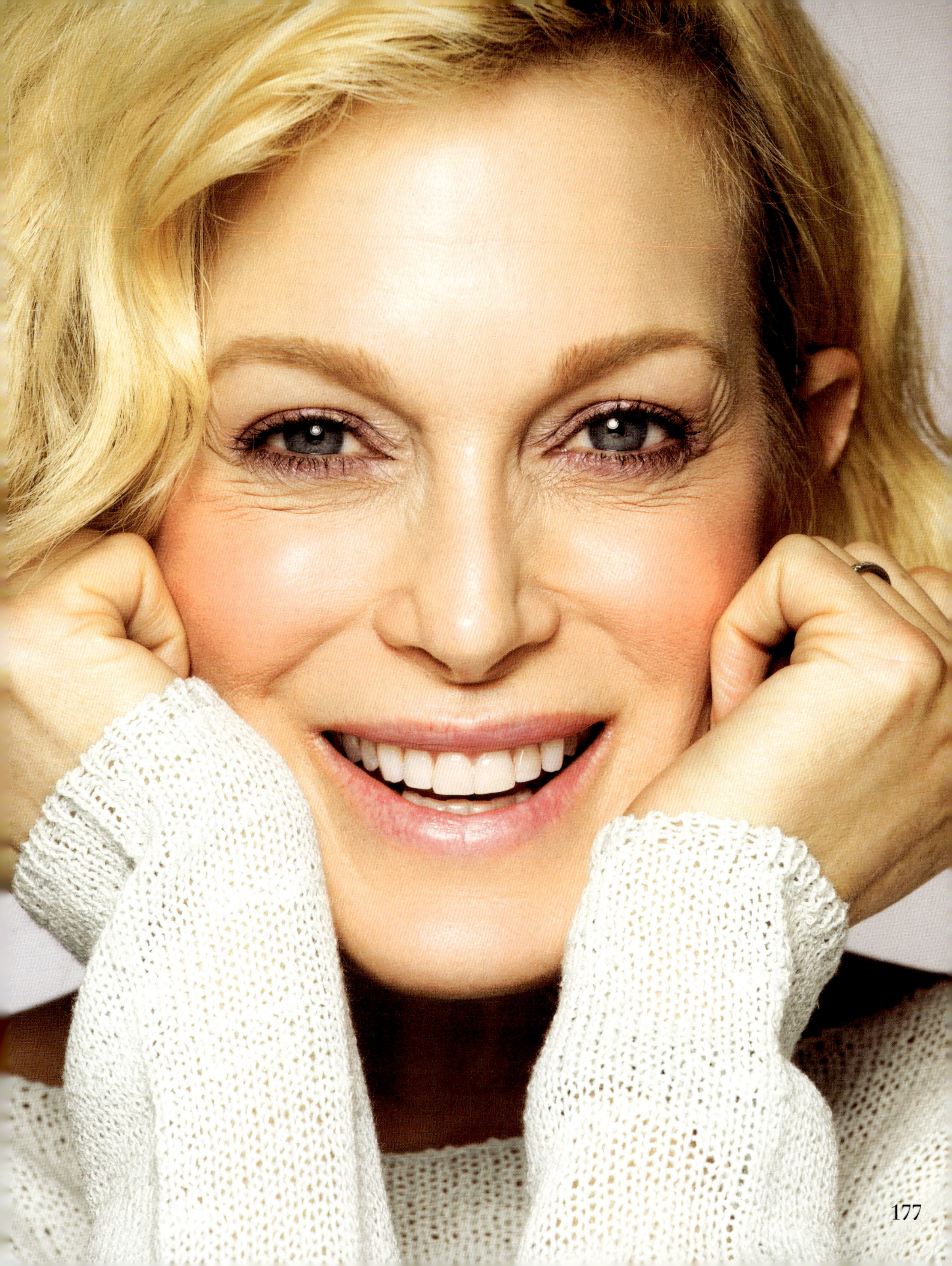

29 *BOLD RED*

"A statement lip is all you need to dress up any look. A swipe of bold red color in glossy, matte, or any texture in between will work to show off your personality in an instant!"

Eyes

Keep the eyes simple with a wash of color. Begin by applying an eyeshadow primer to the lids and lower lash lines using a flat synthetic bristle brush. Then, with a fluffy eyeshadow brush, apply a matte, flesh-toned eyeshadow on top of the primer. Using a clean eyeshadow brush, apply a soft pink shade to the lid. Create an upward gradation from the top lash line and carry it down the lower lash line. For fun and to serve as a cool contrast to the semi-matte lips, I added a drop of shiny clear lip gloss to the lids.

Tip: Add a couple of coats of mascara to the lashes, then use a concealer brush and concealer to slightly highlight the under-eye area

Before

Cheeks

Use a beauty sponge to apply a pink color to the cheeks by dabbing it over your foundation. For an extra glow, do not add powder. Build the color of the blush by applying in layers to make sure the intensity is a good match for the lips. TIP: In my opinion, when the lips are bold, a strong, dewy cheek is a great complement. However, if your eye makeup is also bold, then you might want to tone down the cheek color so that the three looks are not competing with each other. Remember, it's all about creating a harmonious focal point.

Lips

Take a semi-matte, textured red lipstick and swipe it over the lower lip. Press your lips together, then repeat the process. This will give you a very natural lip line that looks modern and not too perfect. Next, using a pointed smudger brush, carry the product to the outer parameters of the lips, concentrating on the lower lip line and the cupid's bow. If you'd like for the lipstick to look more matte and have a longer-lasting effect, use a concealer brush to tap a tiny bit of translucent powder over the lips.

Tip: A bold lip is a great look for pictures, but if you wear it for the day, keep in mind that it will crease. So just embrace it and have fun!

179

SMOKEY LOOKS

30 SMOKEY GRAY GAZE

31 COPPER SMOKE

32 AQUA SMOKE

33 VIOLET SMOKE

34 ICY GRAY SMOKE

181

30 SMOKEY GRAY GAZE

"With a look like this, it's easy to let your eyes do the talking. Eyes are the most expressive facial feature and enhancing them the correct way is key. I designed this look to let your gaze—not your eyeshadow—steal the show."

The Tools
The right brushes will allow you to create a seamless smokey look that lifts and enhances the eyes. You will need a fluffy eyeshadow brush, a pointed smudger brush, a crease-enhancing brush, and an eyeliner/eyebrow brush.

Lashes
Using an eyelash curler, curl the lashes and hold for about 20 seconds. Repeat a couple of times for maximum lift. Comb through with a lash primer to add volume, then follow by swiping mascara in an upwards motion to the top lashes..
Tip: One trick is to place the mascara right at the base of the lashes and blink a couple of times onto the brush. This coats the base of the lashes, as well as combs the product through to the tips.

Eyes
The key here is to use the correct shades to highlight and enhance to create a bright, open eye. Begin by applying eye primer all around the eyes, or use concealer if you need to color correct the eyelid area. Follow by using an eyeshadow brush to dust a matte highlight color all over the eyelid, concentrating on the area from lash line to crease. Swipe the same brush on a tissue to clean off the eyeshadow, then apply a warm brown shade from lash line to crease.
Tip: On eyes with little or barely visible lids, concentrate the application on the outside corners of the eyes and carry it down the lower lash line.

Continue by adding more depth all around the eyes, using a pointy tipped smudger brush to create a very soft halo-like effect around the eye. Use a darker brown or soft gray matte eyeshadow and once again concentrate on the outer corners, making the color almost disappear into the inner corners of the eyes. Line your upper lash line with an angled brush using a black, matte eyeshadow.
Tip: If you prefer, you can use your favorite type of eyeliner instead of the eyeshadow. If you do, remember to keep the application very thin and as close to the base of the lashes as possible so that there are no spaces within.

Before

182

Cheeks and Lips
Use a cheek brush to brush on an apricot shade of blush. Blend well. On the lips, use a semi-matte or slightly creamy lipstick to ensure the focus is on the eyes.

31 COPPER SMOKE

Eyes
With a fluffy eyeshadow brush, encircle both eyes with a shimmery copper-brown cream eyeshadow. Begin right at the lash line, blend up to the crease, then apply to the lower lash line.

Tip: Cream eyeshadow works really well for this look because it doubles as an eyeshadow primer. Using an eye crease brush, define the crease with a matte hazelnut eyeshadow, then blend seamlessly with the copper-brown cream shadow on the lid and carry on the lower lash line. Use a clean brush to blend any hard edges. Use the tip of a smudger brush to apply a dot of light gold shimmer shadow to the inner corner of the eyes. Fill the brows with a soft brunette brow pencil and set them into place using a brow gel.

Cheeks
Use a matte contour powder to define the cheeks and warm up the complexion.

Lips
Use a nude lip liner all over your lips and top it off with a shimmery gold lip gloss.

AQUA SMOKE 32

Eyes
Using a gel cream eyeliner and an eyeliner brush, draw a line from the inner corners to the outer corners of the eyes. With an eyeshadow brush, dust a shimmery blue shadow onto the lid, smudging it into the eyeliner. With a smudger brush, line the lower lashes with a dark matte blue eyeshadow, then blend well. Finish with another layer of gel eyeliner, winging the line out a bit on the outer corners for a lengthening, cat-eye effect. Curl lashes and apply a couple of coats of black mascara. Fill in the brows and define their shape with a soft brown brow pencil. Blend with an angled brush.

Cheeks
Using a cheek brush, dust a soft warm blush onto the cheeks and blend in upward and downward motions until the shade is almost undetectable.

Lips
To keep the focus on the eyes, line the lips with a nude lip liner and follow with a matte nude lipstick.

33 VIOLET SMOKE

Lips
To keep the focus on the eyes and enhance your natural lip color, use a light nude gloss on the lips.

Before

Eyes
Begin by dusting a matte flesh-toned eyeshadow onto the lid. Next, create a fun effect using a black eyeliner to tightline the whole upper lash line and the inner and outer corners of the lower lash line. Smudge the line using a smudger brush or a Q-tip.

Tip: To create a bright doe-eyed effect, don't apply eyeliner to the lower middle lash line area (which is right under the iris when looking straight at a mirror).

Take a violet purple eyeshadow and apply to the lid and the lower lash line using a using an eyeshadow brush. Blend well with a clean brush. Apply a few coats of lengthening mascara to further enhance the bright-eyed look.

Cheeks
Dust a matte pink blush onto the hollows of the cheeks using an angled cheek brush. Blend using upward, circular motions.

34 ICY GRAY SMOKE

Eyes
Outline the eyes with a black pencil eyeliner, keeping as close to the lash lines as possible. Smudge using a smudger brush or a Q-tip. Use an eyeliner brush to apply a shimmery gray eyeshadow on top of the eyeliner and blend to just under the crease (but make sure you can see the shade when your eyes are open). With a brown matte eyeshadow, define the eye creases using a crease brush. Blend well up and out, making sure all of the edges look soft and are not too far up from the crease. If desired, add a golden-toned shadow to the inner corners. Apply a couple of coats of black mascara to both the upper and lower lashes.

Cheeks
Dust a golden salmon cheek color onto the cheekbones and blend in upward round motions toward the ears and temples.

Tip: Applying with round motions ensures that you don't apply too much blush on any one area.

Lips
Use a medium nude lip liner to line your lips and correct their shape. Use a matte lipstick with a nude pink undertone to finish the look.

Before

189

THE METALS

㉟
GOLDEN GARNET

㊱
GOLDEN TOPAZ

㊲
ROSEGOLD

㊳
SPARKLING PEWTER

㊴
BLUE PEARL

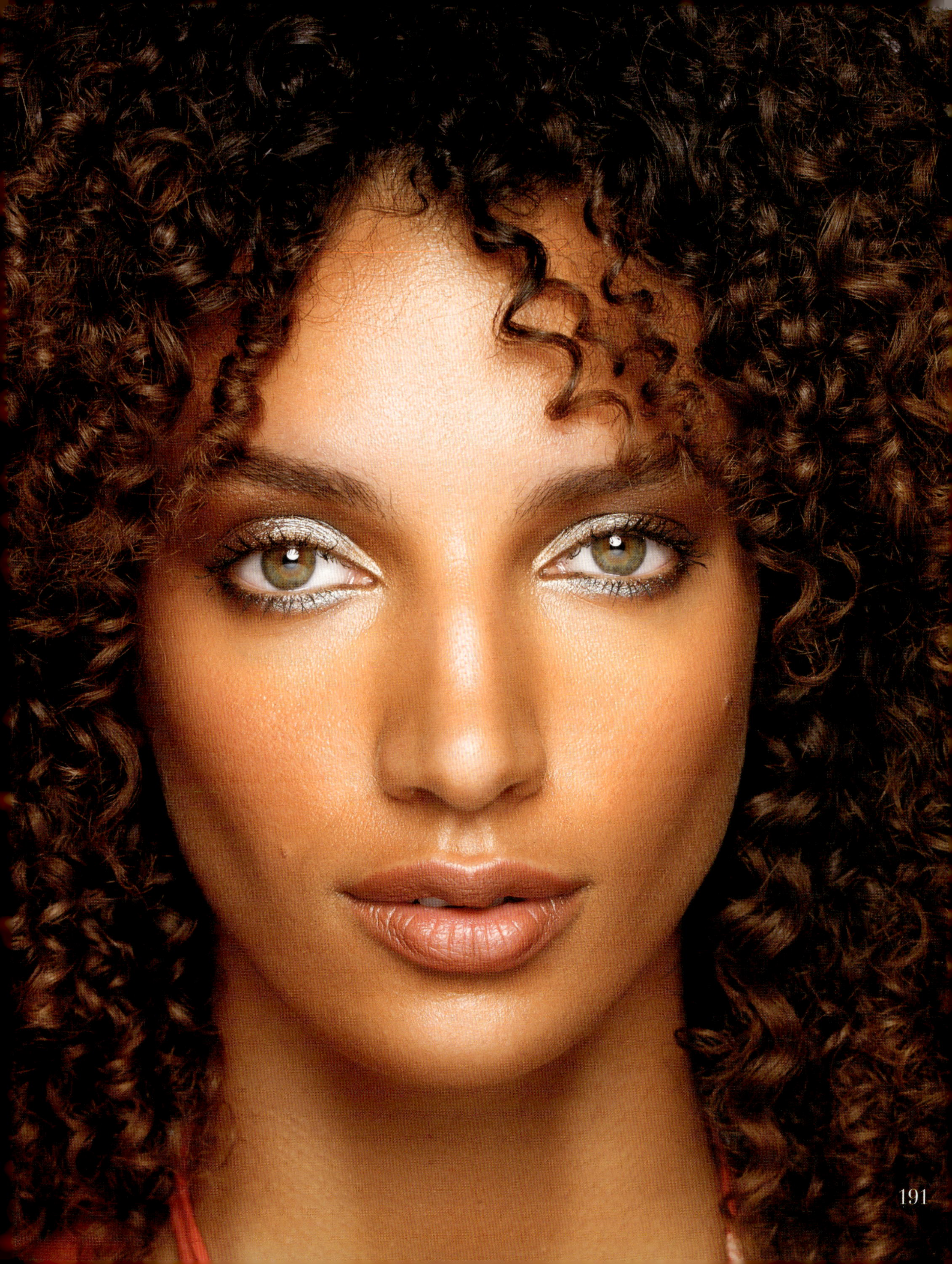

35 *GOLDEN GARNET*

"This lip look takes highlighting to the next level by adding a dab of metallic eyeshadow or lip gloss to the middle of the lips. It's an easy way to give any makeup look a new twist."

Eyes
Apply a bit of concealer under the eyes and at the inner corners. Rub into the skin with your fingertips from inner to outer corner to correct any discoloration on the lids, as well as prep the area for eyeshadow. As a base, apply a flesh-toned eyeshadow to the lids, blending with an eyeshadow brush up to the brow bone. Then, with the same motions you used to apply the concealer, surround the eye with a gold copper eyeshadow shade from the lash line to right under the crease and onto the lower lashes. Eyeliner is optional, but mascara is a must for a look like this.

Cheeks
Go for a bright and natural complexion by using a cheek color that is bright but blends out to a sheer finish. Blend some highlighting powder on the top of the cheeks to give them a pretty glow. Use a cheek brush to blend, lightly caressing the cheeks for a very soft application.

Tip: Semi-matte or semi-shine lip formulas work best as a base to apply other products onto.

Tip: You can also try using a metallic liquid lipstick as your eyeshadow. It will be a little less bold, but will create the same effect.

Lip
Prep your lips with lip balm and blot away any extra moisture. Use a medium-nude lip liner to highlight the cupid's bow by making an "x" shape. Define the bottom of the lips and the corners to create the perfect outline. Follow by swiping on a creamy, soft red semi-matte lipstick. Finish the look by pressing a gold eyeshadow in the middle of the lips, pressing the lips together and feathering with your fingers.

Before

36 GOLDEN TOPAZ

"This is the perfect look for dark brown eyes. The gold color accents the eyes, while the rest of the face is kept looking glowing and fresh. A must-try!"

Eyes

Using your fingertips, apply eye primer to your lids and lower lash lines. Then, using a black eyeliner pencil, draw a thin line along the top and bottom lash lines. Using the same pencil, gently sketch out a "v" shape at the outer corners of the eyes, connecting it to the lower lash lines. Use an eyeshadow brush to diffuse the eyeliner up slightly at the lash lines and in at the outer corners for a smokey effect. Blend a dark brown eyeshadow into the liner to give it a gradated effect. Blend well. Beginning at the inner corners of the eyes, use a smudger brush to apply a dot of warm gold eyeshadow to brighten the eyes. Finish the look by using an eyeshadow brush to swipe the gold eyeshadow from the inner corners until it meets and disappears at the outer "v". Tap the eyeshadow on at first and then blend it well.

Lashes

Curl your lashes and apply a coat of volumizing mascara. Using tweezers, apply individual false lashes along the top lash line, starting at the outer corners. Apply eyelash glue to each lash and let dry for at least 30 seconds. Use your natural lashes as a shelf and place the false lashes right on top, as close to the lash line as possible. Finish the look with a couple of coats of mascara.

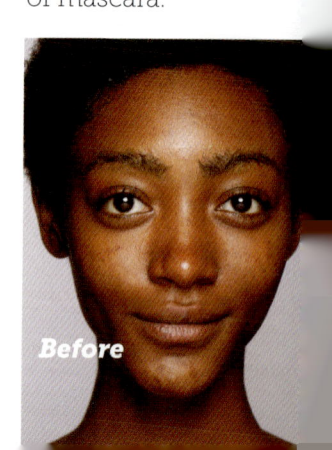

Before

Brows
Use a brown eyebrow pencil to fill in and accentuate your brow shape, then enhance and seal with an eyebrow gel.

Lips
Apply a drop of foundation or concealer to the lips to erase any uneven shades on the lips. Follow a couple of coats of nude, semi-shine lipstick.

㊲ ROSEGOLD

"Metallic rosegold shades and perfect contouring keep this monochromatic look modern and simple."

Eyes
Apply a neutral matte eyeshadow all over the lid using a fluffy eyeshadow brush. With the same brush, add a shimmery flesh-toned eyeshadow on the lid and lower lash line, stopping right under the crease. With the horizontal side of a crease brush, sweep a mauve eyeshadow right on the crease to intensify the socket's shape. Then blend with the vertical side of the brush. Curl lashes with an eyelash curler and apply a coat of waterproof mascara.

Eyebrows
Using a matte taupe eyeshadow and the angled side of a brow brush, fill in any sparse eyebrow areas, then brush them into place with the spoolie side of the brush.

Tip: Use an eyebrow pencil that's a shade lighter than your hairs and add eyeshadow on top to define them. This layering effect will keep the brows in shape throughout the day. Finish with a coat of brow gel.

Before

Contour
With a blush brush, lightly mix a rosy blush with a matte contour powder. Dust the blush lightly on the hollows of the cheeks and blend in a slightly upward motion.
Tip: Dust a tiny bit of translucent powder over your cheeks to tone down cheek color that is too bright.

Lips
With a rose-color lip liner, line the lips using soft, feathery strokes. Define the lips and fill them in with the lip liner. Follow with a metallic-copper lip gloss dabbed right in the middle of the lips.

38 SPARKLING PEWTER

"Get ready to sparkle at any occasion with this simple yet powerfully sophisticated metallic look."

Skin
Apply a thin layer of matte foundation to the face, then blend well with a damp sponge. Use an undereye corrector to brighten under the eyes, then follow by concealing any areas on the face you'd like to camouflage. With a powder brush, use a press-and-roll motion to apply translucent powder whenever needed. The goal is for the skin to have a fresh texture that looks elegant and polished.

Eyes
Prep the eye area with primer or concealer, then use an eyeshadow brush to apply a neutral pearl eyeshadow over the entire eye area. Beginning at the outer corners of the eyes, apply a silver shimmer eyeshadow to the lids, blending well toward the inner corners. Use a smudger brush to line the bottom lash line with a dark gray or black matte eyeshadow, carrying the line outside the outer edges to create a smokey, elongated effect. Blend into the silver eyeshadow. Curl the lashes and finish the look with two coats of mascara on both top and bottom lashes.

Cheeks
With a cheek brush, apply a brownish-pink cheek color to the tops of the cheeks. Use a contour powder to contour under the hollows of the cheeks and at the temples.

Lips
Give the lips a natural effect with a semi-matte lipstick in a natural shade. Finish the look by applying finishing spray all over the face in an X and then a T shape for even coverage. Repeat for a long-lasting makeup effect.

Before

198

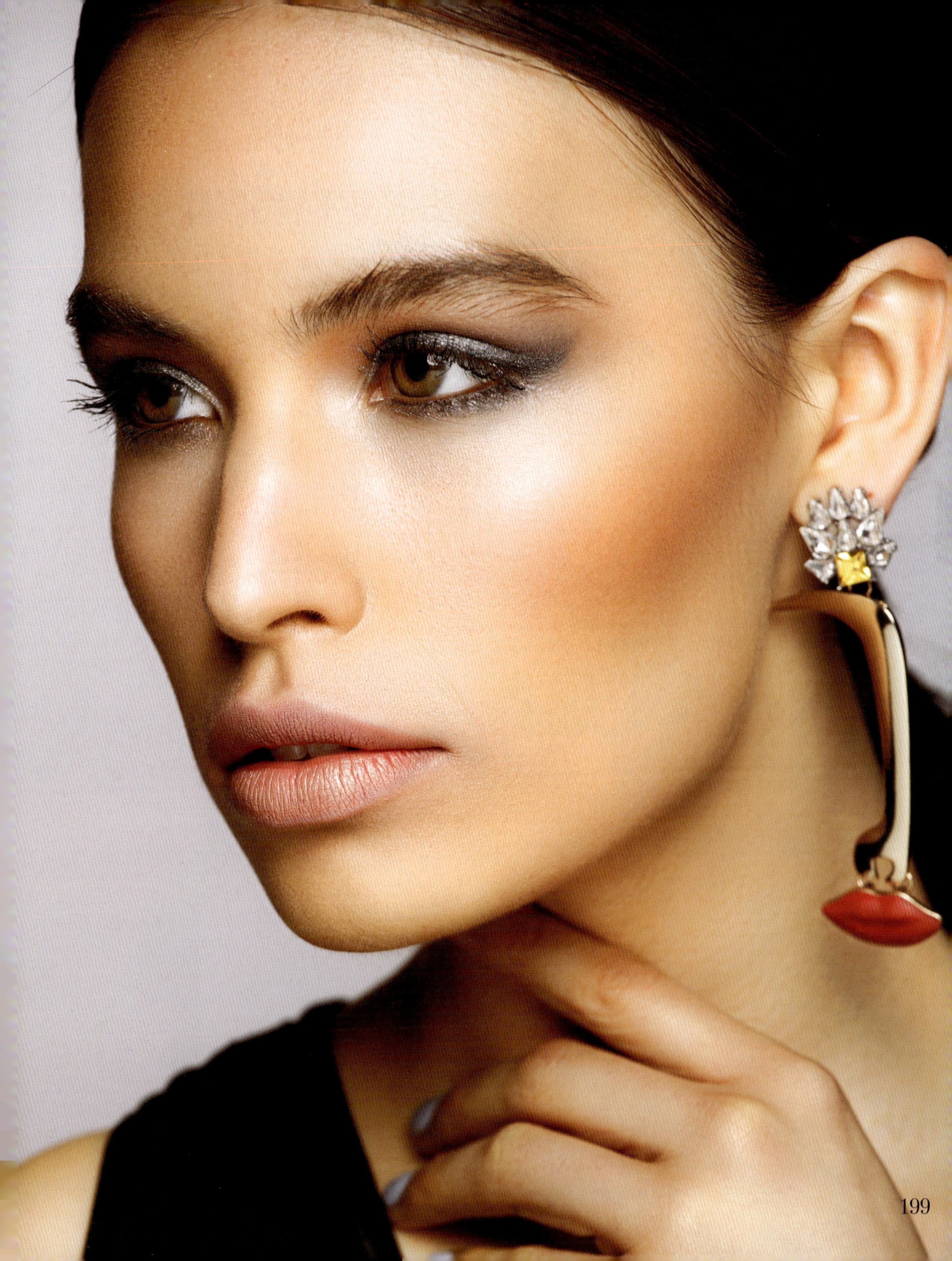

③⑨ BLUE PEARL

"Get ready to sparkle at any occasion with this simple yet powerfully sophisticated metallic look."

Skin
Here, you'll use two foundations to contour and highlight the face. Apply a darker matte shade to the areas you'd like to recede (under the hollows of the cheeks, the sides of the nose, the jawline, etc.) and add a luminous skin-toned shade to the other areas of the face. Apply with a foundation brush and blend with a damp sponge. Add powder where needed. Apply a warm rose blush to the tops of the cheeks.

Eyes
Using a cream color brush, tap a silvery/aqua shimmer eyeshadow onto the lids, starting at the inner corners of the eyes and letting it blend out as you carry the color toward the outer corners and down the lower lash line. Apply a warm brown eyeshadow shade to the crease with a crease brush.

Using a smudger brush, apply a chocolate-colored eyeshadow, starting from the outer corners and bringing the color in sofly to meet the silver eyeshadow. Blend with a clean eyeshadow brush.

With a brown eyeliner, tightline the upper lash line to add dimension and impact to the eyes. Curl the lashes and apply two coats of a lengthening mascara.

Tip: When creating a shimmery eye, clean up the under-eye area after you finish the eyes and then apply concealer once any eyeshadow fallout has been picked up.

Before

Lips
Using your fingers, dab a nude lipstick on your lips and repeat the process.

THE PARTY LOOKS

40
CLASSIC CHIC

41
24-KARAT MAGIC

42
GARNET GOLD

43
PARTY GLOW!

44
BRONZE SMOKE

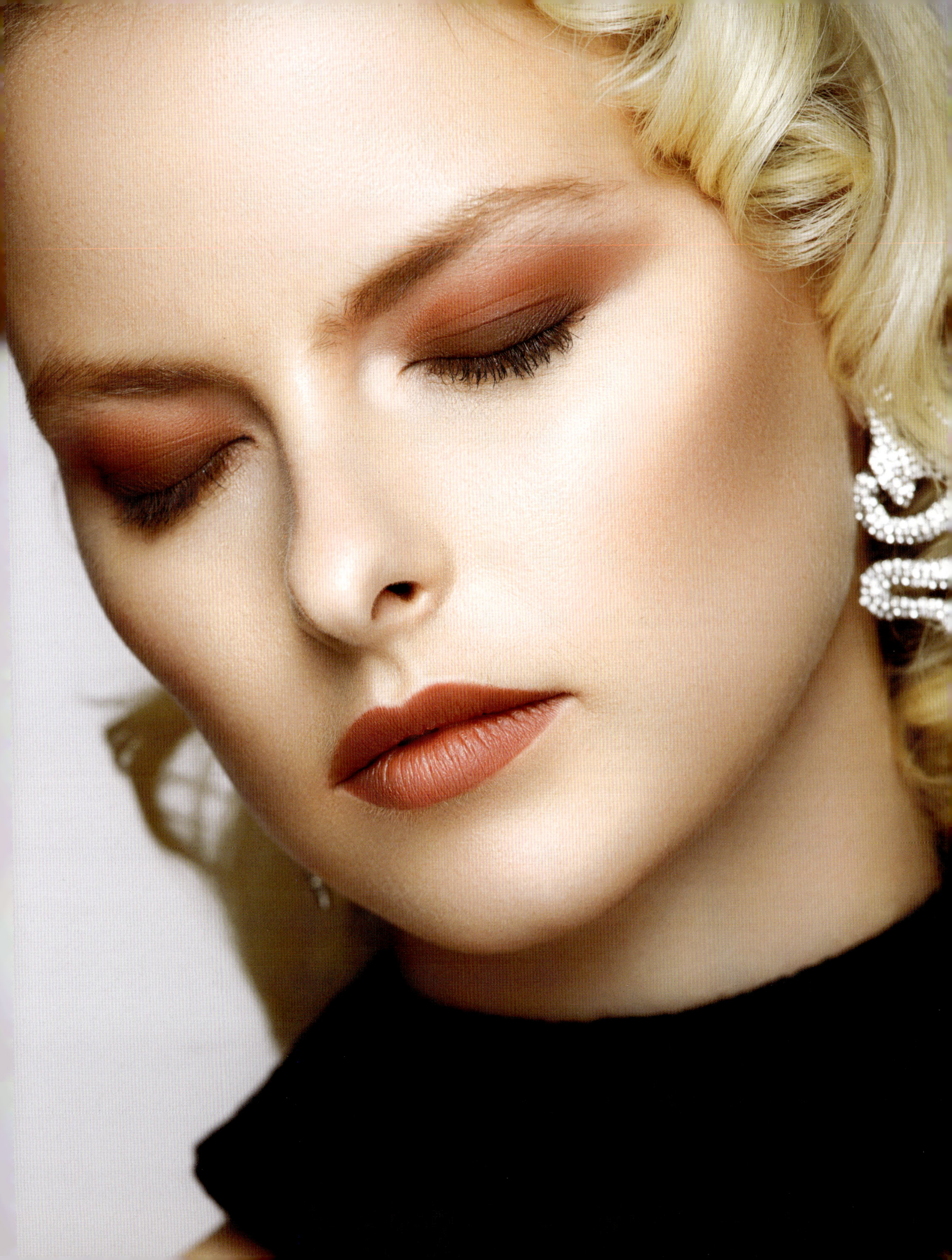

40 CLASSIC CHIC

"Matte neutral shades work harmoniously to create the perfect subtle-yet-defined look that shows off your best features."

Cheeks
Use a cheek brush to deposit a warm peach cheek color onto the apples of the cheeks, then bring the color down into the hollows. Use a larger powder brush to blend away any hard edges.

Tip:
If your cheek color looks too strong, you can tone it down by applying a bit of translucent powder over the cheek color when blending.

Lips
Use a nude lip liner to correct and enhance your lip shape. Follow with a swipe of natural nude, semi-matte lipstick.

Eyes
Begin by applying an eye primer to the lids and the lower lash line for a long-lasting effect. The texture of the primer will also make it much easier to blend matte shades. With an eyeshadow brush, apply a matte, light-flesh toned eyeshadow to the whole lid as a base. Then, with an eye crease brush, sweep a matte brick-red shade all around the eyes, carrying the color up to the orbital bone. Blend any edges up and out with the fluffy side of the brush. Using a smudger brush, softly line the upper lash line with a dark brown matte eyeshadow, then blend it into the brick-red shadow with an eyeshadow brush. To give your lashes an extra boost, apply a very thin line of brown eyeliner as close to the lash line as possible, making sure there are no gaps.

Tip:
This trick will not only intensify your gaze but also make your lashes look instantly thicker. Curl lashes and follow with an eyelash primer. Finish the eyes with a couple of coats of lengthening mascara.

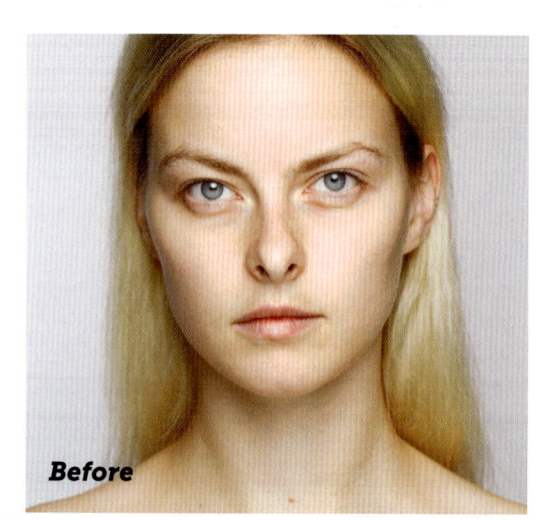

Before

204

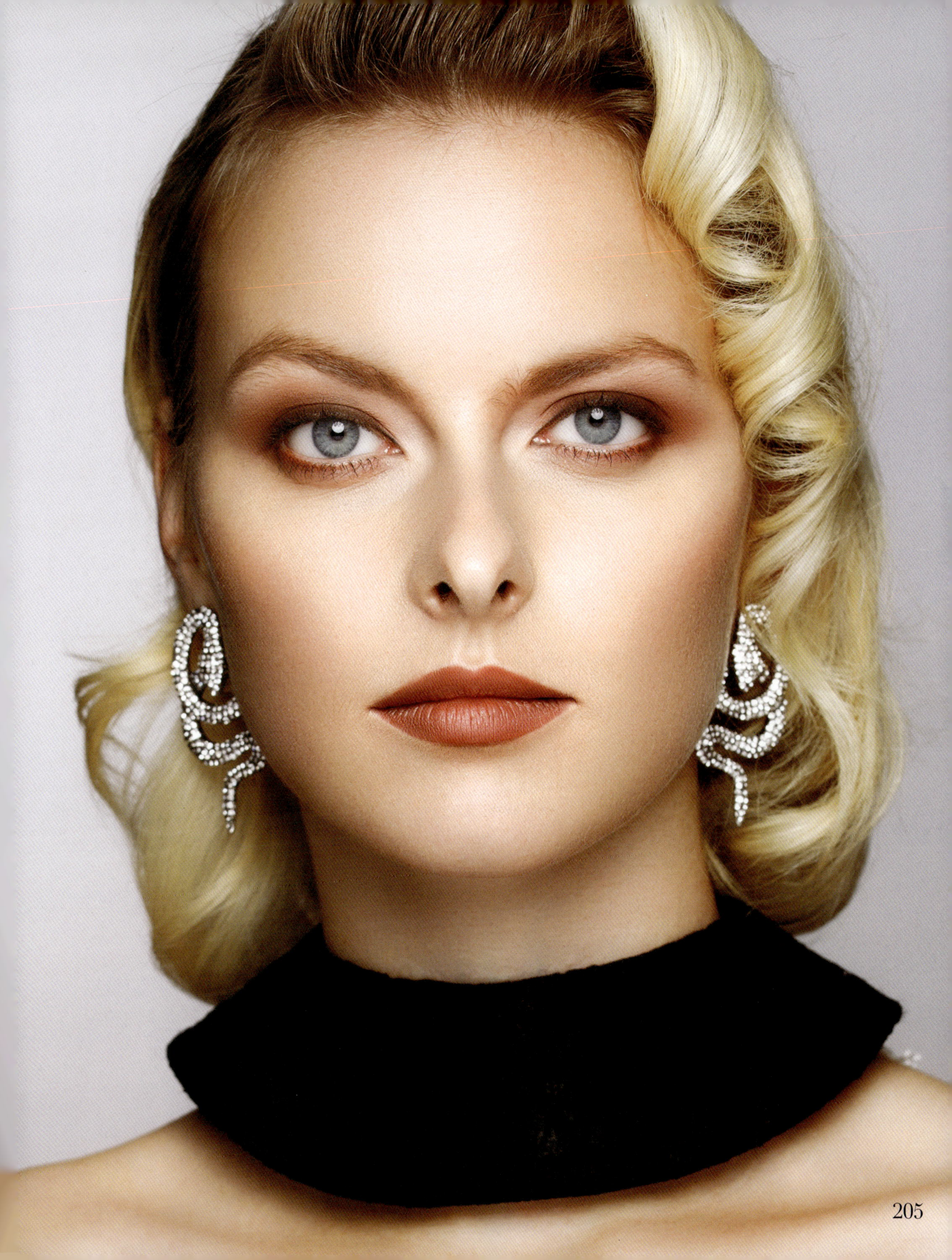

④ 24-KARAT MAGIC

"Inspiration comes from everywhere and sometimes jewelry can set the tone. In this look, the eyes are rimmed in a copper/gold shade that is similar to the color of her earings."

Brows
Use a brunette brow pencil to add more definition to the eyebrows. Comb the brows with a brow gel.

Lips
Apply a natural-toned lip liner all over your lips, then top it off with a shimmery gold lip gloss. Using the lip liner as a base in this way will enable the lip gloss to stay on for a longer period of time.

Eyes
Using your fingertips or a cream eyeshadow brush, swipe a shimmery light copper brown cream eyeshadow all over the eyelids (to serve as a base) and on the bottom lash lines. Define the crease by applying a hazelnut eyeshadow to each crease with an eye crease brush, then blend under the lower lash line. Using an eyeliner brush, define the lash line all around the eye with a dark brown shimmery eyeshadow. Blur the lines with a clean smudger brush. For a brightening effect, use the tip of a smudger brush to dot a light apricot gold shimmery shadow into the inner corner of the eyes.

Cheeks
Define the cheeks by applying a dark matte contour powder to the hollows of the cheeks, then add a sparkling golden-brown cheek color to the tops of the cheeks for added glow.

GARNET GOLD 42

"Inspiration comes from everywhere and sometimes jewelry can set the tone. In this look, the eyes are rimmed in a copper/gold shade that is similar to the color of her earings."

Eyes
Using a synthetic, cream-color brush, apply a copper-gold cream eyeshadow to the lid from the lash line to the crease. Blend up with your fingers to a bit above the crease, then carry the color on to the lower lash line. Apply a matte brown shade over the cream to create depth, starting from the outer corners and concentrating on the outer V of the eyes.
Tip: If you don't have a cream eyeshadow, apply a generous amount of eye primer to the lids, then dust on copper-gold powder eyeshadow. Curl lashes and apply waterproof mascara to both top and bottom lashes.

Lips
For a festive, stained look that will last, take a red lip liner and smudge the shade on the back of your hand. Then dab a creamy, semi-shine red lipstick on top and blend into the lip liner. Apply this mix to the lips using your fingertip or a brush. To finish, add more of the lipstick to the middle of the lips to create extra fullness. Repeat the process for longer wear. Finish the look with a couple of sprays of finishing spray.

Cheeks
Softly contour the cheeks with a soft brown matte powder.

207

㊸ PARTY GLOW

"This look will take you from daytime to glam-time by using some simple, tried-and-true techniques. It's totally modern and totally YOU!"

Brows
Fill the eyebrows with a precision pencil that is slightly paler than your natural eyebrow color. Use light, feathery strokes, making sure to accentuate and elongate your features as much as possible. Then, use a brunette tinted brow gel to brush the hairs into place.

Skin

Apply an oil-free moisturizer to your entire face and dot eye cream around your eyes. Follow with a pore-reducing primer and a matte foundation.

Tip: On darker skin, you might need a darker foundation for the outer perimeters of the face, as well as a slightly lighter one for the inner areas of the face. Apply with a foundation brush or your fingertips, then blend with a damp beauty sponge. To conceal dark circles, dot concealer under your eyes. Press the concealer gently onto the skin and blend with a concealer brush. Dot concealer on any other areas of concern on the face and blend well. Finish with a setting powder.

Eyes

Use an eyeshadow brush to apply a light matte shade to the lids, starting at the inner corners and making it disappear just above the crease. Blend well in up and outward motions. This shade should be about one to two shades lighter than your skin tone. Carry the color under the eye right at the tear duct and stop. Using a crease brush, apply a matte brown shade at the outer corners of the eyes and blend it into the lighter shade. Blend into the crease, then with a clean crease brush, blend to create a seamless contour.

With a smudger brush, line the lower lash line with the same matte brown eyeshadow. Then, create a very thin line of black gel eyeliner with an angled liner brush, apply it to the very base of the eyelashes from the middle of the eye and going out. Use a slightly bigger brush or a Q-tip to blend. Finish by using the smudger brush dipped into a matte black eyeshadow to intensify the look of the gel eyeliner. Smoke it out very close to the base of the lashes. Curl lashes a couple of times and use a lengthening and waterproof mascara.

Before

44 BRONZE SMOKE

"A perfectly placed highlight in the inner corners helps to brighten and enhance the whites of the eyes. It's an easy wake-me-up tip for any type of look!"

Skin
After going through your chosen skincare routine, blend a few highlighting illuminating drops or a liquid highlighter into your foundation for overall luminosity. Apply all over the face with your fingertips, then blend with a damp beauty sponge. Add extra luminosity to the tops of the cheeks by adding another drop of illuminating liquid to the areas that you'd like to accentuate.

Cheeks
Luminosity is key for this look, so use a slightly shimmery highlighter on the tops of the cheeks, then follow by adding a warm bronze contour shade to the hollows of the cheeks and blend it seamlessly. Use a cheek brush for both of these steps, then use a new, clean brush to make sure everything is perfectly blended.

Lips
Exfoliate and hydrate the lips with a lip scrub, then follow with a moisturizing lip balm. Wipe away any extra moisture from the lips, then apply a matte nude liquid lipstick. Re-apply for a longer-lasting effect.

Eyes
With an eyeshadow brush, apply a shimmery gold eyeshadow from eyelash to just above the natural lid. You can use either a cream or powder eyeshadow, but the bit of shimmer is key. Concentrate the gold at the inner corners of the eyes by using a slightly damp pointy smudger brush that's been dipped in the gold eyeshadow. ***Tip:*** Use this wet eyeshadow technique only when using powder eyeshadows (never when using creams). With a crease brush, apply a matte brown eyeshadow to the lid, creating a rounded shape and bringing it to the outer corner just a little. Follow with the same shade on the lower lash line. With an angled eyeliner brush, use a black gel to line the upper lash line, staying very close to the lashes. Create a line that goes straight out toward the temples, making sure you can still see it when your eyes are open. Using an eyelash curler, give the lashes a little lift before applying a lengthening mascara. ***Tip:*** Heat up the eyelash curler with a blow dryer, test it on your hand to make sure it's not too hot, then curl. A hot eyelash curler does its job even better.

Before

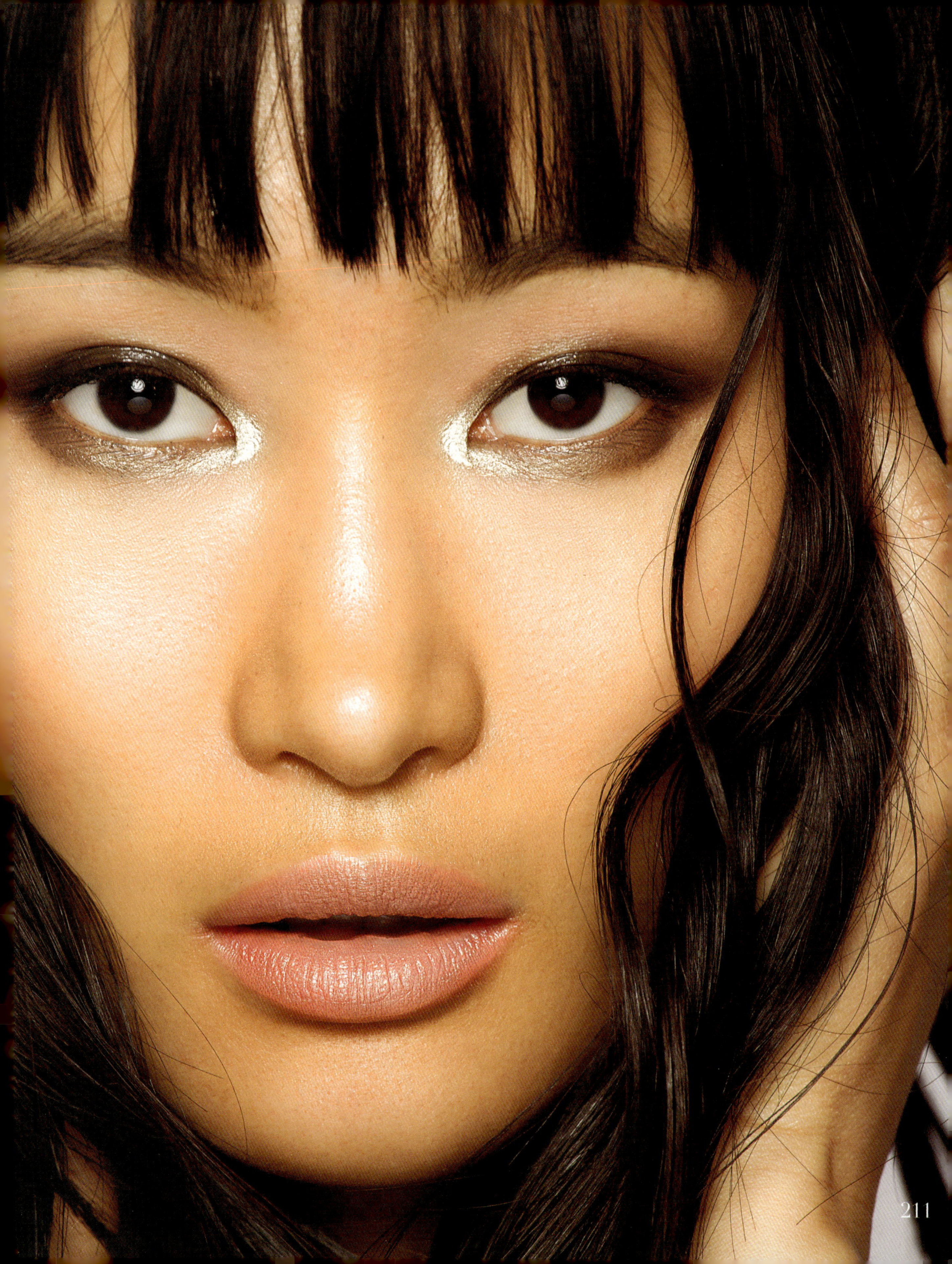

THE BRIDAL LOOKS

45 *PRETTY IN PINK*

46 *SOFT ROMANCE*

47 *BITTEN LIP*

48 *CANDLELIGHT*

49 *SWEET CHAMPAGNE*

213

45 PRETTY IN PINK

Skin
When prepping for a special event, it's very important to begin with a foundation primer. Use it after applying your skin care and before foundation. It will even out the skin surface, decrease the look of pores, and blur out any fine lines. Find a foundation shade that is as close to your overall skin tone as possible *(see page 25)*. For this look, use a medium coverage liquid foundation and apply it with a foundation brush. The right foundation will hide any unevenness in the skin tone and give your skin a flawless finish. Conceal specific areas of concern with a concealer that is also close to your skin tone. Use a slightly lighter one under the eyes. Use a translucent powder (with no color) to set the foundation and make it last. The powder will also minimize the look of pores while keeping the color of your foundation true for a seamless finish. Use the powder only where you need it, then spritz a few mists of finishing spray all over the face to set the look.

Tip: After you apply the makeup spray, lay a tissue over your skin for a second to give it a natural look that still glows and looks like you are not wearing much makeup. Repeat the process.

214

"Colors can speak in a thousand different ways, but pink really says romantic and girly. This look is a celebration of all things pink!"

Cheeks
Using a cheek brush, swipe a sparkling rose hue onto the apples of the cheeks, then blend a bronze contour powder below the cheekbones for definition. Blend the two together for a seamless look.

Eyes
Begin by applying an eyeshadow primer using a synthetic bristle flat brush all over the lid and the lower lashline. Using a fluffy eyeshadow brush, use a matte flesh tone eyeshadow on top of the primer. Using a clean eyeshadow brush, apply a soft pink shade creating a gradation from the lash line upwards and carry it down the lower lash line.

Tip: With mono-lids (eyes that lack space between the lash line and crease) make sure to check your work with your eyes open looking straight ahead. It might mean you need to carry the eyeshadow a little higher on your crease so that you can actually see it. If desired, use a smudger brush to apply a deeper pink/violet matte eyeshadow to the outer corners of the eyes. Blend seamlessly with the lighter pink. Follow by applying black gel or liquid liner to tightline (meaning lining right at the base of the lashes) around the eye, concentrating on the outer corners.

Lips
Fill in the lips with a nude lip liner that's close to your natural lip color. Dab and blur away any visible lines with your ring finger. Next, apply a pink semi-matte lipstick straight from the tube onto the center of lips. Use a flat Q-tip to blend the color out to the lip corners. This will create a beautiful, stained look.

Tip: Use a makeup-specific Q-tip that resembles the one in the picture. They normally have a pointy and a flat end. Blot with a tissue and repeat TWICE for a long-lasting effect.

Tip: To keep the lips feeling soft and creamy, begin layering with a semi-shine or creamy lipstick, then add a layer of a matte shade.

Tip: To make your eyes look larger, apply the eyeliner right at the inner corner. Just a little bit of liner in that inner corner will add further length to the eyes.

215

46 SOFT ROMANCE

"Neutral shades like these work on any skin tone. They enhance the features you want to bring out and keep the focus on you. If you don't know what look to try or are afraid of looking too made up, then go for a look like this!"

Skin
Moisturize the skin with an oil-free moisturizer, then follow with a skin primer (concentrating on any large pores and the t-zone. Apply a light layer of powder to the t-zone with a puff brush, then buff it out toward the rest of the face using a large powder brush.

Eyes
Use your fingertips to dab eye primer to the lids and lower lash lines. Dust a matte ivory eyeshadow all over the lid and blend it up to the brow bone. Apply an eyeshadow shade that's about two shades darker with an eye crease brush, sweeping it back and forth through your crease to softly deposit the color. Carry it slowly onto the lower lash line.

Tip: It's fine to take your eye color above and below the crease, as long as the eyeshadow is well blended. Use two clean brushes — one to blend and one to apply. Using the same sweeping motions, apply a darker brown shade right at the crease to further intensify the look. Tightline the upper lash line by softly applying a black eyeliner to the base of the lashes. Follow with a liquid eyeliner to perfect the line and fill in any gaps. Apply a coat of waterproof mascara, then apply individual false eyelashes right at the base of the lashes.

Tip: An easy way to get the look of individual falsies is to take a strip of lashes and cut into similar size clusters. Apply the clusters the same way you would apply individual lashes. The clusters will make the lashes look a lot more natural and make them much easier to apply.

Cheeks and Lips
Apply a rosy-brown cheek color to the tops and hollows of the cheeks using a cheek brush. Use a similar shade of lip color to line and fill in the lips.

BITTEN LIP 47

"This is a fresh and modern look that's perfect for a special day. It combines a metallic silver eyeliner with a pretty just-bitten look on the lips."

Eyes
Apply a coat of mascara to the corners of the lashes, concentrating on the tips.
Tip: Start by smudging the mascara right at the base of the lashes to add depth.

Skin
Illuminate the complexion by using a powder brush to apply highlighter to the tip of the nose, the cupid's bow, and tops of the cheeks.

Lips
To create a fun gradient effect, use a dot of concealer to blur any lip lines. With a lip brush, apply a hot pink semi-shine lipstick to the center of the lips. Blend the lipstick up using the same lip brush or a Q-tip. Smack your lips together a couple of times, then finish the look with lip balm or clear gloss, if desired.

48 CANDLELIGHT

"This look provides you with an easy and wearable way to create a 'halo' effect on the eyes. It creates a light-to-dark shade with gradient."

Eyes
To create a halo eye effect, begin by applying eye primer to the lids. Dust on a rosegold eyeshadow from the top lash line to the brow bone using a fluffy eyeshadow brush (making sure to evenly cover the lid and from corner to corner). Apply a matte brown eyeshadow with a crease brush and define the outer corners with a slightly rounded V. Then, sweep that same shade on the lower lash line from the outer to the inner corners. The idea is to surround the eye with a "halo" of color. Using your fingertips, add a bit of the rosegold color to the center of the eyelid and blend, making sure that the edges of the lighter color merge seamlessly with the color on the lid. Crease by blending with a clean eyeshadow brush.

Skin
Prep the skin first with a brightening facial mask, then follow with moisturizer and primer. Apply a luminous finish foundation, concentrating on the middle portions of the face and feathering it out with a wet sponge. Powder the t-zone and mist on a couple of layers of finishing spray.

Lips
Exfoliate and hydrate lips, follow with a nude semi-matte lipstick.

SWEET CHAMPAGNE 49

"This look is all about showing off gorgeous, radiant skin. A blend of shimmer and matte powders make this look a stand out!"

Brows
Use a precision eyebrow pencil to fill in any gaps in your eyebrows, then use a spoolie brush to blend. Follow with eyebrow gel to brush the brows into place.

Eyelids & Eyeliner
Apply a wash of gold-copper eyeshadow to the lids and lower lash lines with an eyeshadow brush. With a matte-brown shade eyeshadow and a crease brush, outline the outer corner of the eyes and blend. Use a clean brush to continue blending and diffusing so that the color dissipates at the edges. Finish by using a smudger brush to apply a light champagne shade of eyeshadow right under the brows and blend well. Use a dark brown eyeliner to tightline all around the eye, smudging the liner softly at the outer corners. Finish with a coat of waterproof mascara.

Lips
Exfoliate lips to remove any dead cells, then moisturize with a balm. Use a coral lip liner to line all around the lips. Follow with a coat of pink lip gloss.

Cheeks
With a cheek brush, begin by contouring the cheeks with a matte brown contouring powder. Then, using circular motions, blend the powder up and out to diffuse.

THE RUNWAY LOOKS

50
ADDICTED TO LOVE

51
AU COURANT

52
MESMERIZING

53
DRAW THE LINE

54
CATWALK GIRL

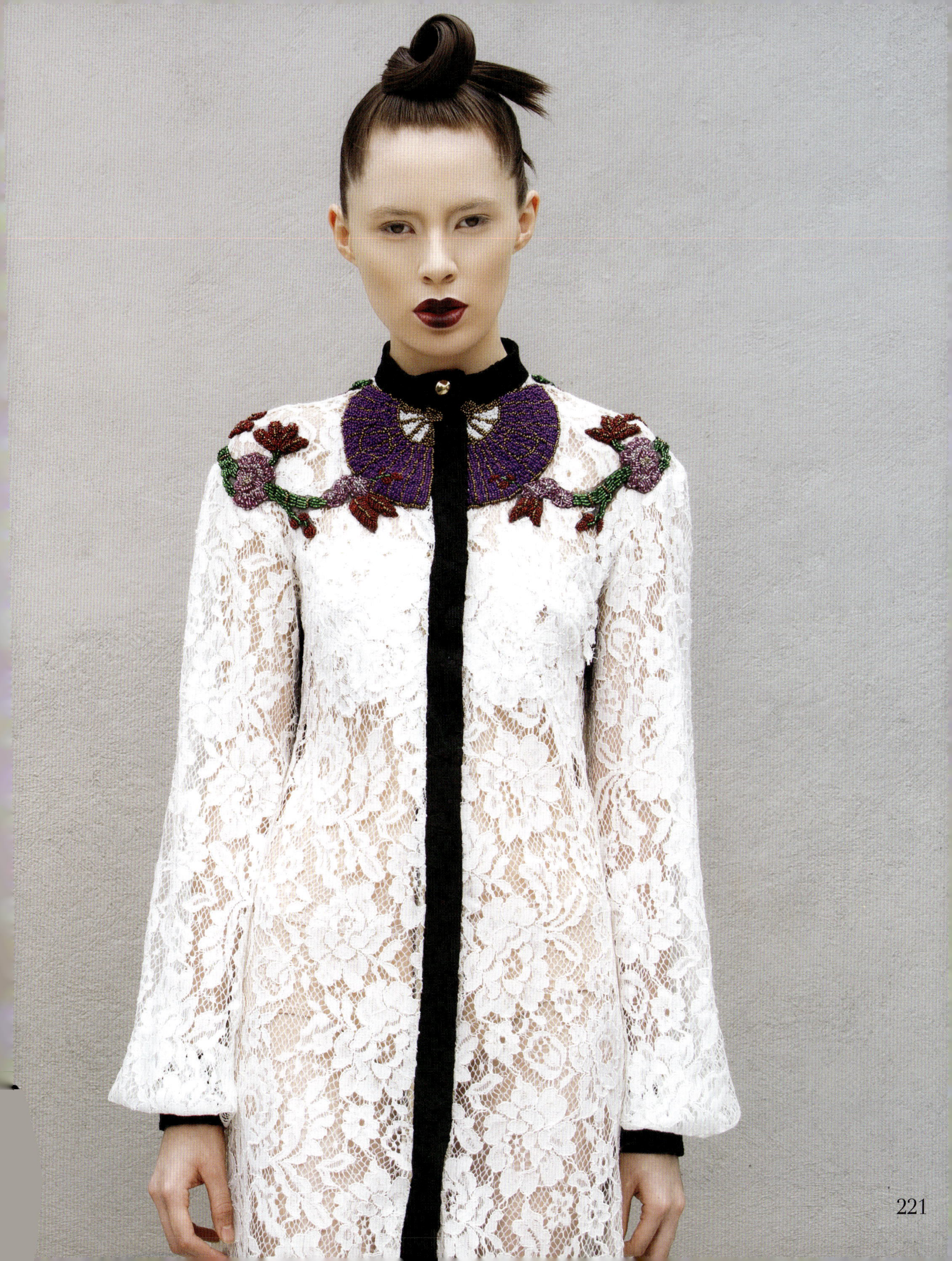

50 ADDICTED TO LOVE

"An easy way to build up the Aqua Smoke look *(page 176)* is to add a glossy lid, perfectly lined red lips, and radiant skin. These elements make this look a very modern version of early 80s glam."

Skin
To begin, refresh the skin by applying one or two coats of finishing spray.

Eyes
The eyebrows are further intensified and perfected. Use a precision eyebrow pencil to intensify and perfect your brow shape, then follow with a clear or slightly tinted brow gel. Create a cat-eye by using a black eyeliner pencil to draw a diagonal line from the outer corners of the eyes. Use the same pencil to line your lash line. Next, draw a second diagonal line from the outer corners of the eyes at a slightly higher angle to create a small triangle with the lower eyeliner line. Using your eyeliner, fill in the triangle to complete. Add more blue eyeshadow on top, if desired. With your fingertips, tap a tiny drop of clear lip gloss or lip balm to the middle of your lids. **Warning:** the gloss will crease after a while, but don't worry, it's supposed to. To avoid a sticky mess, stop applying the gloss or balm right below the crease. This will help prevent your lids from sticking together.

Tip: You can use a shimmery cream eye color instead of gloss or balm for a more user-friendly alternative.

Tip: Add a coat of waterproof mascara on both top and lower lashes.

Lips
Using a red lip liner, start at the center of the bottom lip and apply color halfway to each side. Then apply color from the corners of the mouth to the middle of the bottom lip. To line the upper lip, draw a small X shape right at your cupid's bow, then connect and line down to the corners of your lips. These steps should give you a perfect lip-lined look. Finish by applying a semi-shine red lipstick with a lip brush.

Before

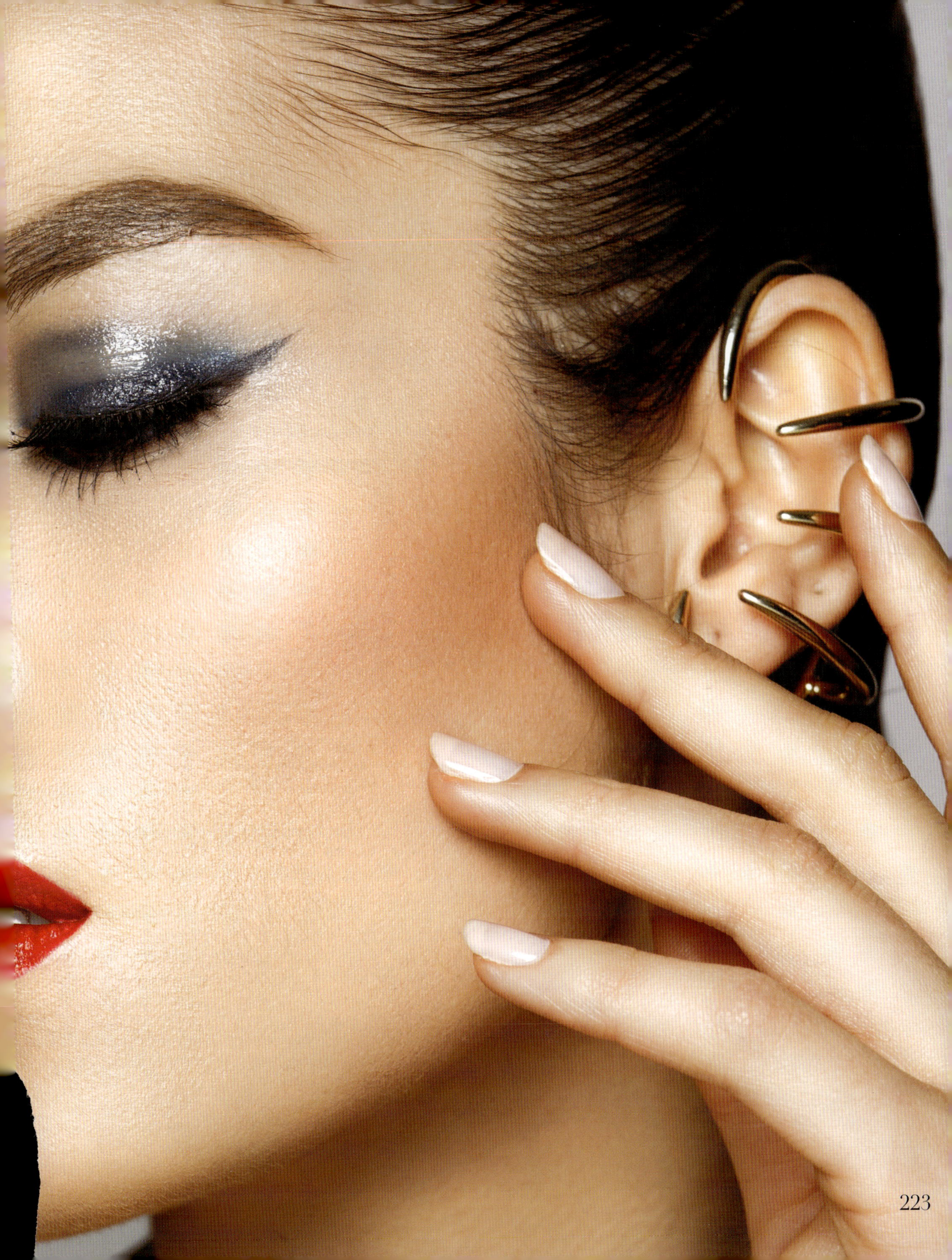

51 AU COURANT

"Strong, bold, and graphic — those are words I use to describe this look. Wear it as is or adapt it to your own personality. No matter how you apply it, the results are quite stunning!"

Before

Skin
Hydrating the skin is a must for this look. Begin with an antioxidant-rich serum to help plump the skin, then give yourself a facial massage with a soothing and brightening moisturizer. Hydrate the eyes with a hydrating eye cream and prep the lips with a scrub to exfoliate any dead cells. Smooth on a balm to moisturize.

Foundation
Using your fingertips, tap a dot of luminous foundation onto your cheeks, forehead, tip of nose, chin, and any other areas where you'd like more coverage. Follow with a foundation that's about two shades darker to contour the hollows of the cheeks, the temples, and under the chin. Use a foundation brush to blend. Follow with a corrector to erase any dark areas (at the sides of the nose, on the eye lids, etc,) and a concealer to hide any blemishes. Perfect the look by blending and diffusing with a damp sponge. Skip the powder until the rest of your makeup is applied and remember that there's usually no need to apply powder everywhere — target shiny areas only.

Eyes
Brush your eyebrows into place with a brow gel, then dust a light, slightly shimmery pearl eyeshadow onto the eyelids. Curl the eyelashes and apply a light coat of mascara.

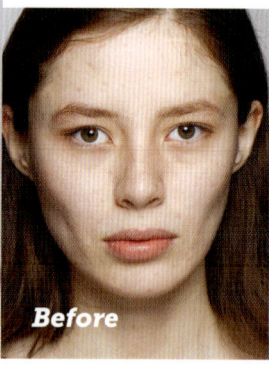

Lips
It's very important that you choose your colors carefully when it comes to ombré lips. Whether you're going for a bold look like this one, or a softer, more subtle finish, you want to make sure that the shades of lipstick you use are complementary and blend well together. Here, I used a deep-berry tone combined with a deep red. Be sure that you have an angled brush and a smudger brush with a small rounded tip on-hand before you attempt to apply ombré lips. You'll need the angled brush to create defined, precise lines around your lips, and the rounded brush to blend the multiple shades of lipstick together. Begin by applying the deep red shade all over the lips and lining them with the angle brush. Next, apply a dark cherry shade to the center of the lips and use the smudger brush to blur the lines and create a gradient effect. Line the darker area with the angled brush and then press your lips together to blend.

Tip: You can create different effects by playing with the application (try applying the lighter shade in the center of the lips, for instance). Just make sure the colors are well-blended and diffused.

224

225

ⓔ² MESMERIZING

"Understanding simple techniques for shading, color placement, and seamless blending are essential when it comes to creating a look like this. With a little know-how, you can master this look for any eye shape and with any color!!"

Eyes

Start by applying eye primer, which is a must for this type of look. Take a pointy smudger brush and apply a gold eyeshadow to the lids, starting at the inner corners of the eyes and blending it with an eyeshadow brush toward the middle of the lid. Let it dissipate above the crease. With an eyeshadow brush, apply a green eyeshadow to the middle of the lids and blend out toward the outer corners of the eyes. Then, with a smudger brush, use a matte blue shade to rim the lower lash line and further define the outer "V" of the eyes. Curl your lashes and apply mascara on both top and bottom lashes.

Lip

Use a nude lip liner all over the lips and top it off with a light nude semi-matte lipstick.

Contour

Use a creme-to-powder foundation that's two shades darker than your skin tone to define and contour any areas you'd like to recede (the hollows of cheeks, the chin, or the forehead, for instance). Apply your usual shade of foundation everywhere else, then blend the two together with a damp foundation sponge. Dust a warm peach cheek color onto the tops of the cheeks.

Before

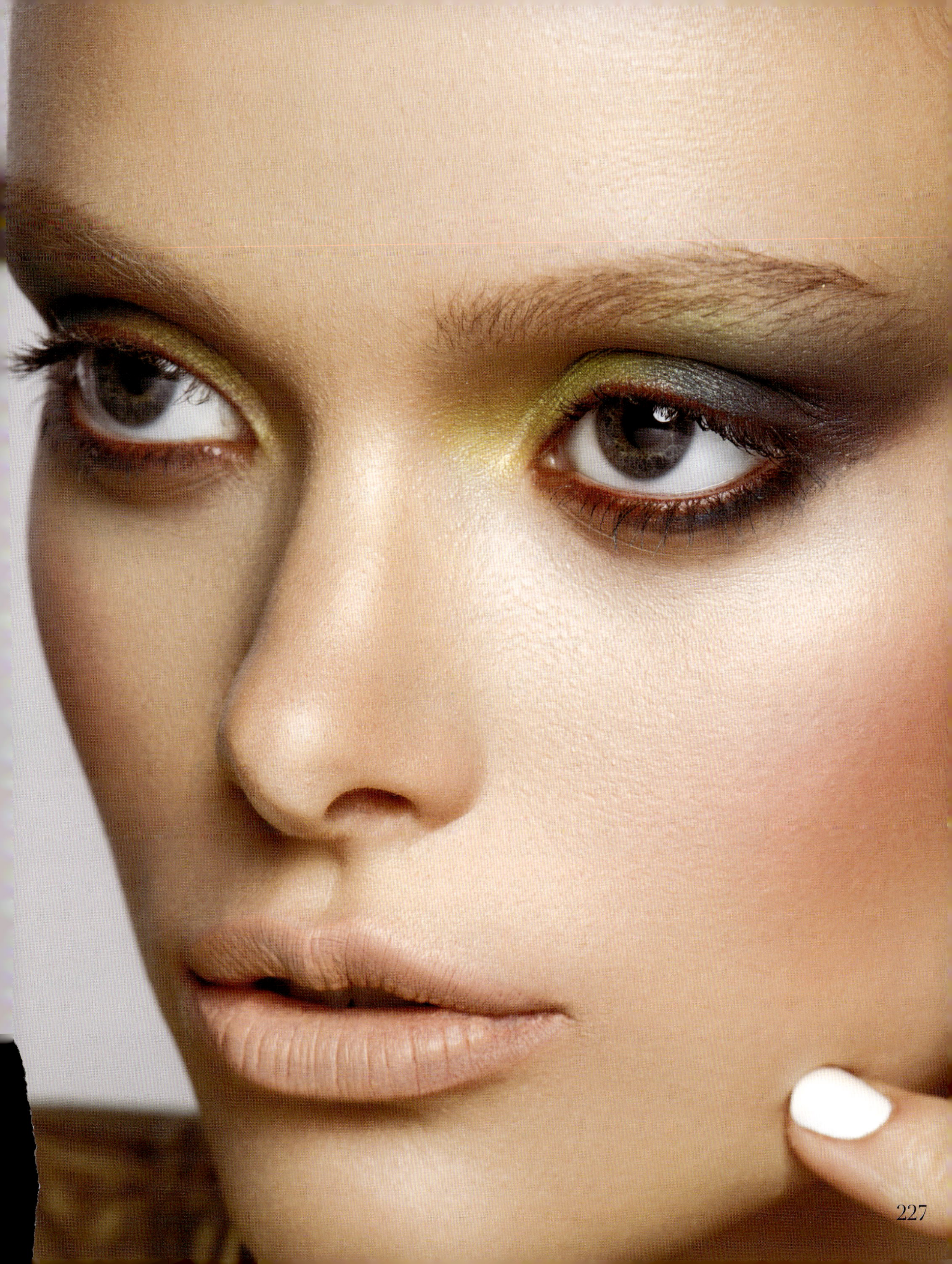

㊷ DRAW THE LINE

"This is a nude look that's accentuated by a feline-style eye. It's simple, but the play on different textures all around the face makes this a really exciting and flattering look for most people"

Skin
Don't be afraid of a little shine, and remember that if you want to mask your pores, a smoothing primer is a huge help. Also embrace highlighters, but make sure to apply them to the highest planes of your cheekbones and to blend toward your temples (instead of letting the hue sit near the middle of your cheeks).

If you do start to get really shiny halfway through the day, consider using blotting papers instead of a powder to touch-up. Oil-blotting sheets are easy to use and allow you to target only the areas of your face that you want to mattify.

Lips
Apply a nude matte lipstick that matches your skin tone or is one shade deeper. This will highlight the lips in a very subtle way.

Eyeliner
With a gel eyeliner and an angled brush, draw your line (as skinny or as thick as you like) across the top lash line, stopping just at the outer corner. Then, place the pointy edge of the angled brush where you want the tip of your wing to be. Angle it back to where you want it to connect with the rest of your eyeliner. Connect and then line the lower lash line.

Tip: If you like the look of a cat-eye created with liquid liner, but feel that your hand isn't quite steady enough, try using a combination of liquid, gel, and/or pencil liner. Apply liquid eyeliner to the inner and outer corners of eyes (which is where you want precise detail), then use a gel or pencil liner to fill in the areas where you want a thicker line.

CATWALK GIRL 54

"Having a specific color stand out as a prominent focal point can add a big impact to any makeup look. Here, I applied a light blue shade to the outer corners of the eyes and a pink shade to the inner corners. They both create the perfect pop of color!"

Eyes

To create this simple, sultry look, begin by priming your eyelids. Use a fluffy eyeshadow brush to dust a light neutral shade over both of your lids. That shade can have a bit of shimmer, if preferred. Using a smudger brush, apply a light blue shade in a sideways "V" shape to the outer corner of your crease. Using the same brush, dot a small amount of warm pink eyeshadow to the inner corner of your eyes. Curl your lashes and apply two coats of volumizing mascara.

Cheeks and Lips

Apply a pink semi-shine lipstick to the middle of the lips, using your fingertips to tap the product on. Feather it outwards using a lip brush.

THANK YOU

I want to thank the following people who have inspired, encouraged,
and supported me through this process that has taken a few years to put together.
I couldn't have done it without you!

Sheryl Adkins-Green, Holly Baker, Daisy Casco, David Ferron,
Emily Gradess-Hartman, James Hickey, Stephen Kamifuji, Yaya Kosikova,
Jenny Laible, Madeline Leonard, Susan Linney, Rose Mailutha, Ciara Moriarty,
Abigail Nieto, Brian Parillo, Tino Portillo, Betsy Rhodes, Barbara Sagami,
Frank Sebastian, Veronica Soto, Shannon Summers,
Preston Wada, Lorraine Young,
and so many more...

And to all those beautiful faces that will always keep inspiring me
to *CREATE*....